ADVERTISING *INSIDE OUT*

ADVERTISING INSIDE OUT

Philip Kleinman

W. H. ALLEN · LONDON
A Howard & Wyndham Company
1977

Printed and bound in Great Britain by Butler & Tanner Ltd, Frome and London for the publishers W. H. Allen & Co. Ltd, 44 Hill Street, London W1X 8LB

ISBN 0 491 01678 6

CONTENTS

FOREWORD

In July 1976 the Barons of Adland—chairmen and directors of advertising agencies, of publishing and broadcasting groups and, above all, of the manufacturing companies which spend money on advertisements—gathered together at London's Queen Elizabeth Hall for the golden jubilee conference of the Advertising Association. Their mood was at the same time hopeful and truculent. The hopefulness arose from an unexpectedly strong recovery in the level of advertising activity after the two depressed years which followed the 1973 boom. The truculence was caused by their realisation that, despite a series of efforts to tighten up voluntary controls of advertising, and to convince the advertising industry's critics of their effectiveness, they were still threatened with the possibility of statutory intervention. In particular they were worried and annoyed about a draft directive on advertising issued by the EEC Commission in Brussels. The principal provisions of the draft were: that legal sanctions should be brought to bear on advertisers, agencies and media responsible for publishing 'misleading or unfair advertising'; that such sanctions should include the power to order publication of corrections; and that consumers' groups and other bodies be enabled to take legal action against offending ads.

The draft was, of course, only a draft, and implementation might be years away, but the assembled admen (including some adwomen) felt it was time for their industry to reassert itself and to proclaim the belief that advertising was an indispensable element of a free society, a belief underlined by several speakers. One speaker, and one only, appealed to the audience to meet the critics halfway and cooperate in establishing a system of statutory control. That was Eirlys Roberts, deputy director of the Consumers' Association, and when Angus Ross, chairman of the Advertising Association, rebuked her for it in a burst of unrestrained fury, he got the biggest applause of the conference.

Miss Roberts had never hidden her own criticisms regarding 'the contemptuous attitude to people shown by advertisers who fill them up with all these dreams'. Her opponents, upholders of the dream business, deplored in turn her failure, and that of the Brussels authors of the draft directive, to acknowledge the value of the 'subjective satisfactions' supplied by advertising.

Controversies over the morality and utility of advertising have been going on for a long time and will continue for a while yet. Perhaps both sides tend to exaggerate the industry's importance; nevertheless it *is* important, on both the economic and the cultural levels, and it may be conjectured that even its critics are influenced by its productions. It is an interesting paradox that a public opinion survey published at the time of the AA conference showed a growing majority of people in Britain both to be critical of advertising and to express general approval of it.

Controversies apart, advertising is a fascinating business, situated as it is at the crossroads of commerce, art and sociological investigation. This book attempts to communicate some of that fascination.

P.K.

SHATTERING EFFECTS

I

Remember the snazzy young man in the sepia photograph, wearing a wide-brimmed hat and leaning against a lamp-post? There was a caption, 'Accountancy was my life until I discovered Smirnoff. . . The effect is shattering.'

Some accountants didn't like it, back in 1970, but many did and so did a lot of other people. They liked the other advertisements in the series too. Remember any of them? There was the sexy girl in the negligé: 'I've crossed a few bridges since I discovered Smirnoff.' The man riding a rickshaw through an Eastern street: 'I'd set my sights on a day trip to Calais until I discovered Smirnoff.' The girl looking coyly around as she pushes open a smart front door: 'Rumour has it she's discovered Smirnoff.'

The effect was always 'shattering' but only once shattering enough to cause a row. That was when London Transport refused to accept a poster showing a couple who might, from what could be seen of them, be presumed to be copulating. 'I used to catch the 7.29 until I discovered Smirnoff.' The girl's breasts were bare, and that also upset the board of International Distillers and Vintners, the company which makes and markets Smirnoff vodka in the UK, through its Gilbey Vintners subsidiary.

Tim Ambler, Gilbey Vintners' marketing director (now in charge of all IDV's UK marketing) got a rocket. Cut out the nudity, he was told, and from then on he did, though he later recalled that 'I personally was in favour of nudity. I think it's entirely right when it makes a relevant point. But nudity for its own sake, just to titillate, is entirely wrong.'

Even Ambler, however, had balked at the first picture

which advertising agency Young and Rubicam had proposed for the campaign. It showed a naked blonde on horseback. She'd been an ordinary housewife until she discovered Smirnoff. 'We turned it down,' said Ambler, 'because we thought it would cause a storm. But it set the style for the others.'

The 'discovery' campaign or, as its authors called it, the 'potency' campaign, was judged a great success by the client company, the agency and the advertising industry generally. It was visible, it was memorable and—nudes or no nudes—it was titillating. The erotic innuendoes which made it so didn't occur by accident. Dennis Auton, chairman of Young and Rubicam's London office, admits that the campaign was designed as a 'leg-opener'. (The phrase is in fact a quotation from one of the young people who took part in a series of discussion groups organised, before the campaign started, to probe their attitudes to drink.)

However, neither IDV nor Y & R is in the entertainment business, and still less in that of changing sexual mores. If the ads were entertaining, which they were, and their style in keeping with the permissive trend of the times, which it was, the reason was that client and agency were agreed that those qualities would help to sell vodka.

To the casual observer the campaign might have appeared frivolous, but advertising frivolity is invariably based on painstakingly serious analysis of the market. To the same casual observer the product itself might have appeared to be of no particular importance, like many other advertised products. It is true that society could get along pretty well without vodka, but the fact is that between 1969 and 1975 sales of the stuff in the UK trebled to about 4½ million gallons a year. Smirnoff, with half the market, stayed well ahead of all other brands on this rising tide.

So to those who were involved in making and selling Smirnoff, or indeed any of its competitors, what went into its advertising was of some consequence. Whatever the casual observer might have thought, no professional marketing man (or woman) would have been surprised to learn that the 'discovery' campaign had emerged not from a burst of whimsicality among IDV executives or

Y & R copywriters but from an agonising reappraisal of the brand's competitive position.

In 1969 sales were growing relatively slowly. Y & R had been in charge of Smirnoff advertising for two years. Its first effort had featured a picture of a haystack with the copy line 'Is it true what they say about Smirnoff?' Subsequently the agency had resorted to stylised graphics, keeping the same copy line. After a while the client became convinced that this approach wasn't getting the brand anywhere.

Such convictions arise not only from sales figures, which can obviously be influenced by many factors of which advertising is only one, but from research. All big consumer goods manufacturers are compelled to carry out research of various kinds—or to have it carried out for them—if they wish to stay competitive. We shall have more to say about the general subject of research in a later chapter. Suffice it for the moment to point out that the major questions any advertiser wants his research to answer are: how many and what kind of people use his product (and rival products); what they think of it; and how their attitudes and purchasing behaviour can be, or have been, influenced by his actions, including his advertising. (Be it noted also that evidence about the effect of advertising on consumer behaviour is notoriously difficult to evaluate. But let us not at this stage get bogged down in that problem!)

IDV's research revealed two principal facts about general attitudes to vodka:

1. Although it is one of the weakest of the hard liquors, it is commonly thought of as one of the strongest. No doubt the stereotype of the butch vodka-swilling Russian—fostered by novels and films—has something to do with that.
2. It is perceived as a 'clean' spirit, largely because it is flavourless and makes the drinker's breath stink somewhat less than other forms of alcohol. This is a point which Smirnoff's rival Cossack (made by the Distillers Company) has made some play with. For

reasons of brand differentiation, Smirnoff's advertising has steered clear of it.

Instead it was decided that Smirnoff should try to exploit the illusion that vodka has some special potency. After discussions between client and agency, Young and Rubicam produced a 'creative work plan' embodying the policy which copywriters and art directors were to follow. This was submitted to, and approved by, an *ad hoc* committee consisting of Ambler, George Bull, managing director of Gilbey Vintners, and Ian Lockwood, brand manager in charge of Smirnoff. The document read as follows:

1. Key Fact
Smirnoff is the brand leader in a relatively small but growing and fashionable liquor category.

2. Problem the Advertising must Solve
Although the budget of around £100,000 is high for a vodka brand, it pales considerably when viewed against the background of £8.5 million of liquor advertising spread across other brands.

3. Advertising Objective
To firmly establish the brand's modern and fashionable image as a potent and exciting drink in a way that commands attention.

4. Creative Strategy
A. Prospect Definition
1. Young working-class consumers who are just being introduced to 'hard' drinks. Heavy emphasis on females.
2. Upper and middle-class consumers of all ages who see vodka as a 'trendy' drink.
B. Principal Competition
All other vodkas, principally Cossack. Also gin, white rum and fashion drinks like Campari.
C. Promise
Smirnoff is a very potent drink, particularly effective in banishing day-to-day inhibitions.

D. Reason Why

Research shows that Smirnoff has perceived qualities of potency (despite a lower proofage than gin or whisky) and has powerful associations of modernity, excitement and virility.

5. (If necessary) Mandatories and Policy Limitations

We are in no way permitted to mention the product's Russian or Polish origins.

(Regarding that last point, it ought to be explained that the brand started in Russia but that, after the Revolution, the Smirnoff family moved itself and its business first to Poland and subsequently to France. The brand was eventually bought by the United States firm of Heublein, and it was under licence to Heublein that Gilbeys started making Smirnoff in Britain in 1953.)

Responsibility for turning this brief into words and pictures was given, according to what has become normal ad agency practice, to a team of two people: one copywriter and one art director. (An art director is not actually a director in the managerial sense. The term has in recent years replaced the earlier one of 'visualiser', which was perhaps more precise, though less glorious.) The copywriter was John Bacon and the art director David Tree.

Tree, who was later to move to senior jobs with Y & R in Stockholm and Tokyo before returning to the London office in 1976 as creative director, recalls how the pair of them struggled for weeks to get the right answer. Their original efforts were based on the idea of comparing the excitingness of Smirnoff with the boringness of other drinks. It was too negative an approach. If they had any doubts about whether they were heading up a blind alley, these were settled by Tim Coles, the account supervisor (the agency man responsible for liaison with the client), who rejected their first draft ads.

The breakthrough came by an accident of the kind well known to advertising creatives. One day, after a fruitless session, Tree was leaving for lunch when he happened to glance at a magazine pin-up adorning the wall of the office he shared with Bacon. 'If we really get stuck,' he quipped, 'we can always say "I was a boring housewife in Southgate until . . ." ' (Southgate was where he was living at the time.) As he spoke the unconsidered words, both of them suddenly realised they'd found their solution. Coles, later to become managing director of Y & R, agreed.

Although they cooked up the new campaign between them, Bacon and Tree were by no means the only people to produce ads for it. Almost everyone in the agency's creative department got his or her finger in the pie at some time or other. One doesn't need to know much about advertising people to understand that it was a popular account to work on.

The ads were distinctive not only because of their provocative humour but because of their layout. At a time when the normal drink ad featured a picture of a bottle, with the advertiser's story underneath the picture, Y & R did away with pack shots (i.e. photographs of the product) and lines of explanatory copy and merely used half of Smirnoff's picturesque label as a kind of sign-off.

Incidentally, the part of the label which was reproduced bore the legend 'Purveyors to the Imperial Russian Court 1886–1917', so the ban on mentioning the brand's origin was less strictly interpreted than the brief approved by the client might have suggested.

Another feature of the layout was that the pages on which the ads appeared were all 'bled', i.e. no margin of white paper was left. This normally gives any magazine picture more impact.

The general style of the campaign was very much linked to the client's decision to go as strongly as possible for the youth market. 'Trendiness', that magic attribute referred to in the creative work plan, is easier to talk about than to define, but in the late Sixties people like David Tree, himself a trendy youngster at the time, perceived that it had something to do with a certain elegant nonconformism, a stylised rejection of the older generation's social and sexual conventions, a (to use a famous oxymoron) radical chic. Trendiness was not—oh dear me, no—the same as revolution but it did have a bright streak of anti-establishmentarianism. Those were, after all, the years when young men were letting their hair grow long and young women cutting their virginity short.

The IDV Board were agreeable that the language of youth be used to recruit young consumers, but at the same time the directors were anxious that the campaign should not go beyond the bounds of respectability. In particular they laid down that, as Ambler put it, there should be no 'encouragement of indolence'. Nonconformists yes, drop-outs no. And that's the way it was.

By the summer of 1975 it began to be felt that the cock-snooking had gone on for long enough. Times were changing and the campaign, client and agency agreed, was beginning to look a little tired. There was, however, a more precise reason for thinking that a new approach should be evolved, and that reason was to do with the work, and the growing importance, of the Advertising Standards Authority.

The ASA is one of those curious British institutions—the BBC is another, more important example—which occupy a halfway house between private enterprise and State control. The BBC is an independent body which relies on the State for its financing. The ASA is a creation of the advertising industry, wholly financed by that industry but amenable to pressure from the State regarding the application of a supposedly voluntary system of control of the content of advertisements.

We shall have more to say about the ASA later on. Let us just note that, as part of a general tightening up of the British Code of Advertising Practice administered by the ASA, new rules regarding the advertising of alcoholic beverages were introduced in early 1975. The Code had already laid down that alcohol ads should not be aimed at young people and that they 'should not contain any encouragement, whether direct or indirect, to over indulgence'. The new rules added in particular that 'advertisements should neither claim nor suggest that any drink can contribute towards sexual success'.

That this provision was intended to be taken seriously became perfectly clear shortly afterwards when the ASA publicly stated that an advertisement for Courvoisier brandy contravened the Code. The ad, part of a humorous series which pictured characters from Napoleonic times, showed an officer stealing into a lady's bedroom through a secret panel while she waited for him in bed. While the ASA's adjudications do not have the force of law they are normally adhered to by advertisers and their agencies. In the case of Courvoisier there was a good deal of grumbling among admen about the alleged narrowmindedness and humourlessness of the Authority. Nevertheless, the agency concerned, Sharps, did as it was told and, in subsequent ads, restrained the licentiousness of its fictional officers.

It was also laid down that 'advertisements should not emphasise the stimulant, sedative or tranquillising effects of any drink' and that 'advertisements should not give the general impression that a drink is being recommended mainly for its intoxicating effect or that drinking is necessary for social success or acceptance'.

No formal complaint was addressed to the ASA about Smirnoff's advertising, unlike the case of Courvoisier, although informally the Health Education Council expressed disapproval of it even before the new rules were adopted, on the grounds that it was clearly aimed at young people. Whether a complaint that the campaign was in breach of the 'stimulant' ban would have been upheld is difficult to guess. The rules, as can be seen, were sufficiently vaguely worded to make interpretation all-important. However, the example of Courvoisier held out no hope that the ASA's interpretation would err on the side of indulgence.

Considering that judgment was in practice delegated by the Authority to a committee of people drawn largely from the advertising industry (advertisers, advertising agents and representatives of the media), such severity might appear surprising. But these people, whatever sympathy they might feel for fellow toilers in the commercial vineyard, were intent upon proving that the voluntary control system was no mere sham. They believed that, unless they succeeded in doing so, the industry would be saddled with a much more disagreeable system of statutory controls.

IDV was not slow to respond to the more restrictive atmosphere which developed in 1974–5. Holding that discretion was the better part of advertising valour, the company began to tone down the 'potency' campaign while denying stoutly that there was anything wrong with it. The erotic suggestiveness disappeared, the appeal to youth was made less obvious.

Among the new-style variations on the old theme turned out by Young and Rubicam was an ad with no people pictured in it at all, just the inscription on a whitewashed wall 'I thought St Tropez was a Spanish monk until I discovered . . .' You couldn't get much more discreet than that.

Meanwhile the search began for a new campaign which would be just as compelling as the old one while less provocative to anti-alcohol vigilantes. Over the months a succession of ideas was put up to, and knocked down by, Tim Ambler. Finally he gave the thumbs-up, and in June 1976 the first ads of the new £400,000 campaign (inflation had done its work) were unveiled.

Visually and verbally the derivation of the new stuff from classic Smirnoff was plain to see, but in place of the earlier exoticism the jokes were downbeat. An elegant young man lounged on a pile of cushions. 'They say Smirnoff can't make you an overnight sensation. That's OK, I'm busy tomorrow.' A pretty girl quipped: 'They say Smirnoff won't put hair on your chest. Well, that's good news for me.' (The model was a black girl, and IDV had researchers check out beforehand that the immigrant community wouldn't take it amiss.)

The new punch line, even more downbeat, was 'You drink it for what it is', which could be held to mean almost the opposite of the old 'The effect is shattering' slogan. Some admirers of the 'potency' campaign expressed disappointment, but client and agency declared that their research indicated that consumers responded to the new ads even more positively than to the old ones.

The Smirnoff story just told, though necessarily briefly, is not about one of the biggest of advertising campaigns nor one of the most important products advertised. Other campaigns we shall mention could be said to have made a greater impression either upon advertising practitioners or upon the consuming public. Furthermore, the Smirnoff campaign was untypical of modern advertising for mass-produced repeat-purchase goods in that it made no use of television. (This, incidentally, was because of a long-standing gentlemen's agreement between British drinks firms to keep all hard liquor off the small screen.)

Nevertheless, it's a good story to start with not only because the ads gave much pleasure but because it illustrates neatly a number of interesting points about the ad industry. These, listed in no special order, are as follows:

1. Advertising always has a serious commercial purpose but it has also become to quite a large extent a form of entertainment.

2. Advertising seizes upon general social and cultural developments and endeavours to exploit them for its own ends.

3. As the most visible channel of communication between business and the consumer, advertising has become a subject of great public and political concern.

4. The creation of advertising involves a high degree of skill—analytical and artistic—on the part of specialists.

5. Although the evidence is not clear-cut, it is generally agreed that advertising does in fact do what it purports to do, i.e. affect the volume of sales of the product.

6. Advertising campaigns are influenced by a continual process of discussion between people on both the client and agency sides. In this process sharp differences of opinion can and do arise.

7. Successful campaigns nevertheless maintain a consistent approach over a long time, years or even decades. It is this consistency which justifies the use of terms such as 'brand image' or 'brand personality'.

8. The image of a brand, as created by advertising, is undeniably an important, if intangible, part of what people pay for when they buy it. In other words, they go for the sizzle as well as the steak, the dream as well as the reality.

Indeed, in the case of many heavily advertised products, including alcoholic drinks, it is the dream rather than the reality that the customer cares about. The image he has of the brand overlaps with the image he has of himself—or would like to have.

9. Though comparatively few people are knowledgeable about advertising as an industry, almost all of us take some interest in advertisements, which are after all woven into the fabric of everyday urban life. The more successful advertising slogans quickly work their way into popular speech, journalese and even graffiti. This certainly happened to Smirnoff's 'potency' campaign, with public lavatories sprouting lines like 'I thought fellatio was an Italian opera until I discovered Smirnoff'.

10. In the light of the above, and in particular of point 8, it may be conjectured that advertising plays a greater role than it is sometimes given credit for in shaping the way in which we in late twentieth-century Britain perceive the world about us.

2 WHO ADVERTISES AND WHY?

But enough of abstractions, for the moment. Let's find out exactly what kind of an industry it is that is responsible for the shattering—and not so shattering—effects just mentioned.

First, it should be explained that the term 'advertising industry' is a somewhat ambiguous one compared with, say, 'motor industry.' The latter covers all those—and only those—companies which are mainly engaged in the manufacture and distribution of motor vehicles or components thereof. Those who speak of the 'advertising industry', however, are commonly referring not only to companies whose *main* business is the production and distribution of advertisements—i.e. advertising agencies—but to the advertising activities of all companies, whatever they produce, which attempt to communicate with the public through ads. They are also referring to the advertisement departments of the newspapers, television stations and other media through which such communication is channelled.

And, while we are defining our terms, the word 'advertising' itself will bear a little closer scrutiny. It covers a multitude of sins as well as of things which even the severest critics of the ad industry would be hard put to it to think of as sins. For instance it covers classified advertising, the small ads which fill a large part of many newspapers and magazines, especially local papers and trade journals, and which are frequently ignored in any debate about the rights and wrongs of the industry.

Classified accounts, however, for a sizable chunk of the advertising cake. In 1975 total advertising expenditure in media was £967 million, of which £218 million, or nearly a quarter, was accounted for by classified. Roughly a half of the figure, incidentally, went on job ads.

Excluded from the £967 million figure is all of what is known as 'below the line' advertising, or alternatively as sales promotion. These phrases cover such activities as direct mail, point-of-sale displays, sports sponsorship, trading stamps, consumer competitions, gift offers and other promotional stunts—in other words any form of commercial publicity which does not go through the 'main media' of press, television, radio, cinema and posters.

The amount spent 'below the line' is very much harder to quantify than is media advertising expenditure. There are no entirely reliable figures, but the best estimate comes from a sales promotion company called Harris International Marketing, which, together with the (unrelated) Louis Harris research firm, runs regular surveys of consumer reaction to various sales techniques. According to HIM, total 'below the line' spending in 1975 was about £680 million. This is a huge sum, but it includes the cost of cut-price offers which, though they come out of the same promotional budgets as do companies' ad campaigns, are far removed from what most people call advertising. According to HIM, price reductions in 1975 accounted for £425 million.

Returning to the media, the 1975 total of £967 million represented 1·54 per cent of consumers' expenditure and 1·04 per cent of the gross national product, a sharp drop from two years previously, when the corresponding figures were 1·95 and 1·39 per cent. But 1973 was a boom year for advertising, the last of a kind which in the Fifties and Sixties the industry had come to regard as normal.

Not much more than a third of the £967 million (to be precise £387 million) was spent on what the industry calls MCA, manufacturers' consumer advertising, a clumsy but useful expression which covers all campaigns by private sector manufacturers for branded consumer goods. MCA, although it amounted in 1975 to only 0·42 per cent of GNP (down from 0·58 in 1973), is indeed what most people think of when they hear the word 'advertising' and is certainly what most criticism of the much-criticised ad industry is concerned with.

Of course, £387 million is still a lot of money. In 1975 it included £89 million spent on advertising food, £73 million on drink and tobacco, £87 million on household and leisure goods, £53 million on toiletries and medical products, £33 million on cars and other automotive products and £12 million on clothing.

It will readily be deduced that different types of manufacturer devote very different proportions of their turnover to advertising. At one extreme clothing ads represent only a fraction of one per cent of consumer expenditure on garments; at the other producers of toiletries and medical products spend over five per cent of their industry's retail income on advertising.

The biggest category of display (i.e. non-classified) advertising apart from MCA is retail advertising. In 1975 chain stores, local shops and mail order firms spent £163 million between them, double the figure of three years before. Trade and technical advertisers spent £65 million on display advertising in the specialist press (in addition to £21 million of classified ads in trade and technical journals). Financial advertising, including company reports and ads by banks and insurance firms, accounted for £36 million. Government advertising totalled £21 million in addition to £18 million spent by the nationalised industries.

Just one more figure, and then we'll take a rest from statistics. In 1974 a total of £236 million was spent on television advertising, the vast bulk of which fell into the MCA sector. For most well-known brands of packaged and bottled goods, except as we have seen spirits, TV has become the preferred medium. The reasons for this development are its mass audience and what is felt to be its communicative power as compared with the press. This latter point is one which still arouses vigorous controversy among advertising people, particularly those directly concerned with the buying and selling of press space and broadcasting airtime.

Irrespective of whether advertising money ends up in the hands of newspaper or magazine publishers or TV companies, how does it get there? Well, obviously the process starts with the advertiser. And here one must trot out two truisms which to any denizen of Adland are boringly familiar but which, taken together, the outsider may be forgiven for finding rather odd. These truisms are: (*a*) companies advertise because they believe that doing so induces people to buy their products or services; (*b*) they are seldom sure how well any particular ad campaign is going to work or even, after it is over, how well it has worked. Point (*b*) we have already touched on apropos of Smirnoff, and we will come back to it. Let's concentrate for a moment on point (*a*).

Consider, to begin with, the testimony of Arthur Lines, advertising director of Kelloggs UK from 1945 to 1976, in which capacity he became almost as well known as in his other capacity as one of Adland's favourite after-dinner wits. Kelloggs, with half the British breakfast cereal market, of which 30 per cent is accounted for by its Corn Flakes brand, is a major advertiser. 'We know,' says Lines, 'that advertising is effective, even though we have never found any precise way of assessing its effectiveness.'

His faith, and the faith of others, in advertising is based on evidence like the result of the experiment which Kelloggs carried out in the Tyne-Tees television area. There the company doubled the volume of advertising support for its Frosties brand of cereal, and after two months sales increased. 'One could say with 90 per cent certainty there was a causal relationship,' comments Lines.

Looking at the question the other way round, he is 100 per cent certain that, if Kelloggs were to halt all advertising, sales of its products would decline, although no change might be visible for six months. Such certainty is based not on hunch but on observation of other campanies' setbacks. Notably Force, once a famous name in British breakfast cereals, practically disappeared from the market after a period of promotional weakness. And America's giant General Mills company tried to introduce a number of its brands into the UK in the mid-Sixties but, for lack of advertising back-up, all were squeezed out within a year.

Similar stories come from other product areas. A 1975 study by the Television Consumer Audit, a research operation conducted by the Audits of Great Britain company on behalf of the major ITV contractors, analysed the effects of various promotional activities on sales of certain toothpaste brands. According to the report, TV advertising increased market shares of the brands advertised during the week they were advertised and for up to four weeks subsequently. This finding applied to both new and established brands.

An earlier TCA study, on the soft drinks industry, showed that when manufacturers reduced advertising in favour of cut-price promotions, it resulted in a decline in their share of the market, with over 40 per cent of sales being captured by retailers' 'private label' brands. 'Private label' goods, also known as retailers' 'own brands', are often supplied to the supermarket chains by the same factories which turn out proprietary brands. The marketing difference is that the retailers, like Sainsbury, Tesco or the Co-op, rely for the sale of their own brands not on advertising but on price advantages (plus their own reputation for quality).

Another famous case history is that of the comparative fortunes of Andrex and Delsey toilet paper. In 1963 Andrex held 22 per cent of the market and Delsey 16 per cent. Pressure from retailers forced both brands to reduce their prices, and the reaction of Kimberly-Clark (manufacturer of Delsey) to this situation was to try to recoup the money lost by cutting the brand's ad budget. By the end of 1965 Delsey had virtually stopped advertising, but Andrex carried on doing so. The outcome was that, while sales of cheaper brands of soft toilet paper grew, so did those of Andrex, and by 1969 its share of the market had risen to 39 per cent. Delsey on the other hand went into a sales decline, and attitudinal research surveys indicated that, after its advertising ceased, its reputation among consumers declined too.

Cadbury Schweppes maintains that 'by the judicious use and timing of advertising' it was able to reduce seasonal fluctuations in the consumption of Cadbury's Drinking Chocolate. To quote John Beasley, chairman of Schweppes, speaking in 1974: 'This product historically peaked in sales in the winter. May to September, which without seasonality would attract 38 per cent of annual sales, accounted for 29 per cent of sales in 1958. We have now lifted that to 33 per cent with consequent benefits to production and employment.'

So belief in the usefulness of advertising is well established among manufacturers, particularly those in the mass consumption, repeat-purchase sectors. To put that belief into practice such companies employ people knowledgeable about advertising techniques, and these people are nowadays normally, though not always, part of an integrated marketing department, in which problems of general promotion, pricing, distribution, packaging and product innovation are considered in relation to each other as well as to advertising policy.

A common arrangement is for each brand in a multi-brand company to have a brand manager responsible for administering all these activities under the supervision of a product group manager and, higher still, a marketing director. As far as advertising goes all these gentlemen (occasionally ladies) perform principally as clients. Usually, though not invariably, the day-to-day work of actually devising campaigns and arranging when and where the ads are to be published or screened falls upon an agency. Or indeed agenc*ies*, for big manufacturers with a variety of brands often use the services of two or more.

Economically speaking, agencies are very small beer compared with the client companies for which they work. One famous pre-war agency man, Ashley Havinden, is reputed to have defined advertising as 'a boil on the arse of commerce'. To complete his elegant metaphor one might add that the agency business forms merely the head of that boil. But for most people who are at all involved in advertising, agencies and what goes on in them constitute an endless topic of conversation. This is because, in their own oft-repeated cliché phrase, they constitute 'a people business', in which even the biggest firms employ little fixed capital but depend for their living on the ideas, character, brainpower, reputation and panache of their staff.

This 'people business' is also, perhaps more than any

other, a volatile business in which firms and individuals can rise and fall with sometimes astonishing rapidity. It is a business with more than its fair share of poseurs, bull-shitters, eccentrics, whizz-kids, backstabbers and rumour-mongers. It also contains a high proportion of people who, while perhaps not as clever as they think they are, manage to appear very clever indeed.

3 THE AGENCY GAME

There are thought to be about 600 ad agencies in the UK but many of this number are very small outfits consisting of perhaps only a couple of people. Almost all the agencies of any size belong to the Institute of Practitioners in Advertising, and these numbered 276 in 1975. Between them they handled about 90 per cent of display advertising expenditure and employed 13,300 people (down from a peak population of 20,000 in the mid-Sixties).

The vast majority of even IPA agencies are very small fry. Nearly two thirds of all their employees are to be found in the 50 biggest agencies, and over one third in the top dozen alone. In 1975 the biggest agency in Britain, J. Walter Thompson, had a staff of 800 (in prosperous 1973 it had been close on a thousand). By and large big advertising accounts are handled by big agencies, while small advertisers use the services of small agencies, but there are many exceptions to this general rule. Indeed, many agencies now in the big league began their growth when, as lean and hungry small firms, they were entrusted with a major account by an advertiser which felt it would get better service from them than from their older and fatter rivals.

Another general rule is that advertisers with a large number of different brands employ a number of different agencies to handle them, although here again there are exceptions. For example, Kelloggs channels all its annual British advertising expenditure of £3 million through J. Walter Thompson and has done so for many, many years. Not that such cosy arrangements are guaranteed to last for ever. Even Arthur Lines says: 'A company our size could do with more than one agency, say three.'

Advertisers tend to feel that competition between agencies is a good thing and keeps them on their toes. A manufacturer using several agencies is likely from time to time to review their comparative records and to reward those felt to have done good work by giving them extra chunks of business taken from those considered to have performed less well.

It is not, however, only agencies which share a client with other agencies which find their performances thus scrutinised and evaluated. Part of the job of every marketing director, be his company big or small, is to keep the work of his agency or agencies under review. Some companies make a habit of inviting presentations from agencies which do not work for them just to keep in touch with the state of the game—in other words, to know which agencies might be worth hiring in case they decide to dispense with the services of the one currently handling their account.

Since advertising is only one element in what is known in business jargon as the 'marketing mix', and since it is rarely possible to establish with any degree of certainty how far a particular campaign has contributed to the success, or indeed lack of success, of a given brand, an agency cannot be sure whether and when a client will conceive the notion that a change of agency will do him good. Even the longest and closest client-agency relationships are subject to sudden upsets, and the switching of accounts occurs often enough to keep the advertising trade press full of news and agency executives in a state of constant alert. This kind of precariousness is what gives the agency business a large part of the fascination it exerts over those who get involved with it. There is a wealth of anecdotes to illustrate the point, and as this book proceeds we shall have occasion to retell some of them.

The agency, then, works for the client company and its fortunes rise or fall in accordance with advertisers' satisfaction. It is worth explaining for the benefit of those who know little of the history of advertising (most people in the country) that this has not always been the case. Agencies first came into being at the beginning of the last century as space brokers. Their principal function was to sell advertising space on behalf of newspapers. They were paid by way of a commission from the newspapers and periodicals they served, who were their clients. Services to advertisers, such as writing their ads for them, developed as a way of attracting their business. James White, who set up an agency in London in 1800 to sell space for provincial newspapers, employed his friend Charles Lamb (the essayist) as a freelance copywriter, devising ads for Government lotteries. In the course of time this space-selling function of agencies withered away. There are still a few dozen firms in London which specialise in selling space, largely for overseas publications, but these firms are known today as advertisement representatives, not advertising agencies. There is no doubt whatsoever today that the agency's client is the advertiser, not the newspaper or TV station which carries the ad.

But, and it is a very big but, the remuneration of agencies has continued to be based on the commission system, and this is really a very strange state of affairs, even though it is common throughout the Western World. Let us be quite clear what this means. Agencies take a commission on the money paid by the advertiser to the advertising media—15 per cent in the case of TV and national newspapers and magazines, 10 per cent in the case of trade and technical publications. So the more the advertiser spends the more the agency earns, irrespective of how much effort or talent of its own it contributes.

To take an extreme, but not absurd, example, if an advertiser chooses to fork out a million pounds on a heavy TV campaign making use of only one or two different commercials, the agency will get £150,000 commission, exclusive of production costs, e.g. fees paid to a specialised TV production company and air fares for models, camera crew and director to a Caribbean location. Such costs are normally borne by the advertiser.

On the other hand, if an advertiser spends £50,000 on a series of complicated press ads, all of them different—giving details perhaps of changing stock and prices available at a retail chain's stores—the agency will make only £7,500, though it may have had to devote many more man-hours to its campaign than did the agency with the £1 million TV account, and though it may have done its job just as competently or even much more competently.

The man in the street might conclude from this that agencies must be strongly motivated to attempt to acquire large accounts rather than small ones, and the man in the street would be right. He might also conclude that agencies once having got an account, would invariably try to persuade the advertiser to spend as much money as possible. Here he would be wrong. It is a point of pride with agencies to seek the best bargains for their clients, i.e. to squeeze the biggest discounts they can out of the advertisement departments of the media they deal with. In doing so they automatically reduce their own commission, but this is not quite so altruistic as it might sound. As we have already seen, the agency business is intensely competitive, and any agency which got the reputation of boosting its own profits at the expense of its clients' profits would pretty soon find itself without clients.

Also it is necessary to add some qualifications to our two hypothetical examples. First, despite the fact that the commission system has survived remarkably well in the face of much criticism from within the ad industry and frequent unfulfilled forecasts of its disappearance, it is not the only form of remuneration open to ad agencies. In the last few years there has been a growing tendency to charge the client fees either instead of commission or, more frequently, in addition to it. Thus if the £7,500 of income in our second example was agreed to be inadequate payment for the amount of work done the client would be asked to supplement it with a service fee, and this is what happens in many such cases.

So in practice the agency in example two is likely to be making more profit out of its client than might at first glance be thought. Contrariwise, the agency in example one may not be coining it quite as easily as it appears to be doing. This is because a big agency—and to be handling a million-pound account it most probably is a big agency—traditionally supplies its clients with a range of services other than the making and placing of ads. For example, it will have its own research department, which will have investigated both the likely level of demand for the client's product and the relative impact of different advertising approaches. It may well have a department specialising in the design of packaging and of point-of-sale display material.

Running ancillary services costs money. In the palmy days of the Fifties and Sixties, when the ad industry in Britain was mushrooming, big agencies would supply clients with the extras for free. Nowadays fees are normally charged for them, but a big-spending client still has first call on the services of all his agency's various specialists. It can be assumed that in some cases where the account is particularly valuable to the agency, and the latter is not too certain of being able to keep it, the client will be able to pressure it into doing gratis various things it might prefer to charge for.

By the same token it can be assumed that in some cases agencies work in effect for less than the official rate of commission. This happens when a strong client is able to pressure a weak agency into rebating to the client some of the commission it is entitled to. The evidence that this sometimes happens is all hearsay, since rebating is never acknowledged to take place. It is in fact prohibited under the rules applied by the media bodies which grant recognition to agencies.

The last sentence needs some explanation. The bodies referred to include the Newspaper Publishers Association, the Newspaper Society, the Periodical Publishers Association, and the Independent Television Companies Association. Each has certain rules with which agencies must comply if they are to be 'recognised' and hence eligible for commission. Many of the rules are concerned with the agency's financial security, for another of the oddities about the organisation of advertising is that, although all their business is conducted on behalf of advertisers, agencies are treated financially as principals. That means that they are responsible for payment of the debts incurred in placing advertisements even when—and this is by no means unknown—their client goes broke without paying for them.

Under the rules only a recognised agency, then, is entitled to buy advertising space and airtime at a discount, other purchasers are not. An advertiser, in other words, who pays £1,000 to a newspaper via an agency (of which the agency keeps £150) will still have to pay £1,000 if he elects to deal direct with the newspaper without employing an agency. In theory there is thus nothing to be gained by not going through an agency.

As often happens in this wicked world, however, theory and practice are not entirely the same thing, and a certain amount of bending of the rules does take place whereby advertisers can dispense with a conventional agency and yet keep part of what would be the agency's commission. This happens through the use of a recently established type of company known as a media broker. Media brokers are an interesting addition to the fauna of Adland, and we shall come back to them in a later chapter, but they are as yet only a minor species.

The media broker specialises in buying advertising space and time and performs this function either for a full service agency or for an advertiser. Some media brokers have in fact the status of agencies, even though they do not create advertisements or TV commercials, and are entitled to commission. The theory is that when they work direct for advertisers whatever part of the commission they do not keep is spent on creative services, also available from specialist companies, so that the client pays out as much as he would do if employing an agency. In practice, as we have said, it is an open secret that this is not always true.

The observant reader may be wondering whether the habit of some agencies, referred to earlier, of charging fees instead of commission is not also against the rules. The answer is no, provided the fee is no smaller than the commission would be, so that there is effectively no rebate by agency to client, however they decide to regulate their financial relationship.

Another way of bending the rules is for an advertiser to operate his own house agency. The IPA frowns on this, but it is up to the media whether to grant such an agency recognition—and commission. No difficulty was ever experienced in this respect by the most famous of house agencies, Lintas (an acronym of Lever International Advertising Service), which was originally set up as a Unilever subsidiary to handle all the giant group's brands. It is noteworthy that over the years Unilever has reduced its equity share in Lintas, although it retains a majority, and has also drastically reduced the agency's share of the group's advertising accounts. Lintas now competes for Unilever business like any other agency. The fact that such a huge advertiser should find its needs are catered for more efficiently by independent, competing agencies helps to explain why such a lot of these are still alive and kicking. (Since Lintas was put on a comparable footing with other agencies the IPA has admitted it to membership.)

Advertising agencies are, as they are fond of repeating for the benefit of their clients and potential clients, dedicated to the aim of selling. What they less often emphasise is that the first thing they are out to sell is themselves—to those same clients and potential clients. In the agency business, more than most others, reputation is crucially important. Agencies' reputations wax and wane because of a number of factors, some tangible but others much less so. Personalities are important, so is the style of advertisements produced. Organisational structure can count for a lot, as can business efficiency. But the first thing anyone in the industry wants to know about an agency is entirely quantifiable: how much does it bill?

The word 'billings' refers to the amount of clients' money spent annually through the agency. It is not, of course, the same thing as the agency's income, which is a very much smaller amount. Most agencies, however, are rather coy about disclosing their incomes while eager to tell the world about their billings. The reason is that a company's annual income is a precise figure which it is not easy to lie about, unless one is both unscrupulous and imprudent. Billings are easier to inflate without actually lying. This happens in several ways, but the main one is the now normal practice of 'grossing up' fees.

'Grossing up' means pretending that the fee is a 15 per cent commission on media advertising expenditure and calculating what that expenditure would have been, i.e. multiplying by six and two thirds. Thus a fee of £15,000 for, say, helping to develop a new product (an area of activity which big agencies are frequently involved in) would be grossed up to £100,000, and this would be included in total annual billings, as communicated to, and printed by, the trade press as part of the regular end-of-year league table of agency performance. These figures are read avidly both by all agencies and by advertisers, even though everyone is aware of the pitfalls in compiling them.

Some agencies jack up their billings figures by including expected annual spending figures for accounts which they have in fact only just acquired and forgetting to subtract those for accounts they have lost. Furthermore, when the official cash value of accounts and their real value diverge, there is a strong suspicion that it is the larger (official) sum which is often included. Such discrepancies occur when, by successful bargaining, the agency is able to buy advertising space and time at less than quoted rates, but also when agency and advertiser concur in pretending that more is being spent than is the case. There are quite a few people who are ready to try to boost their business prestige in this way, although clearly it is not true of all agencies at all times.

Another trick some agencies resort to in order to increase their billings is to include the grossed-up fee income of separate subsidiaries, such as sales promotion and public relations firms. Again not all agencies do this, so if you're interested in comparing the performance of two agencies you have the problem of determining whether they are using comparable methods for calculating their billings. Some gross up even their expenses, i.e. the price, chargeable to the advertiser, of artwork and TV production, others do not.

A final pitfall is that when two or more agencies are in common ownership they may choose to present their billings separately or together. There are a number of agency groups which have offices throughout Britain, and their rank in the league table looks very different according to whether they follow one or the other practice.

Is there any way of verifying the billings figures issued by agencies? In the long term, yes. They have to deposit trading records with Companies House like any other firm. In the short term the answer is also yes, but only up to a point. Independent figures for agency billings can be derived from the reports of advertising expenditure compiled by Media Expenditure Analysis Ltd (MEAL). These reports monitor spending according to brand names and are designed primarily as a service to the advertiser wanting to know whether his competitors are devoting more or less money than he is to promoting their products. An agency's own billings figures are sometimes very different from what MEAL shows it to have spent, but the discrepancy is often to be accounted for by one of two perfectly legitimate reasons: (1) MEAL monitors only television and the main press media, leaving out most provincial papers and most periodicals as well as posters, radio, cinema, etc.; (2) expenditure is calculated at card (i.e. official) rates and takes no account of the wheeling and dealing which results in newspapers and TV companies selling much of their space and time at cut rates.

So as agencies jostle for position in the billings pecking order, it is not always easy to discern which is really growing faster than its neighbours. But some facts are beyond dispute—for instance that half of the top ten, as of the top twenty, agencies in the UK are American-owned and that by far the biggest agency ever since the end of the Second World War has been J. Walter Thompson. In 1975 it billed nearly £42 million, about £10 million ahead of the runner-up, Masius Wynne-Williams. In the next few chapters we'll look at these and some other interesting agencies.

WHERE NIGHTINGALES SING 4

J. Walter Thompson—JWT, as it is universally known in Adland—is a firm of such markedly British character that it is difficult to remember that it is a wholly owned subsidiary of a New York agency. Things were not always thus. JWT's London office was originally opened in 1899, though it didn't amount to much until the 1930s, and was run by a series of Americans for nearly half a century. Its original claim to fame was that it was the first agency to import modern methods of market research into Britain from the United States, where the parent company was already strong on them.

An American cartoon of the early Thirties showed a man at the door of a house saying: 'The J. Walter Thompson company would like to know if you are happily married.' Research provided the basis for much of the agency's British advertising of that era, including the 'night starvation' campaign for Horlicks, which sprang from the discovery that people slept better on a full stomach. Research also led the agency to advise Lever Brothers to market soap through grocers instead of, as previously, chemists' shops. The British Market Research Bureau, a JWT subsidiary, was formed into a separate company in 1933, becoming one of the first firms of its kind in this country.

The first non-American to head JWT London was Colonel Douglas Saunders, who became managing director in 1935 and chairman from 1946 to 1959. Saunders was not only an Englishman, he was a gentleman and indeed something of a snob. Under him JWT became increasingly British and increasingly gentlemanly. This was largely because Saunders was one of the first London agency bosses to make a deliberate policy of recruiting university graduates. Given the educational patterns of those days, the inevitable consequence was that a high proportion of its executives were from upper middle-class backgrounds. And thus there developed the legend of JWT as a home of Old Etonians with carnations in their button holes and as a lovely place to work if only your father could afford to send you there.

The legend—well, perhaps legend is the wrong word, since there was originally a lot of truth in it—was powerfully reinforced by JWT's move at the end of the war to its present headquarters at 40 Berkeley Square. Before the war it had been domiciled at Bush House and its wartime staff found temporary premises at Watford and elsewhere. But for the last 30 years it has been difficult to separate the image of JWT from its beautiful Mayfair surroundings.

When the agency grew too big for No. 40, it expanded into Berger House next door and Hill Street, round the corner. A proposal to move to Holborn was turned down because, say the wags, that would would have been too far from the Guards Club and the Cavalry Club, not to mention good hairdressers for the lady members of the staff.

This image of social superiority applied principally to the account handling side of the agency. At this point we shall have to digress for a moment or two to explain something about ad agency organisation. All agencies have their own little organisational idiosyncrasies, but in general they all employ three main categories of advertising professionals: creative, media buying and account handling.

The creatives—a pretentious, jargon word but there is unfortunately no substitute—are divided into copywriters and art directors. The latter term is also pretentious jargon and refers to people who a few years ago used to be known as visualisers. Creatives are the actual ad-makers, they write the slogans and the captions and the TV scripts and decide what the pictures should look like. Up to the Sixties copywriters and art directors usually worked apart from each other and were organised into separate copy and art departments, but in recent years the usual practice has become to team the two kinds of specialist up with each other in an effort to produce ads in which the visual and verbal components will be integrated from the outset.

Heading the creative department is a creative director, whose function is not so much to be creative, despite his title, as to supervise the creative efforts of others. Then there are lesser hierarchs, creative supervisors in JWT terminology, though other agencies call them creative group heads, who combine administrative and creative functions. Creative, please note, is used here in its technical sense, meaning of or pertaining to the creation of advertisements, not original and/or artistic.

The media department is concerned with deciding when and where the ads go—which newspapers on which days, which TV stations at which hours and so on and so forth—and with negotiating the price to be paid. There are media planners who work out the schedule (as the list of whens and wheres for any campaign is called) and media buyers who do the actual haggling. There is a media director with beneath him a hierarchy of numerate people who tend to be happier with graphs than with ads but who know precisely the cost per thousand viewers of buying a 30-second spot at 8 pm on Thames Television or how many housewives under 30 are likely to read next Friday's *Manchester Evening News*.

Account handlers do not form a separate department of their own. They are the agency's tick-tack men (or occasionally women, but less often so than in the creative department). They liaise between the client and the agency staff working on that client's account, i.e. the creatives and media people and the various other specialists, such as those in the research and TV production departments, who are to be found in a big agency though not in a small one. The account handler is himself a generalist rather than a specialist, and he comes in several sizes, of which the biggest is called account director.

The account director is responsible for the agency's total handling of a client's business. It is he who will take charge of the presentation to a client of a new campaign. It is to him that a client's complaints will be addressed whether they concern creative, research or any other aspects of the account. The account director is likely to have more than one client to look after, but smaller sizes of account handler, to wit the account supervisor and the account executive (known at JWT as the representative), are there to back him up.

Are account handlers necessary? In the past a number of agencies have talked about doing without them, on the grounds that it is better for clients to deal direct with the specialists who are actually making and placing their ads than to have their instructions and criticisms filtered through a protective human layer. Creatives often bitch about the weak account man who comes rushing to tell them that the client wants the copy changed and who fails to put to the client their arguments as to why it should stay as it is. Some small agencies have indeed tried to do without account handlers, but as soon as an agency gets to any size it finds that the liaison job is just too important and too time-consuming to be left to people who are preoccupied with other matters, whether they be writing more ads or working out a media schedule.

In fact most of the board directors of most agencies are also account directors, though not every account director is on the board. It is the account handlers who, by the nature of their work, develop the closest ties with the clients, and this tends to give them the most clout within the agency, since without clients there is no agency. Keeping clients happy is their business. In one case that used to mean sexually servicing the wife of a certain client at the latter's request, but nowadays it normally means displaying a high degree of understanding of marketing conditions generally and of the client's business in particular. That being so, it is not surprising that there is a good deal of job-switching between the account handling side of agencies and the marketing departments of manufacturing companies. An agency account director is quite likely to have started off as a brand manager in a big packaged goods firm. The marketing director of such a firm is just as likely to have spent some time working in an agency.

Keeping clients happy, however, is not simply a matter of

mutual professional understanding. The social rapport or lack of it also counts. Not so very long ago it used to count for a great deal more in dealing with British businessmen than it does now. In the days when much of British industry was run by men of the Colonel Saunders stamp, men to whom breeding meant more than—or at least as much as—brains, it paid for an agency to employ account handlers with the right social background.

Certainly JWT was by no means alone in the early post-war years in hiring well-bred young men, but other gentlemanly agencies have failed to maintain their positions near the top of the tree, whereas JWT has stayed right at the top. Its success has not been due only, or even primarily, to gentlemanliness, but gentlemanliness has played its part. As one senior executive of a client company said, 'Their concern for the client's comfort is paramount. They take you to the agency doors to say goodbye, and for a big meeting they're waiting at the doors when you arrive. Because of their blue blood they keep clients happy. After all, how can a client be rude to a gentleman? And in times of economic uncertainty what could be more reassuring than establishment figures telling you everything is all right?'

The upper-class image is not broken by the personality of the agency's present managing director, John Lindesay-Bethune, the Old Etonian heir of the Earl of Lindsay. But there is no reason to doubt that Lindesay-Bethune's success has depended more on brains than breeding. And breeding is certainly no part of the career history of his predecessor Denis Lanigan (who was managing director for ten years) or of JWT group chairman John Treasure, both grammar school products, though well-spoken ones.

John Treasure merits a few paragraphs to himself both because he typifies JWT's real strength, which for a long time now has lain in its intellectual rather than its social resources, and also because he has become so well known as a spokesman for the ad industry that the label of 'Mr Advertising' sticks naturally to him.

John Treasure, born in Monmouthshire in 1924, trained

as an economist and started his career in fact as a university lecturer in economics. He first got involved in the ad industry as a part-timer, doing research for JWT's British Market Research Bureau, to help him support himself while reading for his doctorate at Cambridge. His thesis was on 'Problems of the British Export Trade'. What had started as a sideline grew to interest him more and more, and in 1952 he joined BMRB, becoming its managing director five years later. In 1960 he joined the board of the agency itself as research and marketing director.

This was at the invitation of Tom Sutton, an ebullient German Jew who had been installed as managing director of JWT in 1959 with the object of shaking the English gentlemen there out of their complacency. This Sutton proceeded to do with gusto, though stories of a great purge of effete old-school-tie-wearers were much exaggerated. 'If he put Old Etonians up against the wall,' quips Lindesay-Bethune, 'the bullets must have missed me.' Sutton's watchword was 'business discipline', a concept somewhat foreign to many agencies in the fat Fifties when all they needed to do was wine and dine clients at the right restaurants while the general expansion of advertising looked after the billings.

Sutton left for New York in 1966, and the chairman of the London agency, Bill Hinks, who had succeeded Colonel Saunders, retired shortly afterwards. As part of the changing of the guard Treasure became chairman and remained so until 1975. In that year he moved up to the new position of group chairman with authority over the main agency and its several old and new subsidiaries, including BMRB, Lexington Public Relations, Lansdowne Marketing (specialising in both sales promotion and advertising), Contract Advertising (specialising in small accounts) and agencies devoted respectively to pharmaceutical, financial and recruitment advertising. In effect he remained what he had been, boss of JWT's UK operations and vice-chairman of the New York parent company.

As chairman (whether of the agency or the group), Treasure has always been chiefly concerned with external relations and the long-term future both of JWT and of the advertising business as a whole, leaving day-to-day administration to others. He has made many speeches, written many articles, talked to many important people. Talking to important people is easy for a chairman of JWT, which has a tradition of entertaining groups of high-powered industrialists and politicos in its Hill Street dining room.

He was one of the first senior advertising executives explicitly to welcome the advent of the consumerist movement which many others in the industry feared like the plague. 'In the advertising business the more checks and balances we have the better,' said Treasure in his quiet, urbane, rational-sounding voice with the slight and engaging Welsh lilt. He is such an obviously rational man that it comes as a surprise to hear him express the opinion that there may be something in astrology—this while musing on the possibility that his character may have been influenced by being born on the cusp between two zodiacal months. But perhaps this willingness to consider even nonsense seriously is simply another mark of intellectual moderation.

Treasure's somewhat donnish persona is shared by a number of other men at 40 Berkeley Square, in particular two who have, with him, helped to establish JWT's reputation as the most academically clever of London agenices. These are Jeremy Bullmore, the agency's chairman and previously for many years its creative director, and Stephen King, who heads its research side. Both Bullmore and King are in their mid-40s, both were educated at Harrow, where they were classmates. Both have hammered away in print and speech at certain shared ideas about their trade, such as that it is not what admen think they have put into an ad that counts but what the consumer gets out of it.

This sounds simple and obvious enough, but if it is a truism it is one often ignored by agencies which are reluctant to check the communicative effects of their flashes of creative inspiration. It should be remembered that people who write ads tend to be younger, richer and better read than most of the people who see them, and their sense of humour may be very different.

To take just one example, which Bullmore likes to cite,

JWT some years ago made an experimental commercial for Polo Mints. It showed a cyclist wobbling about on his machine and explained that the poor fellow's troubles were due to 'mint deficiency'. Research carried out by the agency indicated that a majority of people to whom the commercial was shown failed to see the joke and took the spoof perfectly seriously. The commercial went no farther.

Another JWT belief, expressed most forcibly in Stephen King's book *Developing New Brands*, is in the overriding importance of brand personality. This phrase is, of course, a metaphor for the bundle of thoughts and attitudes consumers may have regarding any brand, but it is a metaphor which JWT researchers have tried to take as literally as possible. Regularly groups of housewives are asked to describe what kind of person they imagine a given brand to be. Respondents talk fluently about such products as Persil—seen by some as a happy contented sort, by others as rather dull—and Andrex. The latter, reports King, is thought of as 'reliable, dainty, clean-living, domesticated, family-centred; she radiates niceness and confidence in her ability to manage'.

If you think such games are childish, try asking yourself why you buy any particular brand in preference to another, and whether practical reasons are not inextricably mixed up with emotional ones. In setting its strategy for the advertising of a brand, JWT constructs a T-plan (a methodological device invented by King) specifying which physical characteristics are to be brought to the attention of consumers, which rational arguments and what they are to be made to feel emotionally.

For the very rational, very well-educated men who run JWT are in no doubt about the crucial part played by emotion in buying decisions. And though the agency prides itself on having no single distinctive style of advertising, what it excels at is the soft sell, the mood commercial, the ad designed to capture the consumer's heart. The corollary, as put by one of the agency's critics in the industry, is that 'if you wanted a campaign for a highly competitive new product you wouldn't go to JWT. Nor would you go to them if you wanted to ram home some very precise product advantage.'

The agency might, in contesting the accuracy of that last remark, point to its work for Gillette's GII shaving system, its 1975 TV commercials for which it incorporated a diagrammatic demonstration of the product's *modus operandi*. (The cartridge holds two blades, one behind the other; the second whips off what is left of the hair after it has been cut by the first.) However, where another agency might have built the whole commercial around this demonstration, JWT made it merely incidental to a human interest situation in which an actor looked in the mirror and was lectured by his face, reflected there, on how to treat it.

Among JWT's many campaigns noteworthy for their human interest (another way of saying emotional involvement) have been those for Persil, Oxo, Kodak's Instamatic camera and After Eight chocolates. Persil in one way or the other has always focused on Mum—a dutiful, tender-hearted caring Mum who, in the 'dirt collectors' series of TV commercials, for instance, is incapable of really scolding her mud-caked little boy. Instead she rushes to wash his soiled clothes, and off he goes again. Sentimental, soppy even, but just sufficiently realistic for actual mums to identify with her. With her help Persil has managed to keep its lead in the washing powder market.

Kodak commercials have also dealt in happy family situations, to be recorded by the Instamatic for the family scrapbook. For Oxo JWT went one better and created a whole fictional family which year after year was seen on the box being nourished by the product. It was a product sales of which had been declining for ten years before JWT was hired, an old-fashioned product which might have been thought to have passed the point of no return. In 1958 it was relaunched as an indispensable part of the life of Katie and Philip, a young and supposedly classless (but vaguely lower-rung professional) fictional couple. Five years later the couple had had a fictional baby, and volume sales of Oxo were up by 35 per cent.

In contrast with the cosiness of the domestic situations created for the preceding three products, advertising for

After Eights, a product which JWT helped Rowntrees to develop, presented from the outset a fantasy picture of upper-class dinner parties in country houses. 'Luxury, unashamed luxury' was the original punch line in the commercials, which were not, of course, addressed to the upper classes at all but to the *hoi polloi*. Very few, if any, of the viewers could have identified with the characters in these commercials as they could with those in the Persil, Kodak or Oxo slices of life. That didn't prevent After Eights from selling very well, however.

Indeed, when an attempt was made to democratise the chocolates and show them being consumed in *petit bourgeois* surroundings, Oxo country, results appeared to show that this was the wrong approach, and JWT brought back the country house and the fake aristocrats. There is no reason to suppose that anyone took them seriously, but the fact that the advertising of After Eights was understood to be a bit of a joke did not prevent consumers from being persuaded that the stuff did after all have a touch of class. The purist might say Rowntrees and JWT were exploiting snobbery, but Stephen King would say the advertising conferred upon the product an 'added value' which increased the consumer's enjoyment of it.

The best comment on the campaign's success, however, has come from two non-JWT research men, Jack Potter and Mark Lovell, in their book *Assessing the Effectiveness of Advertising*. They wrote, in words which deserve to be pondered by anyone concerned with advertising: 'Contrary to some opinions, we hold that complete credibility is probably a disadvantage, and for the advertising to take hold on the imagination—which it must if the campaign is to be effective—a phenomenon known as "curious disbelief" is desirable. This means that, although the consumer feels that what is claimed for the product may be rather improbable, he is intrigued about it nonetheless and eventually may try it out.'

5 CONFESS AND GROW RICH

The terms 'brand image' and 'brand personality', to all intents and purposes interchangeable, were invented not by J. Walter Thompson but by David Ogilvy, a New York adman who, like a number of other New York admen, has had a huge influence on the agency business in Britain.

He is a New York adman despite the fact that he is not an American and no longer lives in America. He is a Britisher, or as he would say 'an Anglo-Scot', and lives in a French chateau. But the agency which it was his principal achievement to build up is in New York, and it was there that he spent his most productive years. Like J. Walter Thompson in New York, it is the centre of an international network of agencies. But the London end of Ogilvy's business was acquired, unlike JWT's, by takeover. Taken over, one after the other, were the two British agencies which had financed his New York debut in 1948, Mather and Crowther and S. H. Benson.

Both these firms were formerly among the top five British agencies. In 1960, it is worth recalling, these five (with their approximate billings in brackets) were as follows:

1. J. Walter Thompson (£15 million).
2. London Press Exchange (£14½ million).
3. S. H. Benson (£11 million).
4. Colman Prentis and Varley (£9½ million).
5. Mather and Crowther (£9 million).

All the above companies, with the exception of JWT, were British-owned. All, with the exception of JWT, have since been taken over; all are now American-owned. In place of

Mathers and Bensons there is now a single Ogilvy Benson and Mather agency, which in 1975 ranked fifth in the billings table, after JWT, Masius Wynne-Williams, McCann-Erickson and the Saatchi Compton group.

David Ogilvy, now in his sixties, became one of advertising's international stars by a roundabout, picaresque route. As a young man in the Thirties he worked, after being sent down from Oxford, as a cook in a Paris hotel and a door-to-door salesman in Scotland before becoming a copywriter at Mather and Crowther, which agency was run by his elder brother Francis. It was one of London's oldest agencies, having been founded in 1850. It was a family-owned business presided over by three generations of Mathers, but Francis Ogilvy was in effective control of it for 30 years (barring wartime service) until his untimely death from cancer in 1964 at the age of 60. Like his younger brother he was a clever, humorous man, a good copywriter and a strong personality.

According to an old friend of both of them, David differed from Francis chiefly in being somewhat harder and more calculating. He was, believes the same friend, bent on emulating and indeed surpassing his elder brother's success, and this may have been one of the motives which prompted him to set up his own agency in New York in 1948. He had left Mathers for the States in 1939 to work first for George Gallup's research firm and later for himself as a tobacco farmer in Pennsylvania. When he did decide to move to Madison Avenue (the advertising agency district of Manhattan) it was with the enthusiastic support of Francis, who had long before predicted that the British would one day invade the American advertising market.

Francis got together with his friend, the late Bobby Bevan, head of Bensons and another charismatic figure in London's Adland, to finance David's new venture, which was called Ogilvy Benson and Mather. Later, however, Bensons dropped out, and the name was changed to Ogilvy and Mather, under which name the New York agency still operates. But though it was backing from London which enabled David to get started, his meteoric rise in the highly competitive world of American advertising was due entirely to his entrepreneurial ability, copywriting flair and—above all—the panache with which he set about publicising himself.

It should be added that to be the one aristocratic-looking, pipe-smoking, elegantly spoken Limey among the fast-talking Brooklyn-accented hucksters of Madison Avenue was, in those days at any rate, a by no means negligible asset when it came to impressing potential clients. The story of how David Ogilvy took his agency in a few short years into the big league of US advertising deserves a book to itself, and indeed it has one, the boss's own best-selling *Confessions of an Advertising Man*, first published in 1963.

This book, considered a 'must' for all aspiring copywriters, is highly readable—provided, that is, you can stand the overpowering odour of self-congratulation. In a recent interview, Ogilvy himself admitted that it was egotistical and that it was 'a barefaced new business pitch, written for no other purpose'. Agency pitches, it should be said, are never strong on modesty even in Britain, let alone America. The book remains influential, however, because of the coherent set of rules it contains on how to make ads.

Perhaps surprisingly for the prophet of the brand image, most of these rules are concerned with the rational, rather than emotional, appeal of advertising. According to this code, ads should be informative, they should make a precise sales promise, they should not be obscure nor indulge in art for art's sake nor attempt to entertain rather than to sell. The ideal ad, like the one Ogilvy wrote for Rolls-Royce, carries a lot of words ('The more you tell the more you sell,' commented the master) under an imaginative but informative headline, in this case 'At 60 miles an hour the loudest noise in this new Rolls-Royce comes from the electric clock'.

Ogilvy's rules, be it noted, are rules for press advertising, not TV; the book was written before TV became the preponderant medium for Ogilvy's clients. They do not explain all of the master's own bright ideas; for instance, the success of one of his most famous ads, for the Hathaway Shirt company, has been universally attributed to the fact that he put an eyepatch on the male model wearing the shirt, which device may not be intended as entertainment but comes uncommonly near it. Further, the rules appear to be in contradiction with a speech by David Ogilvy which predated the book and in which he said that he was astonished how many manufacturers 'believe that women can be persuaded by logic and argument to buy one brand in preference to another'.

In his book Ogilvy laid it down, by contrast, that 'the consumer is not a moron, she is your wife'. Which, *pace* Mrs Ogilvy, is, of course, a *non sequitur*. But the main thing to be said about the rules is that, although many of them constitute perfectly sensible advice, at least for the advertising of certain kinds of products, there is little about them that is original. Ogilvy was drawing upon a body of received advertising wisdom which went back to the teaching of a famous American copywriter of the early part of the century named Claude Hopkins.

Hopkins, too, wrote a book, published in 1923, which he had the temerity to call *Scientific Advertising*. Its contention—that 'advertising in some hands has reached the status of a science'—is reminiscent of a remark of Dr Johnson's nearly two centuries earlier to the effect that advertising had reached such a pitch of perfection that it could scarce be improved upon. In retrospect both statements appear slightly comical, but Hopkins was at least talking about his own experience. Much of this was in mail order advertising, where the effectiveness of any ad could be precisely measured by the number of coupon responses it elicited.

It was Hopkins who first asserted, for example, that humour had no place in advertising because 'people don't patronise a clown'. He also declared that 'fine writing is a distinct disadvantage. So is unique literary style. They take attention away from the subject.' Ogilvy enthusiastically endorsed both opinions.

David Ogilvy's 'Confessions' have some relevance to the kind of advertising which is turned out by Ogilvy Benson and Mather in London today and which is very different from the work for which Mather and Crowther was famous before the merger. This deal was aimed, as far as Francis Ogilvy was concerned, at ending the control of his agency by the Mather and Crowther families. Francis died shortly before the merger was consummated and the family holdings reduced to half the equity of the new company, Ogilvy and Mather International. That was in 1965, and the following year the company went public in New York. The old Mathers was, in the words of a former employee, 'the sort of agency where, if someone thought of a marvellous creative idea which research proved to be wrong, you buried the research'.

According to James Benson, chairman of the London agency (no relation, incidentally, of the Benson family whose name is perpetuated in that of the company), agencies can be arranged—and clients do so arrange them—along a rational-emotional spectrum depending on the character of the ads they turn out and on their general approach to advertising problems. In the early Sixties Mathers was generally considered to be at the extreme emotional end of the spectrum, marvellous at making mood commercials for Players cigarettes (in an age when cigarette advertising was allowed on TV)—loving couples, sunlight through the trees and stuff like that—but a bit short on marketing expertise and not too good at business administration.

No agency, says Benson, should be happy about being stuck at either end of the spectrum, but if it has to be perceived as being near one end or the other, it's the rational, businesslike end which the majority of clients prefer. And that is where OBM stands now; in the jargon of the trade it is thought of as a 'marketing' agency rather than a 'creative' agency. One client specifies: 'They're a very strategic agency, and their creative execution is a good match for the underlying strategic thinking. But it's often lacking in what people call creativity, that is high filmic values, bizarre situations, fantasy.'

The result is that, where Mathers was an agency which attracted a huge amount of copywriting talent—half the creative directors in London seem to have worked there once—OBM is not an agency which today's more self-consciously 'creative' copywriters and art directors would want to work for. That's a big change of brand image for any agency to undergo in a decade. It started when, as part of a new publicly owned American company, struggling to compete with established New York giants, the agency had to engage in a much more deliberate pursuit of growth and profit.

'Before then,' as one director recalls, 'we had just ridden our luck. The agency was run by a bunch of goodhearted chaps who never had to worry about growth. It was our good fortune that when harder times came we had businesslike people in charge.'

Chief among them was Jimmy Benson, first as managing director, later as chairman. Benson, an economist by training like John Treasure, makes an interesting contrast with JWT's boss. Though, like Treasure, a man of obvious charm and intellect, he eschews the limelight and nourishes no aspirations to perform the role of public spokesman for the ad industry. Born in 1926, Benson is the author of four books about the war, including *Above Us The Waves*, based on his experiences in midget submarines. He took a post-war degree at Cambridge, then joined Kemsley Newspapers, where he became research manager and a client of Francis Ogilvy, who brought him into the agency as research director in 1959. He did not hide his view that the creative side in Mathers had grown disproportionately strong. 'The danger of an agency which is creative-dominated,' he said after becoming chairman, 'is that the creative people want to choose the strategies, at which they're often not very good.'

The difference in emphasis is reflected in the personality difference between the present creative director, Dan Ellerington, and his predecessor, Stanhope Shelton, who retired in 1968. Shelton was an inspirational, seat-of-the-pants man, loved and admired but a terrible show-off. Ellerington is analytical rather than inspirational and, like Ogilvy, has no use for ads which are not clearly dedicated to selling things. His detractors accuse him of exercising too rigid a censorship over the output of the agency's different creative groups.

Among campaigns which exemplify the Ellerington approach at its best are those for Comfort fabric conditioner and Crisp 'n Dry cooking oil. Commercials for both are essentially demonstrations, making use of visual gimmicks, what OBM calls 'advertising properties', to ram the product benefit home. In the case of Comfort it is a glass-sided drawer which allows the viewer to see how springy are clothes washed in the product. With Crisp 'n Dry, the gimmick is the paper towel on to which freshly fried chips are tipped but which remains free of greasy marks.

Intelligent advertising, but nothing to get excited about. No sign of a Hathaway eyepatch. On the other hand, OBM has impressed the ad industry with its research department's work on the consumer effects of inflation, work which resulted in a series of presentations to clients and prospective clients on the marketing dangers and opportunities presented by the changing economic situation.

In tracing the development of the agency today called Ogilvy Benson and Mather, no reference has yet been made to the influence upon that development of the takeover of the S. H. Benson group in 1971. This is because, in terms of OBM's essential characteristics, the takeover had very little influence. And this is rather an extraordinary thing to have to say since Bensons was a large business, and its main constituent, the Benson agency, was physically merged with Ogilvy and Mather, the combined staffs being accommodated at Brettenham House, next to Waterloo Bridge, home of Mathers since 1935. The truth is that few of the senior Bensons people stayed, or were encouraged to stay, very long at Brettenham House. At the time of the merger O and M had 440 employees and they were joined by 200 Bensonites. Four years later OBM's total staff was back to 440, of whom only about 50 had been with Bensons. No member of the eight-member executive committee responsible for running the agency was a former Bensonite.

The decline and fall of Bensons, one of the historic great names in the London ad agency business, still serves as a dire warning to others in the industry who might be tempted to take their own good fortune for granted. As we have seen, Bensons in 1960 was very near the top of the tree as far as turnover was concerned. In prestige it might well have claimed to rank as number one. It was founded in 1893. In the Twenties and Thirties it became famous above all for its humorous ads, e.g. the shipwrecked man in his pyjamas clinging to a giant seaborne bottle of Bovril, which 'prevents that sinking feeling', and a whole series of still remembered campaigns for Guinness (of which more later). It was known, too, as a nursery of literary talent, including that of the thriller writer Dorothy L. Sayers, who based the setting of her novel *Murder Must Advertise* on the Bensons office.

Several factors were to blame for the company's downfall, and to explain them all in detail would take much more space than is available here. (For those who are interested that job has already been done by its last chairman, the late Micky Barnes, in his autobiography *Ad.*) But they included an unwise pattern of expansion, a prolonged and disabling series of management upheavals and, most important, the vulnerability concomitant upon having become in the last few years of its life a public company with large unrealised property assets in the shape of its office building in Kingsway.

Only a handful of London agencies are public companies, though some others, notably JWT and OBM, are subsidiaries of other companies which are themselves public. Many more might have taken the plunge and gone for a Stock Exchange quotation if it had not been for the example of Bensons and, shortly before it, another agency called Dorland Advertising. The latter, with its subsidiary W. S. Crawford, had had the misfortune to fall into the hands of the young financier John Bentley, one of the outstanding asset-strippers of the early Seventies, when asset-stripping was all the rage.

Bentley made a killing with Dorlands, the share price of which, he had the good sense to realise, greatly undervalued its property holdings. Within three short months in spring 1971 Bentley had bought and sold Dorlands, an operation which caused howls of rage and pain from other admen, who declared *ad nauseam* that ad agencies, which depended primarily on their human resources, could not be traded in as other firms could without disrupting their whole business. This was true enough, as the departure of some of the Dorland-Crawford executives and accounts showed.

The Dorlands affair thoroughly put the wind up Bensons. Barnes has recorded his surprise that Bentley chose to pick on Dorlands rather than Bensons, where the property assets were even greater. In any case, there were other hungry sharks circling around, and he decided to head for cover. The essence of the ensuing deal was that Rothschilds, acting in concert with Ogilvy, bought the Bensons property for itself and handed the advertising interests over intact to the Brettenham House agency.

Actually, they did not stay quite so intact as the architects of the deal had hoped. As we have seen, a lot of Bensons people left after finding the atmosphere at Brettenham House uncongenial, some of them perhaps because they disliked the tighter discipline, while others may have missed the factional politics which had become such a part of their former lives.

Accounts as well as people left. One of the prime considerations when any two agencies consider getting together is that their account lists should not conflict. This means in simple language that they should not be handling advertising for client companies whose products are in competition with each other. The reason is that advertisers normally refuse to entrust their account to an agency which is already working for a competitor. This unwritten rule is interpreted more or less strictly by different advertisers, according to how worried they are about the possibility of valuable commercial information finding its way via the agency into rival hands—and agencies inevitably get to know a good deal about their clients' business, not merely their advertising plans. In a few rare cases the rule is not applied at all. For instance, the Charles Barker agency was for many years in charge of advertising both the Midland and Barclays banks.

There were very few account conflicts involved in the OBM merger, but more Bensons clients took their business elsewhere than might have been expected. They included such blue chip accounts as Johnnie Walker whisky and British Leyland.

As part of the takeover Ogilvy and Mather International acquired a whole chain of Bensons offices overseas, and OBM found itself master of several subsidiaries which had been part of the Benson group. One, the Harrison Cowley agency, was sold for £431,000, practically half of what had been paid for the Benson group (bar the property), and others were also disposed of. But it kept another agency, Davidson Pearce Berry and Spottiswoode, one of the best of the second division (financially speaking) of agencies, which was to achieve 1975 billings of its own of £11 million. Ex-Bensons men may be forgiven for feeling that their company was flogged off for much less than it was worth.

6 UNCLE JACK AND SUNDRY BEANSTALKS

Number two in the billings table in 1975, as for several years previously, was an agency whose reputation is not dissimilar from the one currently enjoyed by OBM. Masius Wynne-Williams is also reckoned by most people in the business to be stronger on marketing know-how than creative originality. It is, incidentally, usually easier to sum up such reputations than to determine how accurate they are. All big agencies turn out a lot of ads, the quality of which can vary considerably from account to account, whichever set of criteria you take of what makes a good ad.

Masius's reputation is very much wrapped up with that of the man, Jack Wynne-Williams, who ran it on a tight rein for many years until he kicked himself upstairs in 1974 to be international group chairman. The agency is largely his creation, though in a curious reversal of what has come to be thought of as the normal course of advertising events it originated as an American enterprise, the British arm of Lord and Thomas, Claude Hopkins' employer. When Albert Lasker, who owned Lord and Thomas, retired in the early Forties, he took the agency name with him. His business in the States was inherited by Foote Cone and Belding; in London it was bought by another American, the late Mike Masius, and became Masius and Fergusson, which name it bore until 1964.

Wynne-Williams, a big man who in his youth was an amateur boxer, joined Masius in 1951 after a career in selling. He had been an area sales manager for Kensitas cigarettes, managing director of Pepsodent and for five years manager of Mappin's department store in Brazil. He is not an intellectual, and his agency does not go in for much intellectualising à la J. Walter Thompson. Nor, despite its agreeable location in Mayfair's St James's Square, is it known for JWT's social airs and graces. Masius men are generally thought of as a hard-nosed bunch, specialising in down-to-earth advertising for mass consumption goods like Colgate's toothpaste, Ribena, Pal dogfood, and Wilkinson Sword razor blades.

Wilkinsons is perhaps a good example of the Masius hard sell in practice. For more than a dozen years the advertising approach was kept substantially the same, with TV commercials which avoided any human interest and majored on the client's 200-year history of British craftsmanship. This brand image has been pushed through pictures of swords (the company still actually makes them), musical fanfares and voices-over declaiming about 'the name on the world's finest blade'. Pompous, repetitive, not a touch of wit or humour, nothing calculated to attract attention to the copywriters and film-makers involved but, in the opinion of the client, very, very effective.

Nevertheless there are a number of more self-consciously 'creative' agencies which wouldn't have had the nerve to persevere with such a monotonous message for so long. They wouldn't have insisted, as Wynne-Williams did, that 'our creative people don't create for their own amusement'.

It is difficult to speak of Masius without speaking of Uncle Jack, as some of the agency's staffers call him, even though he has now relinquished the chairmanship to Tony Abrahams, the dapper Harrovian (he claims to have fagged at school for JWT's Jeremy Bullmore) who served him for many years as managing director. In his day Wynne-Williams was something of an autocrat. He was also a huge new-business-getter. When he appeared on the scene in 1951 Masius billed less than £1 million, and much of its present turnover comes from clients he signed up in the next dozen years. He never, like so many others, sold out to Madison Avenue, but he did form a close financial association with an American agency, D'Arcy-MacManus. Masius's official name is now in fact Masius Wynne-Williams and

D'Arcy-MacManus, but even in Adland, which is accustomed to some pretty cumbersome names, that is too much of a mouthful for anyone actually to say.

Among those British-owned agencies which did sell out were, as has been mentioned, the London Press Exchange and Colman Prentis and Varley. But their fates were, none the less, very different.

The London Press Exchange, which in 1960 was only a hairbreadth behind JWT in billings, was founded in 1892 as a news agency. (In that, incidentally, it was not unique; France's biggest ad agency group, Havas, also grew out of a news agency.) Like Bensons it put a lot of its energies into developing a chain of subsidiaries overseas; at home too it owned a number of companies outside the main agency.

In 1968 the group had worldwide billings of some £60 million, but in London it was losing ground and had slipped to seventh place in the league table after several of its biggest clients, including Ford cars and Worthington beer, moved to other agencies. The board decided, therefore, that this was the right time to capitalise on its assets and do a deal with one of the big American agencies interested in going international but without an international network of its own.

The partner eventually found was Leo Burnett, a Chicago agency famous for its cowboy ads for Marlboro cigarettes and for the copywriting talent of its eponymous founder. The deal was a complicated one in which Burnett acquired LPE's main London agency and its international network. The British shareholders, about 100 of them, got a lot of money, a minority interest in Burnetts and kept their London operations, other than the main LPE agency, these being reorganised under the group name of Lopex, and including agencies specialising in financial and recruitment advertising as well as Interlink, a well-thought-of full-service agency of the second rank.

The main agency adopted for a short time the unwieldy hyphenated name of Leo Burnett-LPE, but then the LPE was deleted, and the familiar initials disappeared from the map of Adland to the accompaniment of a chorus of moans and groans from that land's older and more patriotic denizens. LPE was seen as the first really big and old-established British agency to fall into American hands—apart, that is, from Mathers, but Mathers was different, since it could with some justice claim David Ogilvy, even in Manhattan, even with American stockholders behind him, as one of its own, as a British boy made good.

The day after the announcement of the Burnett takeover, many of LPE's clients received telegrams from a rival agency's chairman calling upon them to 'support British advertising'. This caused quite a row since at that time, in the spring of 1969, the rules of the Institute of Practitioners in Advertising (the agencies' trade association) still forbade direct solicitation of business, though that particular rule was later to be changed. Some clients did indeed desert the repainted vessel, even though the crew remained virtually the same as when it had been under British ownership, with the same strengths and weaknesses. The only newcomer of any importance was Carl Hixon, who arrived at the St Martin's Lane offices from Chicago in 1970 to take over as creative director for the next five years.

And, oh yes, the apples arrived too. Apples? Yes, the common or orchard variety which Leo Burnett for some reason had adopted as both a favourite fruit and a kind of company trademark. A supply of apples is always to be found at any Burnett office, a harmless eccentricity though not one calculated to affect the agency's reputation one way or another. That reputation is not a specially bright one despite the fact that Burnetts has a good new-business-getting record and has managed to stay near the top of the tree—number seven in 1975.

Not that Burnetts hasn't, like most big agencies, got some successful campaigns to its credit—one might mention Beecham's Aquafresh toothpaste which it launched in 1972 and which had within three years captured 11 per cent of the market—but the kind of thing which is remembered against it is its advertising for Watney's Red beer. This was relaunched in 1970 as the 'Red Revolution' with posters featuring Communist leaders—Mao, Castro and Khrushchev—and would-be thriller commercials featuring a subversive character of ill-defined political motivation. Newspapers thought the campaign made good copy, but other ad agencies considered it facile and ill-conceived. The board of the client company also felt uncomfortable about it, and when a subsequent campaign, based on the rhyme 'Red, that's the best thing you've said', was universally derided, the account left the agency.

More distinguished than the work of its creative staff has been that of its research department under Simon Broadbent, another clever academic, like John Treasure, who has found the commercial world more to his taste. Broadbent, who took his doctorate at London University, in statistics, became a director of LPE before the takeover and is widely respected as an authority on media research, i.e. the job of finding out exactly which and how many people are reading and viewing what and how much attention they are likely to be giving it. His department, following American examples, has evolved a method of classifying consumers according to their 'life style' rather than according to the conventional social categories used in most other research. The 'life style' classification is based on attitude responses to over 200 questions covering a whole variety of topics.

LPE/Burnett has done pretty well under transatlantic control, Colman Prentis and Varley has entirely disappeared. Not even a vestige of its name is left, as with Bensons, to remind anyone of its great days. And yet not so very long ago it was probably the one British ad agency which a large number of non-advertising people had heard of.

CPV's public fame—or perhaps notoriety might be the better word—was gained during the late Fifties when it became the first British ad agency to be hired by a political party. The client in question was the Conservative Party, and CPV's slogan 'Life's better with the Conservatives. Don't let Labour ruin it' helped the Tories to electoral victory in 1959.

The agency was run at that time by Colonel Arthur Varley, who had founded it in 1934 and who had become one of the big names, with Bobby Bevan and Francis Ogilvy, of post-war British advertising. Varley, like Bensons and like LPE, decided to go in heavily for investing in overseas offices. CPV's Italian subsidiary was particularly successful and became for a time the biggest agency in its market. 'This,' he admitted in 1961, 'is an immensely costly business, and of course your home advertising suffers.'

The fact is that no British agency has been able to follow the example of the major American firms in the business and succeed both in building up a big international network of its own and in safeguarding its own home territory. The British advertising market being so much smaller than that of the United States, it seems that a London-based agency just cannot generate sufficient money to compete effectively in both.

At all events, while CPV remained an important force in international advertising it went into a period of decline in Britain, hastened by two major breakaways, out of which grew two new agencies each of which was destined to end up near the top of the tree.

The breakaway is a perpetual hazard to all ad agencies, a result of the fact that an agency's capital equipment exists almost entirely of people. You don't need a palatial set of offices, though that can help; it is possible to run an agency successfully from a hotel room, and that's been done more than once. You don't need a computer to help work out the media schedule, though a number of agencies have invested in computers, not always to their entire satisfaction. But you can't do without people. And the people you can least do without are the ones most highly valued by your clients, whether they be creatives or whether they be account handlers.

It is most often the account director who forms the closest association with the client company, simply because his job is to keep in touch with them, and it is most often, therefore, the account director whom the client will be prepared to follow out of the agency into a new one. However, it has been known for creatives also to wind up having certain accounts 'in their pocket' to the extent that when they broke away, the accounts broke away with them. The most dangerous kind of breakaway is when a whole group walks out of an agency, including all the principal people who service any particular account or accounts, and sets up in business on its own.

'You're only in business', runs the adage, 'as long as you've got the business,' and agency bosses have often learned to their great chagrin that the business they thought they had actually belonged to one or more of their subordinates. Agencies go to great lengths to try to prevent breakaways, precisely because it is so comparatively easy for their best people to set up on their own.

There must be more incentives available more quickly to the talented in agencies than in any other kind of commercial company—directorships, associate directorships, profit-sharing schemes, equity stakes—yet breakaways still happen. It may even be that, in a sense, they are encouraged by the speed with which a bright youngster can earn promotion. It doesn't take long for him to start wondering whether he shouldn't climb another rung and become an agency boss in his own right.

John Hobson is one of the many successful agency men who have climbed that rung. Not everyone who leaves one agency to start another takes any of his employer's business with him. Hobson, when he left CPV in 1955, did—and he took plenty. He was assistant managing director of CPV at the time, with a good reputation as a marketing man, and it was not surprising that some of its business, including Cadbury's Drinking Chocolate, stuck to him. A little later Hobson sold a controlling interest in his new agency to the Ted Bates company, one of the big operators on Madison Avenue, which had tried to take over Masius but been turned down. John Hobson and Partners became Hobson Bates and eventually, after Hobson's retirement, plain Ted Bates.

The Bates agency is known all over the advertising world for three letters—USP. These letters sum up the doctrine of Rosser Reeves, former chairman of Bates and one of the foremost philosophers of modern advertising. The word 'philosopher' may strike you as facetious. Perhaps it is, but the companion word 'philosophy' is used as a piece of advertising jargon without any facetiousness at all being intended. Most agencies will tell you with a straight face that their 'philosophy' of advertising is thus and thus. They mean their theory of how advertising works and how it should be constructed. Most respectable agencies, especially in America, would be ashamed to be seen without a philosophy, but not all philosophies are quite as cut and dried as Reeves's.

USP stands for Unique Selling Proposition, and those who work for Bates know that every product has got to have one. Bates, which told America that Colgate toothpaste 'cleans your breath while it cleans your teeth', is a hard sell agency (Rosser Reeves was never a great man for mood and image) and it's probably no accident that it was Bates in London which turned out the enormously successful TV advertising for the *Sun* newspaper, full of pace, punch and promise like a really good Petticoat Lane salesman. No sarcasm intended.

Ironically, the *Sun* parted company with Bates as the result of another breakaway, when in 1975 the agency's managing director and creative director, Leon Lerner, walked out to set up on his own. Two million pounds worth of billing went with him, including the *Sun*. His move followed an acrimonious row with chairman Mike English, who accused him of disloyalty. Declared English, known not to be Lerner's best friend, 'If somebody is in charge of a piece of business, his duty is to the agency and he shouldn't abuse his position by putting it in his pocket and walking out with it.' Such invocations of the Goddess Loyalty are common among those whose business interests are being damaged. The attentive reader need hardly have it pointed out to him that if John Hobson had been as great a believer in loyalty as his successor he might never have started the agency of which Mike English became chairman.

But we digress. Let's go back to CPV, which in 1959 suffered another damaging breakaway, when two of its executives, John Pearce and Geoffrey Tucker, left with the Harvey wine account to help start a new agency called Collett Dickenson Pearce and Partners. Tucker went on to other things, including for a time the publicity directorship of the Conservative Party, but Pearce's firm developed in a very interesting way, becoming the biggest of the agencies held by the consensus of copywriting and art-directional opinion to be 'creative'. As has already become apparent, this word is used not only to indicate a specific set of advertising functions but to imply a judgment about the kind of advertisements an agency produces. We shall return to it in a later chapter when we shall consider the validity of such judgments. For the moment let's just mention a few of the campaigns devised by Colletts, as the agency is known, which may be taken as most representative of its style.

Much of its most admired work has been done for Benson and Hedges cigarettes and cigars. One of its earliest TV commercials for B & H Special Filter cigarettes (in the days when cigarette advertising was still allowed on TV) showed a cat burglar who included the gold-coloured packet of the product in his swag. Instead of a lot of superfluous words there was a catchy and distinctive piece of background music. With the help of such films and of beautifully photographed magazine ads with brief, witty captions on the 'gold' theme, the brand had by 1965 crept up to a 40 per cent share of the king size tipped cigarette market and by 1968 achieved leadership of the sector.

More recent commercials for B & H cigars (which are permissible on the box) have shown a man choosing a hat to fit the length of his cigar and a railway waiter pulling the communication cord to stop a train so that he can light a customer's cigar in comfort. The films are remarkable for their economy of words and gestures and their clever use of music, by Bach. For Hamlet, another Gallaher brand like B & H, the agency produced a series of humorous commercials showing absurd situations—for instance, a ghost carrying its cigar-smoking head under its arm—with the punch line 'Happiness is a cigar called Hamlet'. Again the music, which viewers have learned to identify with the brand, is by Bach, the *Air on a G String*. Hamlet took the lead in its market in 1972.

Proof of the agency's self-confident—some say arrogant—way of doing things is that early research on the Hamlet advertising indicated a negative reaction by consumers.

Instead of being deterred, Colletts pressed on with its ideas, and eventually the consumers changed their minds. The same, as says the agency's managing director, Frank Lowe, was true of its series of extravagant fantasy ads for Heineken lager ('Heineken refreshes the parts other beers cannot reach'). Other leading admen whose opinion Lowe respects told him, when the campaign started, that this time Colletts had got it wrong. But by the time £500,000 of advertising money had been put behind the brand views had changed. Certainly sales of Heineken (in common with other lagers) moved up sharply. Agencies, declares Lowe, should not be afraid to give public taste a lead.

Another well-known example of the Colletts style is the agency's Hovis campaign, nostalgic films of a bygone age with a boy delivering early morning bread, riding his bicycle over cobbled roads and past thatched cottages, and an old man's voice remembering his youth. Again an original and effective use of music, Dvořák played by a brass band. It is a style in which wit, sensibility and aesthetic refinement are at a premium. These are not characteristics which the dry and uncommunicative Pearce exudes himself, but somehow his agency managed to hire a succession of people who do possess them, including creative director John Salmon and, most notably, Colin Millward, a former CPV art director who is today chairman of the agency (under Pearce, who is chairman of a holding company).

While Colletts and Bates were growing CPV was shrinking. In its empire-building phase it had formed an association with Kenyon and Eckhardt, a large American agency, though not one of the largest. Eventually, in 1973, the Americans acquired financial control. The following year they bought an up-and-coming young agency called French Gold Abbott which was reckoned to have the managerial and creative talents that CPV was now short of. The two were merged, and Messrs French, Gold and Abbott were given control of the new set-up, henceforth called French Gold Abbott Kenyon and Eckhardt—another mouthful, but initiates refer to it simply as FGA. And that was the end of Colonel Varley's heritage.

FGA is one of a handful of recently founded 'hot shops',

to use one of Adland's hip Americanisms, which have done very well in the past few years. But before we take a look at them let's round off our survey of the bigger established agencies with three more firms, all American-owned.

A DAY IN DREAMLAND 7

McCann-Erickson ranked number four in the 1973 and 1974 billings lists and number three in 1975. It's been one of the fastest growing London agencies of the Seventies, the credit for which is probably to be ascribed principally to two people, both now in their early forties—former chairman Phil Geier, an eight-cylinder American hustler who got his reward by being promoted to even greater international responsibilities, and Barry Day, vice-chairman, creative director and one-time speech writer for one-time Prime Minister Edward Heath.

McCanns, started in London in the 1920s with Esso as its first client, is regarded in the business as a tough, aggressive outfit and a hard-working one. It does not live by any special 'philosophy' of advertising, which is ironic in a way, since Barry Day is renowned for his ability to hold forth at a moment's notice on the philosophical (in a non-jargon sense) aspects of his profession.

Day is one of Adland's most accomplished speakers and writers about advertising. He may not be as amusing as JWT's Jeremy Bullmore, who when on form can keep an audience in stitches, but he can dazzle the same audience with a display of verbal agility as he fits advertising fashions and social trends into their appropriate places within the jigsaw which is the 'global village'. The significance of the latter expression is that Day first became well known, when he was at Lintas, as an enthusiastic exponent of the ideas of that expression's author, Marshall McLuhan. The sage of Toronto is given to portentous phrases, and it must be said that some people find Barry Day also a shade too portentous for their taste. But his style sells well. At least it impresses many clients.

For several years Day has expressed his thoughts on advertising in a weekly column in the advertising trade magazine *Campaign*. The column took the form of a review of current campaigns and was signed anonymously 'A Creative Director', but his authorship of it was an open secret. It probably did his reputation a fair amount of good as did, businessmen being what they are, his publicity work for Heath. With his Hampstead home, hip talk and occasional reflections on the social responsibilities of business, not to mention his working-class family background, Day could easily be mistaken at first sight for an armchair socialist rather than a Conservative, but in his case, as in Heath's, grammar school and Oxford led to an enthusiastic acceptance of capitalism.

He himself puts McCann's recent success down to the advantages of having a stable team at the top. Its other members are, apart from the now departed Geier, Nigel Grandfield, who succeeded Geier as chairman, and Ann Burdus, the agency's other vice-chairman and research chief, a cool, clever and good-looking lady who can be considered, despite her relative youth, as the doyenne of adwomen. (In passing it should be emphasised that whenever this book refers to admen, the term normally embraces adwomen.)

Day is one of those creative directors who prides himself on the fact that his agency's output has no identifiable style, in the way that Colletts for instance has, but treats every account as a different problem to be solved by, if necessary, different means. Certainly there is little in common between McCann's TV campaigns for, say, Tetley tea bags (cartoon characters demonstrating the efficacy of the bags' perforations) and Martini.

The Martini campaign is a classic of soft sell and brand imagery. It compares interestingly with the Smirnoff advertising which was described in Chapter 1. Both liquor brands plumped for fantasy, but where Smirnoff's press ads have their tongue in their cheek the Martini films are not played for laughs at all.

Both the Smirnoff and Martini campaigns took perceived attributes of their products and exaggerated them. With Smirnoff it was potency, with Martini sophistication. Martini was largely a woman's drink, and women were already half-convinced, pre-campaign research showed, that it was smart, sophisticated, international. But advertising was confronted with a new mass market of young or youngish people much more affluent than their parents had been but uncertain as to how their money should be spent. Crawfords, the agency which handled the product before 1970, had tried to solve the uncertainty problems by dubbing Martini 'the what do you want to drink drink' and by showing the consumer as an elegant lady accompanied by a uniformed chauffeur. This was snob appeal of a rather crude kind.

McCanns decided that to pitch the product directly at the woman drinker in this way was bad marketing strategy; it would be better to position it as a 'his and hers' drink. 'You'll never make it masculine,' says Day, 'but it must be something a man won't be ashamed to be seen with.' A test commercial made in 1970 focused on a glamorous young couple; later it was groups of young people who were seen riding horses into the sunset, skiing, speedboating, travelling in multi-coloured balloons to a romantic castle top.

'We offer the consumer a dream world she knows isn't true,' says Day, 'but she likes to dream and the dream comes back into the product, and maybe it's just a bit true.' Which is as eloquent a summing-up of the way a lot of advertising works as anyone is likely to produce.

Absolutely vital to the advertising effect was the dreamy song, specially composed by Chris Gunning. 'We wanted'—Day again—'romantic music but still modern. We were aiming at the middle ground, talking not necessarily to young people but to people who were young at heart. So it mustn't date. We built the thing to last.'

The words of the song are worth quoting:

Try a taste of Martini,
The most beautiful drink in the world,
It's the bright one, the right one.

There's much more to the world than you guess,
And you taste it the day you say yes
To the bright taste, the right taste
Of Martini. . . .

'The right one'. Yes, indeed. 'We are,' observes Barry Day, 'selling reassurance.'

McCann-Erickson is a very big agency in the States and internationally in its own right. But it is still only one part of an even bigger ad agency group called Interpublic which, with total world billings in 1975 of around $1,000 million, ranks as the world's biggest, ahead even of J. Walter Thompson and the Japanese giant Dentsu. Since Interpublic is a holding company, however, rather than an operating company, one rarely hears it mentioned. In this country, for instance, McCanns operates completely independently of Wasey Campbell-Ewald, the other big Interpublic agency, and they figure separately in all the billings lists.

Waseys (originally Erwin Wasey) opened its London office in 1919 at a ceremony attended by President Woodrow Wilson. After the Second World War it absorbed two other Interpublic agencies, Jack Tinker and Pritchard Wood, and subsequently underwent a difficult period of organisational restructuring, during which it was divided into four 'collaboratives', which were in effect self-contained mini-agencies. The objective was to avoid having a large bureaucratic structure and to strengthen the standing of creatives, traditionally overshadowed by the account handling side at Waseys, by giving them a share in the running of each collaborative. Alas, the experiment was not a success; decentralisation was judged to have gone too far, at the expense of consistent managerial standards, and the four-in-one system was abandoned.

The agency's reputation in Adland was a somewhat dull and unadventurous one, which rendered all the more interesting the 1975 appointment as chairman and chief executive of Colin Goodson, a wise-cracking iconoclast educated at the London School of Economics who had originally joined Waseys as a research man. Illustrative of his mischievous sense of humour is the following incident, which occurred some years ago, when he was managing director.

Walking around the agency's Paddington offices one afternoon with a visiting journalist, Goodson learned from a chance conversation that a couple of executives had spent their lunchtime with their secretaries, celebrating the birthday of one of them. By a further chance he subsequently espied one of the two executives, an account handler, in a corridor. He hailed him and introduced the journalist falsely as an emissary from Interpublic headquarters in New York, come to check up on the staff's efficiency.

The journalist proceeded, in a phoney American accent, to question the executive on how he spent his time and specifically on what he had done that day, displaying special interest in his lunchtime activities. The executive, nervous but determined to give the right impression of the agency to this nosey 'inspector', said he had lunched with a potential client and, when pressed, even described what business this fictitious lunch companion was in.

Meanwhile Goodson had to turn aside to disguise his mirth. The journalist thanked the executive gravely and restrained his own merriment until he was safely inside his host's private office. The lie, if that is what it should be called, was not held against the executive, who Goodson guessed had acted from an honourable motive, and indeed he later promoted him. The author can vouch for the accuracy of this anecdote, having himself been the journalist–*agent provocateur* in question.

One cannot leave the subject of Interpublic without some mention of the extraordinary career of the man who set it up, Marion Harper. Famous for his ambition even in the ambitious world of post-war New York advertising, Harper was another research specialist who rose to be boss of his agency, McCann-Erickson. But not content with that, he determined to make himself the head of the world's biggest marketing services organisation. This was to be done not by the painstaking process of acquiring new accounts and establishing new offices but by buying other firms.

After 1948, when Harper got his hands on the reins at McCanns, he rode off hell for leather on the takeover trail. A number of agencies were bought, including Erwin Wasey, the 1963 purchase of which cost $5 million in cash. The strategy was partly based on the hope that separate agencies within the same group would be allowed to handle conflicting accounts which would never have stayed together within one unified agency. To some extent this hope proved justified, although there were clients who took the view that if their competitors' product was handled by any Interpublic agency they would not do business with the new group.

Harper soon came to be dubbed 'Marvel Harper'. His enemies, who grew in number, regarded him as a megalomaniac. He certainly talked as big as he acted, evolving a curious style of speech in which abstraction was heaped upon abstraction. He also spent big; money ran through his hands like water as Interpublic lashed out not only on subsidiaries but on such extras as group offices (over and above those of the individual agencies) in London, France, Germany and Switzerland, a dude ranch in Long Island where Interpublic executives could get rest and recreation, and a collection of company planes.

As the superstructure grew the profits dropped. In 1967, when the group faced a loss of $3 million and the banks were squealing, the six other directors on the Interpublic board—all hitherto regarded as Harper's minions—revolted and threw the 51-year-old boss out, despite the fact that he was the largest individual stockholder. An era of retrenchment began. It was the end of the dude ranch and other extravagances. There was a certain amount of nervousness about what the reaction of clients might be to the fall of the Monarch—especially Coca-Cola, whose enormous account was and is handled by McCanns internationally after being captured by Harper personally in 1955—but in the event the structure stayed firm.

Ironically, when expansion was resumed Harper was a largely forgotten man. The absorption by Interpublic during the Seventies of the big Campbell-Ewald agency in Detroit and of the Troost network of European ad agencies headquartered in Düsseldorf was Harperism without Harper. He, after a brief period as co-founder of a small New York agency, was lost to the agency scene on which he had been for so long the centre of attraction. That small New York agency, Rosenfeld and Sirowitz, is now not so small, but its two other founding partners found they, too, could get along without Marvel Marion.

It is easy, and indeed pleasurable, to deride Harper as a pompous bighead, but obviously he was something more than that—a man of genuine vision and force of character—or he would never have achieved as much as he did. He also persistently advocated one idea which has fascinated agency people throughout the world, namely that their remuneration should come not in the form of either commission or fees but as a share of the profits which their advertising helped to create for their clients. Clients, it should be added, have in general not been converted.

Until the return of Phil Geier to New York, McCanns was one of only two Top Ten agencies in London which have in recent years been run directly by Americans. The other, Young and Rubicam, we met in Chapter 1 but merits a little more attention.

Y & R opened its London office at the end of the Second World War to service its General Foods business. The agency was run by a succession of Americans dispatched from New York headquarters. During the early Sixties, when it looked as if a native might be given the top job, Y & R suffered a prolonged and nasty bout of office politics as the various contenders jockeyed for position, but this was ended when a new American satrap, in the strong, quiet person of the late Walt Smith arrived to restore order. In the fullness of time Smith promoted himself to group chairman, supervising the work of Y & R's sales promotion, merchandising and public relations subsidiaries as well as that of the agency proper, the chairmanship of which went to creative director Dennis Auton. After nine years Smith moved on—to general European responsibilities—and yet another American, the bouncy young Joe De Deo, replaced him as group chairman.

In this respect Y & R is unusual; most of the American-owned agencies have tried to follow JWT's example in putting natives in charge of their British operations. But, if the top man is still an American, it remains true that almost everyone else in the group is British.

In the States Y & R is one of those agencies known for the strength of its creative department—Raymond Rubicam, its boss for years, started as a copywriter—and in Britain too its reputation depends largely on the creative work turned out for such clients as Heinz (Beanz Meanz Heinz) and Cadbury. Chairman Auton, who kept the creative directorship until 1976, when he relinquished it to David Tree, is a master of 'golden corn', the visually strong but essentially simple type of advertising which appeals to the mass market. 'He has a wonderful feel for the C1 or C2 housewife,' as one admirer puts it.

Trained at art school in Clapham, Auton started his career at JWT, where he worked his way up from 'dogsbody' to art director. Early on he switched to Y & R, where he's been ever since and where he helped to produce for instance the famous SR toothpaste-in-block-of-ice campaign back in the Fifties. He is an enthusiast who has been known to seize a pencil and draw ads on the tablecloth at a client lunch.

One feature of Y & R's working methods is the relative independence of creatives compared with some other big agencies. In many agencies the account group—that is, the unit composed of all the specialists working on a particular account—is under the undisputed authority of the account director. In Y & R, however, members of a product group (the same thing under another name) are responsible only to the heads of their own departments. Within the product group they are free to argue as much as they wish; if the creatives disagree with the account director, it is up to him to persuade them of the correctness of his views. In case of dispute the argument will be settled at a higher level within the agency, but in practice a product group usually succeeds in thrashing out a collective policy without having to resort to arbitration.

8 HOT SHOPS COOL DOWN

So much for the very largest London agencies. Now let's have a look at some of the more dynamic smaller outfits which have been making a name for themselves—the 'hot shops', to use a piece of Madison Avenue slang which such agencies love to hear applied to themselves.

We start with a paradox. The most successful of these newcomers stood in the 1974 billings table at number 19, but by the end of the following year the advertising trade magazine *Campaign* made it number four, after JWT, Masius and McCanns and ahead of OBM. Now that doesn't sound like a small shop, however dynamic, and it's scarcely credible that a newcomer should rise that high, is it?

Well, not to prevaricate, that number four position was allotted (questionably) to a group rather than a single agency—a group which was itself fairly old-established but which, after a 1975 merger deal, was dominated by the men who had been running an agency founded only five years before. Now even in the volatile ad agency business that has to be some kind of a record.

The agency founded in 1970 was called Saatchi and Saatchi, which might strike you as an improbable joke, except that the founders were brothers, Charles and Maurice, and their surname did happen to be Saatchi. Charles Saatchi, the elder of the two and the agency's driving force, first made his mark as a young copywriter at Colletts, where he and art director Ross Cramer were responsible for the first advertising it did for Ford cars. This was a campaign which caused a considerable stir in Adland because it compared the product with named competitors. At that time—the late Sixties—the rules of the Institute of Practitioners in

Advertising still forbade 'knocking copy', as such comparisons are called. However, newspapers judged that there was nothing unethical about the comparisons made, and the ads ran.

Shortly afterwards Cramer and Saatchi, who had both earned themselves the title of associate creative director, quit to set up a creative consultancy, turning out creative work on a freelance basis for a variety of agencies. Cramer Saatchi, as they called their firm, throve. Within a couple of years they had, they reckoned, been given jobs by some 15 of the top 20 agencies in London. They hired a staff of half a dozen to help them cope with the work. They refused to work directly for client companies, since this would have put them into direct competition with the agencies from which their living came. The first exception to this self-imposed rule was the Health Education Council, which originally engaged the consultancy simply to design brochures and posters, not advertising as such.

A little later the HEC found itself able to spend more money on advertising, and Cramer Saatchi devised a most striking newspaper campaign warning cigarette smokers of the dangers to which they were exposing themselves. The campaign was simple but direct, using few words but making every word count. One ad, for example, headed the page with a picture of a saucer full of an oily black substance, captioned 'The tar and discharge that collects in the lungs of an average smoker'.

This campaign cost only £100,000, mere peanuts in comparison to the many millions the tobacco companies were annually spending on advertising. But it was much noticed, much admired and, whatever effect it may have had on the battle against smoking, it certainly did Cramer Saatchi a power of good. It also decided the Health Education Council to renew its advertising efforts and to engage the consultancy as a full service agency, if it would agree to become one. At roughly the same time the Citrus Marketing Board of Israel asked the consultancy to compete for its account, again on the understanding that, if its creative proposals found favour—which they did—it would supply other normal agency services.

The decision to do so was taken, but it marked a parting of the ways between Saatchi and his partner Cramer, who was not attracted by the prospect of helping to run an agency proper and went off to become a director of TV commercials. In his place Charles brought in his younger brother Maurice, who had previously worked as an executive in a publishing company. The two brothers were then aged respectively 27 and 25. With the two accounts they had been promised, plus some smaller clients who elected to join them, they had £1 million worth of billing when the new agency opened its doors.

From then on it went from strength to strength, picking up blue chip clients all the way—among them Great Universal Stores, Dunlop and British Leyland. Rivals sneered that the secret of the Saatchis' success was that Charles was adept at manipulating the press to his advantage. It is true that he chalked up a huge number of column inches of coverage in both the trade press and the nationals, but this was achieved not through manipulation in any sinister sense but through a considerable flair for understanding what would interest journalists and when and for doing the kind of ad which would arouse such interest.

For example, one campaign which the agency produced for its old customers, the Health Education Council, featured the picture of a pregnant man, or rather a man dressed up to look pregnant. The aim was supposed to be to encourage young men to remember to take contraceptive precautions. You can argue about its suitability for that purpose, you can argue about how many times in the past few thousand years jokes about pregnant men have been cracked, what you can't argue about is that such a campaign is calculated to delight the news editor of any popular newspaper. The ad duly got its Fleet Street coverage. Of course, as far as the general press was concerned, it was the work of the Health Education Council, not of Saatchi and Saatchi. Readers of popular newspapers are not expected to be interested in the technicalities of who actually produces advertisements, and most of them probably haven't the faintest idea of how an ad agency works or indeed that such animals exist at all. No matter, other admen, including those working for client companies, knew very well which agency was involved. If in any doubt they had only to read the advertising trade weeklies, of which at that time there were two. It all helped to keep the Saatchi name constantly in front of the inhabitants of Adland.

As it grew Saatchi and Saatchi took over two smallish but much older agencies, George J. Smith and Notleys. These happenings too were brought to the attention of the trade press, as were the brothers' attempts to expand into continental Europe. *Campaign* proudly devoted its front page to their purchase of an agency in France, a story which Charles had given to the magazine as an 'exclusive'. When the provisional deal eventually fell through, which it did, the trade press was left to find that out for itself. *Campaign*'s rival, *Adweek*, now unhappily defunct, did so, but by that time the Saatchis' reputation as an agency of international standing had become established.

Notwithstanding such occasional *contretemps*, very few firms could boast of such a smooth and rapid rise. Five years after it started, Saatchi and Saatchi had annual billings of £13 million, as well as an enviable brand image of its own.

Curiously for the agency business, in which personality has always played a large part, Charles's reputation as a clever go-getter was based almost entirely on what he had done, including his own copywriting work, the competence with which his company's affairs had been handled and his skill at promoting it. It was hardly at all based on the kind of person he was since, unlike many of his counterparts in other agencies, he did not go in for public speaking and writing. Indeed, he disclaimed, with apparently genuine modesty, any ability as a writer outside his own special field of advertising.

It was this agency, widely reckoned to be brash and bouncy but also imaginative and successful, that Adland learned in the autumn of 1975 was to be merged with the publicly quoted Compton UK Partners group to make a new constellation with combined billings of over £30 million. Surprise turned to astonishment when the terms of the deal were learned. Between them the Saatchi brothers were acquiring 35 per cent of the equity of the new holding company. They were also to get the lion's share of the £400,000 in cash which was being paid to the half-dozen shareholders in the Saatchi and Saatchi agency. Charles Saatchi was to be joint chairman of the holding company with Ken Gill, the Compton group chairman. The main agency in the Compton group, Garland-Compton, was to be physically merged with Saatchis, under the managing directorship of Tim Bell, a Saatchi man, and with another Saatchi man, Jeremy Sinclair, as creative director. Managerially, it was clear, the bigger partner in the deal was being taken over by the smaller and younger. How had it happened?

The Compton UK group grew out of an agency founded in 1928 by Sidney Garland, a former *Daily Mail* space salesman. This agency, S. T. Garland Advertising Service, was passed on to his son Leonard Garland, who in 1960 joined up with the American agency Compton Advertising. Thus was born Garland-Compton. But the group's expansion policy, pursued energetically by Leonard Garland's successors, differed from that of the majority of the bigger ad agency businesses. While most of these relied on vertical growth, i.e. the addition of more and more clients and the spending of greater sums of advertising money by existing clients, Comptons went in for horizontal growth, i.e. the acquisition or foundation of more and more separate offices.

This, of course, had been the Interpublic solution too, as previously described. But there was a very important difference. Where Interpublic's UK agencies were all in London and operated completely independently of each other, the new Compton agencies—a whole string of them—were set up in the provinces. And while they functioned autonomously, each of these offices—in Leeds, Manchester, Bradford, Nottingham, Gloucester, Edinburgh and elsewhere—was able to draw upon central research, creative and production services in the capital as and when needed.

It was a formula adopted by certain other agencies, notably the (entirely British-owned) Brunning and Royds groups. Indeed, the success of the formula had been established in the first place by Carl Brunning, a bluff but shrewd Northerner who had started his advertising career in Liverpool and had gone on to found a veritable chain-store agency, with offices in ten cities.

Brunning's example was important for Comptons in another respect. He was the first British agency boss to go for a stock market quotation. He used the accruing capital, incidentally, not merely to strengthen his agency but to build up highly successful non-advertising subsidiaries making boats and selling caravans. Other British agencies which followed him in going public were Bensons and C. J. Lytle (both now extinct), Colletts, Geers Gross, Kimpher (we shall be talking about these latter two) and, last of all, Comptons.

Comptons UK went public in 1972, leaving the Americans with a minority shareholding. In the year 1973 the group made profits of £506,506, its highest ever, but the following year they were down to £446,000. Given the downturn in real advertising expenditure after the boom year of 1973 this was not a discreditable performance, but a public company is bound to pay greater attention to its profit figures than a private one, and the Compton management under Kenneth Gill began to get seriously worried about long-term prospects for their group. Feelers were put out in more than one direction, but it was only after the publication of an *Adweek* interview with Charles Saatchi in which he (cunningly?) expressed admiration for Garland-Compton's creative work on its Rowntree and Procter and Gamble accounts that Gill got in touch with him.

The ensuing merger was praised by all concerned as a sensible and far-sighted arrangement for protecting the best interests of both parties. And no doubt it was. This did not prevent the general impression from being gained that the Saatchi brothers had in effect taken over the older, bigger firm. The American Compton Advertising, it was noted, held 26 per cent of the equity of Saatchi and Saatchi Compton, the new holding company, meaning that the brothers had only to keep in with the Americans to be able to do just what they pleased.

If this outcome was galling to anyone within Garland-Compton or its subsidiary agencies, nothing was said publicly. The deal could not, observers conjectured, be wholly palatable to Graeme Roe, boss of Roe Downton, one of the most successful Compton subsidiaries with offices of its own in both London and the provinces. A handsome ex-athlete, midway in age between Charles Saatchi and Kenneth Gill, Roe might well, it was thought, have nourished ambitions of following Gill as the Compton group's chief executive. But, as the saying goes, that's show business. In many respects showbiz and adbiz are, as you must now have gathered, very similar.

Now let's jump back a few years to 1964, in which year was founded an agency which at the time was regarded as an even hotter shop, even brasher and bouncier, than was to be the case with Saatchis. The agency was Kingsley Manton and Palmer. Its three eponymous founders were, unlike Charles Saatchi, all personally highly visible, since all three had in turn been chairman of the 44 Club, an offshoot of the Institute of Practitioners in Advertising (the club was later renamed the IPA Society) and all had held responsible managerial posts in other agencies. All were then in their mid-thirties. For the student of advertising it is enlightening to learn who they were and what they became.

David Kingsley had been president of the students' union at the London School of Economics and had become an honorary but influential publicity adviser to the Labour Party in 1962 (a role he was to perform until 1970). Most people meeting him are struck, as it happens, by his facial resemblance to Harold Wilson, but there is no foundation to the rumour that the two are related. His Socialist views were not of a kind, however, that ever deterred Kingsley from making a career in commerce and by 1964 he had become an account director and board director of Benton and Bowles, a large American-owned agency, though not one of the very largest.

Michael Manton, whose facial resemblance is to the actor Peter Finch, went to Cambridge, as befitted a brigadier's son, then worked for three years for a trading company in India before going into advertising. He rose rapidly to become a director of Crawfords.

Brian Palmer was the creative man, a copywriter who had risen to be one of the three creatives on the board of Young and Rubicam—the others were Dennis Auton, whom we have met, and Norman Berry, who also left to become a partner in his own agency, now called Davidson Pearce Berry and Spottiswoode.

Again unlike Saatchi, Kingsley, Manton and Palmer chucked in their jobs and set up their new agency without a single account to their name. They set about soliciting clients for business, a practice even more frowned upon by the IPA then than it was when Saatchi and Saatchi was founded six years later.

They drew attention to themselves from the outset by their refusal to join the IPA, their outspoken preference for fees rather than the commission system and the unusual physical arrangement of their offices. They favoured an open plan system, which facilitated ease of communication, and this physical arrangement was reflected in a much more flexible division of responsibilities than pertained at other agencies. The three principals always functioned as a team, sitting next to each other, criticising each other, even 'diminishing each other', as Manton recalls. Although Palmer had the title of creative director, all three were closely involved with the creative work on the accounts they handled. For instance, Kingsley was responsible for the 'For God's sake, care' campaign which KMP did for the Salvation Army and which—like Saatchi's Health Education Council work later on —provedto be a wonderful attention-getter for the agency.

Two years after they started, the trio became a quartet, when they were joined by Len Heath, marketing development director of Birds Eye and a former journalist, copywriter and TV and cinema scriptwriter (he co-authored the screenplays of three Peter Sellers films). It was Heath who conceived the agency's long-running campaign for White Horse whisky, with newspaper ads picturing an actual white horse in a series of absurd situations. This was a campaign which aroused mixed feelings among other admen, some of whom contended that it communicated no product benefit of any kind to the consumer, but readers obviously liked it. In a *Sunday Times* questionnaire to find which were its readers' favourite ads, White Horse scored top marks. In the end the client took the account away, so maybe the critics were right about the campaign's sale effectiveness as far as Scotch was concerned, but it did a great job of selling the agency, or at least of getting it noticed.

In 1969, the famous four decided that, though they had become successful—and billings of £4 million after five years, starting from scratch, certainly qualified as success in the agency game—they also wanted to be big. The way to do this quickly, they reckoned, was by expanding horizontally, in accordance with ideas they had been kicking around between them for several years. To finance their expansion they went public with a new holding company called KMPH (the H was for Heath), a name subsequently changed to Kimpher. The name change came about after a fifth partner, George Riches, had been taken on, but the human chemistry did not work and he did not stay long.

Riches had been acquired together with the agency of which he had been chief executive, an old-established shop called Pembertons, and with its two subsidiaries, one in Australia and one, in London, called Allardyce. In quick succession Kimpher bought a whole series of firms. The details are too complicated to go into, but the upshot was that within about four years the group had come to own, instead of one agency, eight, including five in London and two in Manchester. It also had an important subsidiary called the Media Department, which specialised in buying advertising space and airtime not only for the Kimpher agencies but for a number of clients who wished to do without any agency. Added to this were five market service companies, covering research, design, sales promotion and recruitment and classified advertising, a book publishing company and minority interests in ad agencies in Sweden and Ireland.

It sounds a lot, and it is not surprising that the 1974 league table listed Kimpher at number five, with group billings of more than £23 million. (As with Saatchi and Saatchi Compton the validity of this positioning is open to question; if other agencies under common ownership—for instance, McCanns and Waseys or OBM and Davidson Pearce—were to report group billings instead of, as they do, separate turnovers for separate units, the pecking order would look rather different.) And so they all lived happily ever after, as the heroes of fairy stories and advertisements are supposed to? Afraid not. It was when they'd finally made the big time that the famous four found their real problems were just beginning. Profit problems first, and like other publicly quoted companies Kimpher had to watch out for the way the profits were moving. In the financial year 1969–70 the original KMP agency made £163,000 of profit on its own; in 1973–4 the whole group, with a turnover six times as big, made only £362,000.

Meanwhile the KMP agency stagnated. Its success had been built, perhaps to a greater extent than even the famous four realised, on their own charm and ability and the trust placed in them by clients. As all four withdrew from active participation in making ads into the misty realms of corporate administration, some of those same clients grew increasingly dissatisfied. Pembertons fared even worse, losing some of its biggest accounts, including Haig whisky and the Nationwide building society.

A process of rationalisation was hastily embarked upon, and by 1975 three of the six London agencies in the group, including Pembertons, had disappeared, absorbed into Allardyce—an unglamorous but profitable concern which was chiefly known for its hard sell commercials for Brentford Nylons. Kimpher's management was also rationalised as two of the famous four, Palmer and Heath, quit, Palmer to help run Young's Brewery, with which he had family connections, Heath to start a marketing services business of his own. Manton was left as group managing director. Kingsley, who kept his seat on the board, remained in charge of the publishing arm, Entercom. That same year the group ran into the red, chalking up a trading loss for the first half of £139,000.

Curiously, by this time a 25 per cent interest in Kimpher had been acquired by Christopher Osborne, head of the rival, privately owned Osborne ad agency group. According to Osborne, his shares were simply an investment, but the general suspicion was that if and when Kimpher finally cracked up Osborne wanted to be in a good position to pick up some of the more valuable pieces.

Pessimism about the group's future increased when it published its results for the year ended March 31, 1976. Pre-tax losses amounted to £372,000. Of this sum fully £210,000 was accounted for by one exceptional item, money owed to media on behalf of Brentford Nylons, the big-spending Allardyce client which had collapsed leaving the agency to pick up the bills. Another £72,000 went on 'termination payments' to Palmer and Heath.

Kimpher may yet solve all its problems and fulfil the dreams of its pioneers, as Interpublic did, but few people in Adland would be prepared to bet on it. To date its history would be more likely to be taken as a warning of how fast a hot shop can, even as it grows, cool down.

One of the main difficulties affecting the development of the KMP agency was that of finding a strong second-generation team to replace the famous four. Three young men who would very probably have fitted the bill were Richard French, Mike Gold and Mike Pulman. Instead they quit, amid some acrimony, in 1970 to start their own shop, French Gold Pulman.

Almost immediately they suffered a grievous setback, the death of Pulman from leukaemia. He was replaced as partner and creative director by David Abbott, previously managing director of Doyle Dane Bernbach. This was the medium-sized London office of a very famous New York agency, the reasons for whose fame we will examine in the next chapter. Abbott was also one of the best known and most highly rated copywriters in London. One full-page newspaper ad of his which many people still remember, though it was actually of no commercial importance, was headed 'The board and I have decided that we don't like the colour of your eyes'. It was remarkable not only for its style but for its purpose—it was a recruitment ad for Clive Jenkins's white collar trade union, the ASTMS as it is now called.

We have already met French Gold Abbott, remember?

They were the boys who in 1974 sold out to Kenyon and Eckhardt and, in exchange, were handed the remains of Colman Prentis and Varley on a plate. They followed the merger by gaining more than £2 million of new business and ended 1975 with billings of nearly £10 million, making their agency number 24 in the pecking order.

Slightly behind them, with billings of £8 million, stood an agency called Boase Massimi Pollitt, which in the past few years has made itself one of the most admired in the trade for the wit and ingenuity of its advertising. Among its campaigns have been those for Cadbury's Smash instant potato, Unigate milk and Cresta soft drinks.

Commercials for Cresta, aimed at children, were built around a cartoon bear with a throaty American accent, dark glasses and the punch line 'It's frothy, man'. For Unigate, BMP invented a mythical race of creatures called Humphreys, supposed to steal milk when nobody was looking, and hired such comic characters as Frank Muir, Spike Milligan and Muhammad Ali to take part in entertaining commercials on this theme. The Humphreys themselves were never seen, only the red-striped straws through which they sipped the milk from unwatched glasses. Zany but undeniably funny. The Smash commercials involved the creation of another queer race, this time of robot-like Martians who derided humans for sticking to old-fashioned potatoes.

Despite the family likeness between these campaigns it should not be supposed that they are all intended to do the same kind of job. The Cresta commercials were designed to attract new users, and appear to have worked very well; the Humphreys and the Martians were conceived of as ways of holding on to existing markets, and this accounts for the lack of any specific promises about the products. To make the point clearer, BMP's earlier campaigns for Smash had concentrated on persuading the housewife that the stuff was (*a*) just as tasty as ordinary mashed potato, (*b*) more convenient to prepare. They used a jingle 'For Mash get Smash', calculated to make the brand name synonymous, for the first-time user, with the product category instant mashed potato (there were of course competing brands).

But, as Stanley Pollitt, joint chairman of BMP, emphasises, it is normal for a new repeat-purchase product to have acquired most of its users within two years from the time it is launched. It is also normal for those people who get into the habit of buying it early on to become subsequently its heaviest users. Much advertising of the Smash Martians kind is addressed precisely to these heavy users. Its object, therefore, is not to convince but to reassure, to keep the customer happy.

Pollitt and his partner, Martin Boase, started their agency in the late Sixties as a breakaway from Pritchard Wood, an Interpublic firm later absorbed into Waseys. Smash was in fact one of the accounts they took with them. The third man whose name is perpetuated in that of the agency is Gabe Massimi, who had been creative director of Pritchard Wood. After a while, however, personal rifts developed between Massimi, a handsome, self-indulgent American, and his partners, and he quit to go back to the States.

Most of the campaigns which have won BMP its reputation for good creative ideas have been produced under the supervision of Massimi's successor as creative director, John Webster. It is, by the way, not at all uncommon for agency partnerships to break up in this way; sometimes the company name is changed to advertise the fact, but very often the departed partner leaves his name behind him even when he joins a rival shop.

BMP did change its name—to Boase Massimi Pollitt-Univas—when, in 1976, it sold half its equity to Univas, international arm of the French Havas group, for around £750,000. Boase and Pollitt, now minority shareholders, stayed on as (much richer) joint chairmen.

In 1975 BMP reported billings of £8 million. A little way behind it stood, at £6½ million, a slightly younger agency headed by three partners but bearing the name of only one of them. This is the Kirkwood Company, founded by one of British Adland's best known and most distinctive characters, Ronnie Kirkwood. A one-time professional actor who deserted the stage after a bout of illness, bachelor Kirkwood still carries the stamp of his former profession.

He is tall, graceful, always impeccably dressed (there was a time when no advertising industry banquet was complete without his white dinner suit), extraordinarily boyish-looking, not to say girlish-looking, for his years (he is now in his late 40s) with a face and figure somewhat reminiscent of Dirk Bogarde's.

Such a description may sound malicious, but it is not meant to be. Kirkwood himself has always made the most of his personal charm; he is an outstandingly effective performer at presentations, the ritualised occasions when agencies unveil to clients their thoughts and work. Notwithstanding the many jokes about him, he is much loved and much respected as a clever operator whose actorly ways are only the icing on a pretty solid cake.

He is not, it may be added, the only agency boss to have trod the boards. Kenneth Gill, of Comptons, and Peter Marsh, chairman of Allen Brady and Marsh, a medium-sized but fast-growing shop known for its 'Wonder of Woolworths' and Domecq sherry campaigns, have had acting experience. There is no doubt that such experience is helpful in a business where so much depends on making a good personal impression on the client. And while very few admen may have been actors, a not inconsiderable proportion become actors in the course of their agency duties.

Kirkwood was head of TV at the old CPV and deputy creative director at Bensons before becoming creative director at McCann-Erickson, where he really made his name. He left in 1970 to set up on his own with backing from a merchant bank but without taking any of his employers' business with him. His first move was not to pitch for accounts but to entice a couple of top-rank marketing men into joining him as partners and giving the agency the kind of expertise it needed if it was to get the fast-moving packaged goods accounts which provide an agency with big billings. He found his partners in Gordon Medcalf, a director of Young and Rubicam, and Tom O'Leary, who was running a division of the Heinz company. The partnership paid off, the packaged goods accounts came in, and Kirkwoods started to look like one of the agencies which, amid the blizzards which hit Adland—and everyone else—

after 1973, would still be standing, if any did, in five years' time.

Whether it would be standing on its own was a different question. Twice during 1975 Kirkwood denied rumours that he, like so many successful British agency men before him, was planning to sell out to one of the American majors. The rumours—and most admen have learned by experience to believe all rumours until they are proved false—had Ronnie being wooed by an American lady agency boss named Mary Wells. Ronnie's retort to the rumour-mongers was that they were just good friends who liked to have a drink together whenever he was in New York.

For once the rumour-mongers were indeed on the wrong track. Early in 1976 the expected sell-out took place, but not to Mary Wells or any other American. Instead the buyer was Lopex, the organisation which owned all those companies in the old London Press Exchange group which had not been sold to Leo Burnett. Kirkwoods, it became clear, was to be the Lopex group's new flagship agency. Ronnie Kirkwood and his partners were to carry on running their own show but no longer owning it. The price they got for becoming employees again was a handsome £800,000.

Now this is as good a place as any to tell you something about Mary Wells, without a mention of whom no book on contemporary advertising could pretend to be even half-complete. And although this book is primarily concerned to give you some kind of a picture of what goes on in *British* advertising, you will already have noticed that it is impossible to do even that without fairly frequent references to Madison Avenue. All over the world admen look to Madison Avenue as Moslems look to Mecca. New York is where most of the ideas about, as well as most of the money in, the modern ad industry are concentrated. And most of the larger-than-life personalities too.

London, unfortunately, has no equivalent of Mary Mother of Invention, who in a short time managed to add to the brains and blonde beauty with which she was born a hefty amount of wealth and power. She came from the Mid-West and started her advertising career as a copywriter for a New York department store. After a spell at Doyle Dane Bernbach, the hottest creative hot shop on Mad Ave at the time, she moved on to the Jack Tinker agency, where she really struck oil in the shape of the Braniff airline account. What Mary did for Braniff became one of the classic tales of advertising-led expansion. The most important thing was to make the airline paint its planes in bright colours. Sounds simple, but it hadn't been done before, and brilliant simplicity is, after all, the essence of the best commercial ideas.

With the Braniff account in her pocket, Mary set up an agency of her own, Wells Rich Greene, with two partners who were pretty soon to become back numbers. It didn't take her long either to pocket Braniff's boss, Harding Lawrence. After their marriage her agency stopped doing Braniff's advertising but only to snap up the much larger TWA account in its place. WRG grew fast, aided by a succession of snappy campaigns and Mary's magnetic attraction for clients (in advertising it isn't only male charm that can work wonders), went public and enabled its boss to make herself, by selling her shares, a multi-millionairess. (After share prices fell in 1974, the agency spent $18 million to go private again.)

Wells Rich Greene's American success was not followed by any substantial achievements overseas. The agency has had an office in London for some years, the main function of which has been to service the TWA account in Europe, but without Mary's personal touch hopes of pulling in a lot of other business were disappointed. It is entirely to be expected, therefore, that an attempt will be made to buy the European base which Wells Rich Greene hasn't been able to establish for itself. For these days no ambitious American agency can afford to do without an overseas network to service the accounts of multinational clients.

While we're talking about Americans, let's mention a couple more before we close this chapter. They are Bob Geers and Bob Gross, who built a London agency largely on the basis of one account, Homepride flour, for which they invented the Homepride flour graders, a race of

TV cartoon characters in bowler hats. They made so much money out of this happy device that Geers Gross was able to go public. With the capital gained Gross, the cannier of the two who really runs the business, bought another agency, Thomas Hugo Kettley Browne, and installed an ex-Hobson Bates director, John Hughes, as its managing director.

Geers Gross made itself the envy of other agencies because of its extraordinarily high profit ratio. In 1971, with a staff of only 28, it made profits of £200,000 on billings of £2 million, a ratio of 10 per cent compared with an average profits-billings ratio in large agencies of about 2 per cent. The secret, of course, is to have the kind of accounts where a small staff, producing few separate ads, can cope with the needs of big-spending clients. Nice work if you can get it! In 1973 Geers Gross billed £3·3 million, but profits rose only marginally, to £216,000, signifying a ratio of 6·5 per cent, still the best in Adland but not by such a huge margin as before. The runners-up in the profitability stakes that year—Harrison Cowley, Boase Massimi Pollitt, French Gold Abbott and Saatchi and Saatchi—registered ratios ranging from 4 to 4·7 per cent.

Bob Gross, who looks rather like Dustin Hoffman, is one of the shyer, more reserved agency chiefs. He has not, like some others, courted publicity. But, with profit figures like his, who needs publicity? The danger he has to worry about is that, as Geers Gross billings increase—by 1975 they were up to £6 million—and the profit ratio inevitably falls, he may come under the same kinds of pressures as have beset Kimpher.

The profitability of the whole agency game has in fact declined over the past few years. According to figures released by the IPA, average profits of member agencies in 1960 represented 2·9 per cent of billings and 19·2 per cent of net income. By 1970 the two ratios had fallen to 1·5 and 9·3 per cent respectively. That was a bad year, and they recovered to reach 2·4 and 15·1 per cent in the boom year of 1973. In 1974 they were down again to 1·8 and 11·2 per cent, as inflation and recession hit advertising hard.

Advertisers cut their budgets, and agencies tightened their belts.

Belt-tightening has since then become something of a way of life with agencies, which in the Fifties and Sixties were among the easiest places to make money, both corporately and individually. Nowadays agency staff have to work much harder. In 1960 productivity per head (i.e. total annual billings divided by total number of staff) was £12,000. By 1975 it had risen to £47,000. At the same time salaries declined in relation to other businesses. Up to the early Seventies a bright youngster could earn a lot more in an agency than as an employee almost anywhere else. If a copywriter or account handler in one of the smarter London agencies wasn't pulling in at least £5,000 a year before he was 30 he was really not doing at all well (and that at a time when £5,000 meant something), and remuneration for those in more senior positions was proportionately greater.

The glamorous aura which surrounded agencies during the period of their post-war expansion was generated by their affluence (large rewards for relatively little effort) as well as by their executives' habit of lunching their clients at the best West End restaurants and hiring the prettiest secretaries to impress those clients. The glamour has worn off a bit of late, and the amount spent on entertainment has decreased.

9 MR BERNBACH'S REVOLUTION

So far we have alluded only briefly and in passing to the existence of different 'philosophies' and styles of advertising. Among the philosophers alluded to have been David Ogilvy and Claude Hopkins, who held it to be self-evident that humour was not a paying proposition for any advertiser, and Rosser Reeves, who proclaimed the doctrine of the Unique Selling Proposition. Despite the differences between them they would all have subscribed to the view of John E. Kennedy, who preceded Hopkins as chief copywriter of the Lord and Thomas agency in Chicago, that 'advertising is salesmanship in print'. He wrote that in 1905, when all ads were print ads, so obviously the coming of other advertising media required some modification of his apophthegm. It could be rephrased, clumsily but usefully, as 'advertising is salesmanship in print, television, radio, cinema or any other mass communication medium available'. Does it still ring true?

Well, in one sense, no adman could dissent from it. Clearly no advertisers spend money just for the hell of it. Their ads are always intended (even if they don't succeed) to affect human behaviour and usually, though not always, human purchasing behaviour. Certainly if we restrict the discussion to MCA (manufacturers' consumer advertising—remember?) you can't imagine any advertiser hiring an agency if he didn't think its ads would help to sell his products.

But—there is a but, and a very big one. It concerns the precise meaning of the word 'salesmanship'. As Maurice Smelt, a partner in the London ad agency Dennis and Garland, has pointed out (in an excellent collection of speeches called *What Advertising Is*), Kennedy wasn't using the word as a synonym for 'persuasion'. What his definition meant, to quote Smelt, was: 'Advertising is the equivalent in print of salesmen knocking on doors and selling face to face.' The corollary was that ads should be informative and respectful—showing respect both to the customer and to the product.

This conception of advertising tactics—let's call it the doorstep manner—was the dominant one in agencies for a long time. Not the only one, mind; it certainly didn't fit Benson's old floating Bovril bottle, for example, but if there was any orthodoxy in Adland that was it.

Now it will not have been lost upon the perceptive reader that much of the advertising he or she sees today is very far from having a doorstep manner. The camp snobbishness of After Eight or the risqué flippancy of Smirnoff vodka are not tones of voice you would expect any stranger to adopt when speaking to you on your own doorstep. Yet both are highly successful products, with advertising generally reckoned to have played an important part in their success. However that may be, no professional adman would dream today of criticising such campaigns on the grounds that they were not sufficiently serious or that they appeared to mock the very things they were trying to sell.

The fact is that at the very time that Ogilvy and Reeves were at their peak as pundits, in the early Sixties, a new orthodoxy was emerging. It was dubbed by some of its followers the Creative Revolution, and its undisputed leader was Bill Bernbach, who had been creative director of Grey Advertising in New York before founding his own agency, Doyle Dane Bernbach, in 1949.

Bernbach never formalised his advertising philosophy in the way that Reeves did. He laid down no rules except one: that good creative people should be bound by no rules other than their own taste and judgment. The implication was that the client must accept that they knew best—or take his account elsewhere. At Doyle Dane the creatives ruled the roost. Account handling was seen as a subsidiary function, and Bernbach had little interest in research, which he didn't think was important in enabling an agency to fulfil its purpose, namely to create ads so original and so imaginative that people would be bound to pay attention to them.

Bernbach's importance, though, lay not in what he said but in what his agency did. Doyle Dane created many famous campaigns, but its advertising for one client above all can be said to have contained the essence of Bernbachism, and that client was Volkswagen. No ads have been more closely studied by copywriters and art directors all over the world than these, nor has a style been more widely imitated. Before we go any further, a sample:

> *Once upon a time there was an ugly little bug. It could go about 27 miles on one gallon of gas and about 40,000 miles on one set of tyres. It was just right for taking father to the train or the children to school. But alas it wasn't beautiful. So for any important occasion the poor ugly little bug would be replaced. By a big beautiful chariot, drawn by 300 horses. Then, after a time, a curious thing happened. The big beautiful chariot didn't get any more beautiful. While the ugly little bug didn't get any uglier. The moral being: if you want to show you've gotten somewhere, get a big beautiful chariot. But if you simply want to get somewhere, get a bug.*

The 'bug', if you don't know or haven't guessed, is the VW Beetle, and the above copy was set out under a strip of four pictures contrasting a tiny Beetle with a huge American car, the 300-horse-power 'chariot'. The final picture of the four showed the Beetle driving up to the steps of a grandiose bank.

Now you couldn't get further from the doorstep manner than that. It would probably have given Claude Hopkins a fit. Not only is it funny but, for all its curious syntax, it has to be classified as an example of the fine writing against which Hopkins inveighed. What's worse, its humour is, or at first sight appears to be, directed against the product. What doorstep salesman would start his pitch by saying, 'What I've got here is an ugly little thing which won't do anything for your social standing in the neighbourhood'?

Other VW ads went even further in insulting the product. One famous one captioned it simply as a 'lemon' (American slang for a failure) and left it at that. Even when the car wasn't being insulted its defects weren't glossed over, or at least they didn't appear to be.

The Beetle was, of course, an enormous success in the States. Owning one became a badge of sophistication, a kind of non-ostentatious ostentation. Exactly how far advertising was responsible for that it is impossible to say. Maybe all that Doyle Dane did was to throw its weight behind a social trend—the reaction by some American city dwellers against their country's own breed of big, flashy, thirsty cars. But then nobody would claim that advertising can work against such trends.

In any case, what Doyle Dane demonstrated was that, given the right kind of product and the right kind of market, successful advertising could forget all about the doorstep manner. It could be humorous, allusive, self-deprecating, artistic. In a word it could be sophisticated. And what exactly, you may well ask, does sophisticated mean? Well, in the realm of advertising it means recognising that an ad *is* an ad and not a salesman talking and that the reader or viewer knows that, the said reader or viewer being mentally not a *tabula rasa* upon which a sales message can be written but a person who is accustomed to seeing ads, accustomed to ignoring or discounting them, but ready on occasion also to enjoy them. In Maurice Smelt's felicitous phrase, 'the advertisement itself becomes an entity in the advertising and all the other rules are thereby subverted'.

What Bernbach did—and this is why his example was so inspiring to a new generation of copywriters and art directors—was to take the inverted commas out of 'creative'. Henceforth the 'creative' department, i.e. the ad-making department, was indeed to be the creative department, deserving its title not just as a piece of trade jargon but as an accurate description of its role, which was to give full rein to its powers of artistic originality and imagination.

Of course, such creativity must not be undisciplined. The copy and the pictures could be as funny, as unexpected, as shocking even as you liked, but they had to be relevant to the product. You could make fun of the Beetle in a hundred ways for being small, but only because it *was* small, and this was an important part of the reason why people either bought it or didn't buy it.

For Bernbach did not divorce the artistic content of advertising from its commercial purpose. On the contrary, his acolytes included many of the copywriters who no longer felt that they had to publish novels and poems—or at least to have an unpublished novel in a drawer, as all copywriters were commonly supposed to have—in order to prove that they were really persons of literary sensibility and not mere hacks penning vulgar slogans for even more vulgar products. Now the ads themselves were to constitute their creative output, and although the world at large might not know their names their peers within the industry would collect and discuss their work and confer upon it the critical appreciation which every artist craves, while grateful agencies would shower them with gold in quantities to which, among novel-writers, only very few could aspire.

There was another thing about Doyle Dane advertising, and its Volkswagen campaigns in particular, which stimulated enthusiasm among young recruits to the industry—and remember that we are speaking of a time, the Fifties and Sixties, when it had many young recruits, for it was then a rapidly expanding industry in all Western industrial countries. That thing was honesty. For if the best of those young recruits wanted to feel they were entering a profession in which their intellectual talents would be fully employed, they also, and by the same token, did not want to feel that they were being put under any obligation to behave like rogues or cheapjacks. And as the volume of advertising grew year by year so did the number of those who attacked it for dishonesty and for preying upon the public's gullibility. These were criticisms for which some ads clearly provided evidence. How reassuring to see others which eschewed any attempt to mislead!

Now whether Doyle Dane's Volkswagen advertising was quite so honest as those young enthusiasts took it to be is a moot point. It rather depends on what you mean by honesty. There are degrees of honesty, as there are degrees of dishonesty. And while the style of the Bernbach school was distinctly different from that of older schools of advertising theory and practice, all ads share one characteristic. They are all propaganda. Which, tautologously, is as much as to say they are all ads. They seek to persuade, not to investigate. They may tell the truth, but they will tell only the truths which suit them. They will put the product's best foot forward; if it happens to have a lame foot, they will not draw attention to it.

Obvious? Yes. But perhaps not quite so obvious as all that. At all events it came as something of a shock to quite a number of Bernbachites when, years after the Volkswagen campaigns had been installed in Adland's halls of fame, Ralph Nader came along and accused the Beetle, statistics in hand, of being an unsafe car to drive. The ads had said nothing about safety. They had laughed at the product and pointed disarmingly to some of its defects. Only were they defects? Not in the eyes of potential purchasers. Or, even if they were defects, they couldn't be hidden, and anyway ugliness and smallness were the inevitable price you had to pay for economic petrol consumption and ease of parking, weren't they? And the reliability claims that were thrown in so modestly, they were true. For God's sake who was supposed to guess that its safety record was open to challenge? Anyhow that guy Nader's a fanatic, you can't trust everything *he* says.

But you obviously couldn't trust everything Doyle Dane Bernbach said either. At least not with the kind of trust some had been inclined to place in their advertising. For, lo and behold, that friendly Mr Bernbach was a salesman too. He wasn't standing on the doorstep, he was walking along beside you, laughing and wisecracking and nudging you in the ribs and seeming to spill all the beans. But make no mistake about it, it was your money he was after, and he'd kept a few choice beans to himself.

One of Claude Hopkins's most famous advertising campaigns was for Schlitz beer. It was based on the slogan 'Washed with live steam' and explained that every bottle went through a steam bath to sterilise it before being filled with beer. There was nothing unusual about this, every brewer did it. But only Hopkins was clever enough to advertise it and make it appear to be a special advantage of his client's product. Was he telling lies? He was not. Was he deceiving anyone? Difficult to answer. Let's just say he wasn't undeceiving anyone.

Did Doyle Dane Bernbach tell lies about Volkswagen? It did not. Did its ads deceive anyone about the advisability of buying that particular car as against every other available model? Let's just say they didn't strive to undeceive anyone who might otherwise have suspected that it had defects other than those advertised. But Bill Bernbach wasn't, after all, hired to run a consumers' advice service any more than Claude Hopkins had been.

You know, maybe Hopkins would not, after all, have had a fit if he'd seen the Volkswagen ads. He was a clever man and, being so, would have realised that changing cultural patterns allow for changing sales techniques. Maybe he would have applauded the ugly little bug and realised, though the ads didn't say so, that it had been washed in live steam.

Whatever you may think about the morality of propaganda, commercial or political, most admen would still agree that Doyle Dane's work for Volkswagen was great advertising and that its impact justified the use of all that agency's stylistic tricks. Not even David Ogilvy argues any more that humour is necessarily counter-productive, and indeed his own agency has produced plenty of humorous advertising. But that doesn't mean that controversy has ceased. Rather the controversies nowadays take place on different ground—not which techniques are absolutely right and which are absolutely wrong, but which techniques are right in which situations and wrong in which others.

What is certain is that while Bernbach's creative revolution had a liberating influence throughout Adland, it also set a number of precedents which creative departments everywhere followed at their peril. The trouble is twofold: first, not every audience is susceptible to the same kind of blandishments as worked so well for Volkswagen; second, it's very nice to be original and imaginative and creative (in the non-jargon sense) but if an agency's creative staff (in the jargon sense) are not really up to much, and this is unfortunately more often true than not, their attempts to do a Volkswagen on every product they are asked to handle are going to produce some excruciating results.

Take the first point. Not even Bernbach's agency in New York always got its audience sized up right. For instance, the TV commercials it turned out for Alka-Seltzer around 1970 all portrayed a newly wed couple. The wife kept dishing up freshly learned recipes which the husband hypocritically pretended to love while secretly using Alka-Seltzer to get over their effects. The campaign was cleverly written and skilfully directed and was greatly admired by other admen. But that didn't prevent the client's share of the market from slipping, with the result that Bernbach lost the account to Mary Wells. The sad fact, according to one American market researcher, was that many of the target audience simply did not see the joke. It is not the only evidence that has come to light that jokes which make hip copywriters fall about on their deep pile carpets do not always tickle the ribs of suburban housewives. It is this, and not the Hopkins theory that people do not buy from clowns, that makes humour a dangerous weapon for advertising to use.

The nicest story about humour in advertising is one told by Denis Norden. A long time ago, so long ago that Bensons was still a flourishing agency, it asked Denis Norden to write the scripts for a series of television commercials advertising Omo. Being a humorist by trade, Norden naturally came up with ideas like showing a condemned man being led out in front of a firing squad. Offered a blindfold to put over his eyes, he exclaimed with admiration at its whiteness. Due to Omo, of course. Bensons was impressed. It arranged a meeting at which the campaign was to be presented to the client and asked Norden to make himself available for the discussions which were expected to last all day. A conference chamber was booked at a hotel.

When on the morning of the appointed day Norden

arrived at the scene he saw four tables. One was laden with all manner of good things to eat, two others with drinks and with coffee cups, the fourth was a conference table.

The client was a blunt man. As soon as he had grasped what the theme of the campaign was to be he turned to Norden and put it to him that any use of humour was bound to detract in the consumer's mind from the importance of the product. Poor Norden, who had merely done what had been asked of him, was unprepared for such a question. Being a truthful fellow, as well as a witty one, he replied that he had no evidence that the client was wrong. Whereupon the client got up and departed.

And so the conference ended after only 12 minutes. Instead of staying all day the Bensons team went back to the agency leaving behind all the food, all the drink and three very smug-looking waiters.

Whether or not Norden has embroidered this anecdote in any particular, it is certainly true that washing powder manufacturers have resisted any attempt to make fun of their products. Their fears may be exaggerated, but it is impossible to say that they are groundless. No manufacturer can be happy at the thought of a campaign which amuses some or even many people but does nothing for sales.

One might mention White Horse or Watney's Red Revolution, but the classic example is again an American campaign, for Piel's beer. This featured a couple of cartoon characters, Bert and Harry Piel, who acquired a great following; the beer, however, did not. When you are spending as much on advertising as the soap powder manufacturers (between them Unilever and Procter and Gamble spent nearly £5 million on this category in 1975 alone) you think twice before abandoning a tried and trusty formula for the sake of a joke which not everyone may enjoy.

On the other hand, humour appears to have worked well commercially for quite a lot of products, including Smirnoff, Hamlet cigars, Double Diamond beer, Guinness, Cresta and Brooke Bond PG Tips tea. The long-running series of TV commercials for PG Tips by Davidson Pearce Berry and Spottiswoode, featuring tea-drinking chimpanzees, is particularly interesting, since the humorous device chosen has no basic relevance to the product (there is no more reason for the chimps to plug tea than coffee or sweets or any other product) and is, from the point of view of a Bernbachite Creative Revolutionary as well as that of a Hopkinsite doorstep adman, entirely deplorable. That it works, however, Brooke Bond's competitors are convinced. The brand is market leader and has been since the chimps helped it to knock Typhoo off that perch a dozen years ago. According to John Harvey, marketing director of Cadbury-Typhoo, the chief marketing problem of other tea companies has been to find something to stand up against the chimps. Harvey hoped he had found that something in the shape of the cartoon gnu, devised for Typhoo by its new advertising agency, Geers Gross, and first presented to TV viewers in early 1976. It was the gnu which had helped Geers Gross win the account from the previous incumbent, Young and Rubicam.

But humour was, and is, only one of the weapons in the Bernbachite armoury. It's not, moreover, the only one that can, and sometimes does, blow up in the incautious practitioner's face.

Take the negative pitch, the 'ugly little bug' style of advertising. While nobody can deny that it did Volkswagen no harm, some pretty shrill cries of alarm went up when negativism became a fashion. One of the alarmists was Fairfax Cone, a partner in Foote Cone and Belding. In his autobiography, *With All Its Faults*, published in 1969, the old American copywriter railed against the youngsters who, in their striving after originality, broke what he considered the first rule of good advertising, namely that 'it must immediately make clear what the basic proposition is'.

He was outraged by ads like the one for Volvo which was headed 'this car is for people who don't like cars', and he gave a list of other similar examples: 'Within the course of a few weeks the world is offered a new Lucky Strike cigarette that doesn't taste like a Lucky Strike; Renault (no doubt spurred to excess by Volvo) headlines that our customers are dissatisfied; Ronson advertises table lighters for people who hate table lighters; and Lava soap is presented as the world's worst bath soap.'

Cone continued: 'There is little question that the people who made these advertisements found them offbeat and full of fun. The truth is, each one is ridiculous and, worse than that, wasteful, for it cost as much to publish as a sensible advertisement.'

Well, critic Cone had his own critics. Said one London creative director at the time: 'Cone is of another era. In his day everybody smelled nice, all laxatives worked, all wives were beautiful, ads were full of happy people.'

But the old man nevertheless had a point when he insisted that there was a limit to the extent you could disparage a product and still expect people to buy it. Where in practice that limit should be set it may not always be easy to judge. For example, one campaign that was much admired among British creatives at around the time Cone wrote his book was that produced for Lufthansa by the London office of Doyle Dane Bernbach and written by David Abbott, then creative director of the agency. The trouble about advertising an airline is finding some way of differentiating it from other airlines. Because of International Air Transport Association agreements, they all charge the same prices; because of the obvious physical limitations there's not much that one airline can do to make the passenger any more comfortable than he would be travelling in somebody else's plane. That's why most airline ads tend to focus on national connections (British Airways tells Britons, though not others, to 'fly the flag') or the beauty of the air stewardesses. What they certainly don't talk about is the fact that flying a long way in anyone's plane is bound to be pretty tedious. Abbott decided to take just this negative aspect of flying and make it the central theme of his campaign. So one ad was produced proclaiming 'another madly exciting way to get to Los Angeles'. The picture was the back of an airliner seat. 'The most comfortable way to get to Sydney' was, the picture explained, by ship. Other ads demonstrated graphically how cramping it was to try to sleep in a plane.

Full marks for honesty and for wit. Unfortunately, after the disadvantages had been so cleverly rubbed home, the advantages talked about in the body copy (i.e. the words in small print) seemed pretty tame. As one dubious admirer of the agency said, 'Doyle Dane's honesty does sometimes overstep the mark . . . the only thing the Lufthansa ads offer you is a nappy-changing tray in the loo.' This wasn't quite true, but it was true enough to hurt. Eventually the agency lost the account.

Still, if that particular campaign did err it erred intelligently. Some other examples of so-called creativity are not intelligent at all. When a German manufacturer actually pays for magazine space to tell British readers in large type 'Don't Buy Körting' it is difficult to believe that such an emphatic negative can possibly inspire a positive result, even if the body copy does add 'until your dealer has convinced you that it is the trade mark of the finest colour television and Hi-Fi in Europe'.

Irritating also are the many British ads which slavishly imitate the American colloquialisms or idiosyncratic syntax of transatlantic masters. The short, verbless sentence can, when expertly used, be very effective. But what is one to make of headlines like the following, which appeared over a Colletts ad for Rocola shirts? 'When we make a shirt. We make a shirt.' With full stops after both shirts. For no reason. At all.

This is the kind of trick which has provoked accusations that copywriters are so busy trying to impress each other that they forget that there are a lot of people out there who are so ill educated that they have never heard of Bill Bernbach or read a single copy of the *New York Art Directors Annual* (the Bible of agency creatives the world over) but who are still supposed to be persuaded to buy the client's goods.

GLITTERING PRIZES 10

Why should copywriters, and for that matter art directors, try to impress each other? The answer to that question could be summed up in one word: awards.

While a given campaign may or may not help sell the goods and thus please the client, it can still benefit the creative staff concerned if it wins an award from a jury of their peers. There are a number of bodies which organise award schemes for print ads and commercials, of which the most important in this country is the Designers and Art Directors Association.

Each year the Association appoints a number of juries, members of which are themselves mostly practising copywriters, designers and TV commercials directors, who sift through thousands of entries to pick prizewinners in various categories of advertising. In addition, awards are given for non-advertising graphic design, but basically it's an ad industry affair, and the annual dinner at which the awards are presented is one of the highlights of the advertising year. After the ceremony the best of each crop of entries, including the gold and silver award winners, are published in the *D & AD Annual*.

Taking the 1975 Annual, the 13th published by the Association, one sees that the gold award for the most outstanding newspaper advertising campaign of 1974 was won by Collett Dickenson Pearce for its work on recruiting Army officers. A glance at the ads quickly reveals examples of the downbeat wit of the Bernbach school. 'Any young man who says he wants to be an Army Officer should have his motives examined' is not the kind of heading one can imagine finding favour in Lord Kitchener's day but, given the scepticism of today's potential recruit, it is justified, and the ad is well written and cleverly laid out.

The gold award for the best film also went to a Government-sponsored ad, this time for fire prevention. It made extraordinarily skilful use of sound effects, children's voices calling out in a ghostly fashion, as the camera panned through a home devastated by fire. The punchline: 'Keep matches away from children'. The agency responsible: Thomas Kettley Hugo Browne.

Among silver award winners: commercials by Collett Dickenson Pearce for Benson and Hedges and Hovis, by Boase Massimi Pollitt for Cresta, by Kirkwoods for Vladivar vodka.

The vodka film was one of a series made for the cinema and based on the humorous theme that even Russian brasshats are excited about the vodka from Warrington or, as they pronounce it, wodka from Varrington. It appears, incidentally, to have been one of those humorous campaigns which hit the button. Vladivar's sales shot up to 15 per cent of the market, making it the number three brand behind Smirnoff and Cossack. (Of course, its growth also had something to do with an arrangement reached between the makers, Greenall Whitley, and the Bass Charrington chain of pubs.)

Other silver award winners included a Doyle Dane Bernbach poster for Volkswagen (a picture of the Beetle captioned 'You know what practice makes'), a Saatchi and Saatchi poster for the Health Euducation Council ('Is it fair to force your baby to smoke cigarettes?' over a picture of a nude pregnant woman) and ads by BBDO for Sony TV sets and by Davidson Pearce for Colt International, makers of industrial heating and ventilation equipment.

A high proportion of the material included in the 'Annual' and in all preceding 'Annuals' comes indeed from a handful of agencies—and the name Collett Dickenson Pearce is particularly prominent. The same handful of agencies have also tended to dominate other awards contests. The same TV commercials for Hovis, for example, which won a D & AD silver for Colletts carried off a gold award at the National Broadcast Advertising Festival. And the same Health Education Council anti-smoking campaign which won a D & AD silver for Saatchi took a Grand Prix in the British Press Advertising Awards, sponsored by the magazine *Campaign*. In 1976 Colletts again led in the awards stakes, taking a D & AD gold for its Heineken advertising.

From time to time one hears allegations—occasionally they have even got into print—that there is a clique of people working in the more self-consciously creative (in the Bernbachite sense) agencies who have somehow got their hands on the awards system and turned it in effect into a mutual admiration society. Such talk inevitably contains an element of sour grapes, but it gains substance from the fact that the judges at awards contests frequently come from the same agencies as the prizewinners and are even themselves awarded prizes by their fellow judges. (However impressive their work may be this is bound to raise nasty suspicions of mutual back-scratching.)

One does not, however, have to subscribe to any conspiracy theory to recognise that certain kinds of work are most likely to win awards, even when the organisers conscientiously bring in objective outsiders, such as marketing people from manufacturing companies, to help in the judging. Ideally, the ads which got the awards would be those which were most effective in accomplishing the advertiser's aim, whether this was to gain more sales, maintain the existing sales level or, as it might be in some cases, to deflect public criticism of a company or increase public awareness of Government services. In practice it is impossible to give awards for effectiveness. Quite apart from the general difficulty, to which we have already alluded and to which we shall return, of ever determining the extent to which advertising, as distinct from other factors, has contributed to, say, increasing sales, no awards jury can even begin to assess the likely commercial effectiveness of a given commercial or print ad without knowing a good deal about the precise condition of the market concerned.

Since juries do not have the time or the opportunity, even if they wanted to, to research the background of every ad they are asked to consider, they are forced back on aesthetic criteria—wit, originality, lucidity, tasteful photography, skilful film editing—about which they can form some immediate opinion. They may say, as the rules of the Broadcast Award Festival required them to say, that what they are judging is 'the effective communication of good advertising ideas'. The fact remains that there are certain kinds of commercials, notably in the detergents field, which would never win an award but which have been responsible for—no, let us be cautious, associated with—highly successful sales results. It is by no means certain that advertising which even housewives would commonly dismiss as boring and disagreeable cannot be in this sense effective; on the contrary, there is some respectable research evidence that it can.

So certain types of ad tend to get the awards, both at home and abroad. (For there are international advertising contests too, the most important being the Screen Advertising World Association festivals held alternately at Cannes and Venice.) And certain agencies tend to produce more of these ads than do others, to the disgruntlement of a number of their competitors, who will tell you, with obvious logic, that advertising awards do not sell products and, with slightly less logic, that the awards game is not worth playing.

Indubitably the awards game *is* worth playing—for those individuals who do well at it. Many a young copywriter or art director has seen his market value shoot up in a short space of time thanks to the publicity he has gained within the industry after winning an award or two. For instance, copywriter Chris Wilkins, who made his name in his early twenties working at J. Walter Thompson on its award-winning Guinness campaign, was snapped up by Boase Massimi Pollitt for a salary of £6,000, double what he had been earning at JWT. (That was some six years ago when such sums were not derisory. Later he moved, presumably for a lot more money, to Saatchis.) His immediate superior at JWT, creative group head Tom Rayfield, built his own reputation largely on the same account. He was hired in 1974 to be creative director of Lintas, at a salary not far below £15,000, from which agency he subsequently moved on to become creative director of the Kirkwood Company.

Yes, winning awards does an individual no harm and can do him or her a great deal of good, not least psychologically. Whether it benefits an agency to anything like the same extent is more problematical. Collett Dickenson Pearce's impressive business record has almost certainly benefited; though no advertiser hires an agency solely because it has won awards, winning a lot of them is one way of attracting the advertiser's attention and getting the agency on to the shortlist of those invited to compete for an account. Awards are, in other words, a good advertisement. But, like good advertisements, they don't always sell the goods.

Doyle Dane Bernbach's problem for years after it set up shop in London in 1964 was that it became known as the agency which won all the awards but couldn't make any money. More precisely, the London office failed to attract the big packaged goods accounts which bump up an agency's billing and, for all the prestige won by its creative department, remained a small firm until it bought and merged with Gallagher Smail, a young agency of similar size. Managerially it was a reverse takeover. Tom Gallagher, a breezy but businesslike Irishman, became boss of the London office. Four years later Bill Bernbach summoned him across the ocean to run the parent agency in New York.

Apropos of awards, it should be explained that entering for them costs money, and some agencies take the view that it's not worth paying to take part in an exercise which is basically irrelevant to the proper function of advertising, which is to serve the client. It's an attitude calculated to enhance an agency's reputation with those advertisers who are suspicious of la-di-da creatives, although it sometimes smacks of humbug.

If agencies have reason to question the value of the awards system, no such qualms affect the TV production companies which specialise in making advertising films. They can never be accused of concentrating on a concept which is too arty for the product advertised or too fanciful for the audience the films are aimed at, for the concept is the business of the agency which briefs them. A production company, typically a small partnership, is judged by its execution—lighting, casting, cutting, the whole filmic bag of tricks—and this usually is a determining factor in whether a commercial wins an award.

The awards system has helped to make the names of the film directors involved in the shooting of such commercials familiar to agencies and advertisers. Among the best known are Alan Parker, who directed some of the Colletts films for Benson and Hedges and Heineken (Parker is himself a former Colletts copywriter), Ridley Scott, who made the Hovis films, and animator Richard Williams, who put the Cresta bear on the screen. All these run their own companies, the business success of which is very much dependent upon their own personal reputation. There are in fact only a very few advertising film production companies which are big enough not to have their fortunes tied to those of one or two sought-after directors. The biggest is probably James Garrett and Partners.

Awards or no awards, the aesthetic elements in advertisements are bound to be of considerable importance to at least one category of people, namely those who produce them. No matter how marketing-oriented an agency's creative department may be, no matter how scornful of campaigns designed to appeal more to educated middle-class males (like most of the inhabitants of creative departments) than to ignorant working-class females (like most of the purchasers of branded goods in the supermarkets), it still has its professional pride. It wants its work to be seen as at least craftsmanlike, if not actually brilliant, as original if not recherché, as up-to-date if not avant-garde.

If it were not so, agencies would not get as upset as they do when accused of plagiarising others' ideas. Such accusations regularly enliven the pages of the advertising trade press, and pictures of look-alike ads are assured of gleeful and attentive readership. The usual defence when these coincidences are pointed out is along the lines of 'great minds think alike', denying any conscious imitation. And yet if the likely sales effectiveness of an ad was the only question of any importance, there would be no logical reason for a copywriter not to say, 'sure I pinched the idea, it suits my product perfectly, so why bother with a new one. I'm a salesman, not a man of letters.'

One could fill many pages with examples of this kind of thing, but let's just take two. Coincidence number one: a press ad by agency Cogent Elliott for Climax fork-lift trucks featured a brawny, aggressive-looking workman standing with arms folded under the heading (meant, no doubt, to be mildly shocking) 'The worst thing that could happen to a fork-lift truck'. The visual similarity was striking to an ad which had appeared three years previously, devised by agency Davidson Pearce Berry and Spottiswoode for Colt factory ventilation equipment. The Colt ad featured a brawny, aggressive-looking workman standing with arms folded. The heading (meant to be mildly shocking) was 'You can stuff your 28-day cooling off period, Barbara'. The Barbara referred to was Barbara Castle, and the cooling-off period was part of the pre-1970 Labour Government's attempt to regulate industrial relations.

The reaction of Cogent Elliott's creative director, Bob Nesbitt, when the similarity was pointed out to him, was typical of what happens on such occasions. 'I think it's irrelevant,' said he. 'Anyway we're talking about fork-lift trucks.' Ironically Nesbitt had himself been employed at Davidson Pearce at the time it produced the Barbara ad.

Coincidence number two: as a variation on its After Eight snob-appeal campaign J. Walter Thompson produced in 1973 two punning press ads. They depicted elegant After Eight people in a smart restaurant and on board a yacht. The respective captions read: 'And then Rupert asked if I'd care to lunch Al Fresco. Well, I mean, I've never even met the chap!' and 'How do I like Modigliani? I always think it's best to leave it to the chef's discretion, don't you?'

The copywriter, Adam Rowntree, said he hadn't been influenced by, indeed hadn't heard of, previous campaigns using similar puns, e.g. JWT's own American ads for Ronrico rum ('Ron Rico, Isn't he the Italian film genius. . . ?') and a series by the Streets agency in Britain for Asti Martini ('Asti Martini. Didn't he conduct the Philharmonic?').

So originality is prized, up to a point, as a badge of professional competence. But only up to a point. For, although any agency will be irritated by being accused of copying the details of others' work, all agencies want their ads to be in tune with the mood of the times. This means that they tend to follow the fashions set in other fields—cinema, literature, the press, music, the graphic arts. The pioneer admen are those who jump on the already rolling bandwagon first; others, more cautious, follow later. In this sense they are all plagiarists, but some are more quick-witted in their plagiarising than are others.

Thus sexual permissiveness reared its ugly (or beautiful, depending on your taste) head almost everywhere else before it crept into advertising with campaigns like Smirnoff's. By the time McCann-Erickson was, on behalf of the Milk Marketing Board, asking the British housewife 'Is your man getting enough?' innuendoes which would once have been considered downright obscene hardly raised an eyebrow. Girls running through dappled sunlight became a cinematic cliché before they found their way into TV commercials. The nostalgia boom was already well under way before admen got in on the act with commercials like Dorland Advertising's award-winning evocations of fin-de-siècle France for Dubonnet or the 1930s slice of life recreated for Ovaltine by an agency called TBWA.

The power of fashion is perhaps most obvious in the soundtracks of commercials. The simple, nursery-rhyme-type jingles of the early days of television—'Murraymints, Murraymints, the too-good-to-hurry mints', 'You'll look a little lovelier each day with fabulous pink Camay', 'The Esso sign means happy motoring', etc.—have given way to songs and background music cast in the latest pop styles. Correction, the not quite latest, because advertising never wants to get out in front, it prefers to shove from behind. So Kelloggs Corn Flakes had music deliberately reminiscent of the singer Tom Jones, and for Coca-Cola McCann-Erickson used an original song, 'It's the real thing', by Roger Cooke and Roger Greenaway, which was so right for the times that it was turned into a best-selling record.

It is not only the big shifts in public sentiment which are

reflected in advertising; the sharper creative departments are adept at seizing on events of purely temporary significance and using them for their own ends. J. Walter Thompson, among others, is very good at this. At Christmas 1975 it managed to combine allusions to both the festive season and the recent rise in postal charges into one colour magazine ad for After Eights in which a *grande dame* held up one of the pretty little wrappers containing the chocolates and said: 'As Lucinda so rightly points out, it's the only envelope that doesn't require an outrageously expensive stamp this Christmas.'

When the threat of petrol rationing loomed after the 1973 Middle East War JWT published a spoof ration card for Guinness. When Big Ben broke down in 1976 Colletts was quick off the mark with a newspaper ad showing the clock being 'refreshed' with Heineken.

Such things are the small change of advertising creativity, and it is a moot point how far they contribute to the commercial aims of the advertiser. But when the tricks are performed well, they certainly contribute powerfully to the standing within their trade of the admen who perform them.

GETTING THE CHOP 11

Advertising agency people are a talkative lot, greatly given to bar-room gossip and rumour-mongering. The gossip frequently is about who's in and who's out. Given the talent-intensive nature of their trade and the fact that the recognised way to get on in it is by moving from agency to agency, there is always plenty of news of this kind even in the absence of the rows, bust-ups and breakaways which are bound to happen from time to time when large groups of clever and ambitious people are put to work together. But the gossip which really makes admen prick up their ears is not about who but about what's in and what's out, the 'what' meaning accounts.

There is no question more vital to the livelihood of Adland's denizens than that of which accounts are leaving which agencies for which others and which, if they are not actually on the move, are likely to become mobile. When the accounts are big ones, spending more than half a million pounds a year, interest is particularly keen. A few account gains or losses of that size can make or break a medium-sized agency, and the morale of even the biggest can be markedly affected by news that an important client is hiring or firing them.

And, although it can be shown statistically that the average agency tenure of an account is fairly long (six or seven years), a lot of hiring and firing nevertheless takes place. The wise agency never assumes that any account is permanently safe even when it has worked for the client concerned for many years and produced advertising generally reckoned to be successful. Agencies are always particularly nervous when a client company appoints a new marketing director. The easiest way for him (or, more rarely, her) to make his (or her) weight felt is to change the advertising. Of course that doesn't mean that there may not also be genuine business arguments for doing so.

A case in point is that of Schweppes soft drinks, one of the biggest accounts to switch agencies in recent years. The switch, from Ogilvy Benson and Mather to J. Walter Thompson, took place shortly after Schweppes had acquired a new marketing director, in the suave but pushy person of Keith Holloway, formerly with the Heinz company. The situation Holloway found when he arrived at Schweppes at the beginning of 1972 was that, though the company retained its dominance of the mixer drinks market (i.e. tonic, ginger ale and the other stuff people add to hard liquor to help them swallow it), worth at that time an annual £80 million, its share was being nibbled into by smaller brands, notably Canada Dry. This is not the kind of development any company, even a very big, very rich one, can view with complacency. The first thing Holloway did was review the advertising strategy.

At that time OBM had held the account for some eight years, and its TV commercials for Schweppes were among the best remembered of all advertising campaigns. The theme, or 'copy platform' to use a bit of Adland jargon, was a humorous one, dating from the time that Stanhope Shelton had been creative director and the agency's work had born the stamp of his personal exuberance. The commercials starred (an appropriate word in this case) the actor Bill Franklyn as a spoof secret agent getting into all kinds of weird and wonderful scrapes through which he sailed imperturbably, cautioning the audience about 'Schh . . . you know who'. The catch phrase was unmistakably attached to the brand and, though the campaign is now long over, still is.

But, though Holloway agreed that the 'secret of Schh . . .' made excellent entertainment, he decided that the entertainment wasn't doing anything to convince the audience of the advantages of the individual products within the Schweppes range. According to him, the agency accepted this view and agreed that Franklyn should be dropped but proved unable to come up with the creative goods. OBM people put it a different way. 'We tried all sorts of campaign ideas,' said a director of the agency, 'but we never found anything to beat the existing one.'

By this time OBM was competing for the account with three other agencies, all of which were already working for Schweppes on other business. The three were J. Walter Thompson, which handled the small Rose's Lime Juice account, Boase Massimi Pollitt (Cresta soft drinks, a new range manufactured by Schweppes) and Dorland (Dubonnet, which Schweppes distributes in this country). All were asked to make presentations to Holloway of their ideas for how to advertise the drinks bearing the Schweppes brand name.

In the event JWT won and picked up £800,000 of new billing as a 1972 Christmas present. The advertising world leaned forward with eager anticipation to see how it would cap the 'secret of Sch . . .'.

Many hoots of derision went up when it transpired that the 'Sch . . .' had been dropped in favour of the '. . . weppes'. The word's previously invisible backside reappeared, so to speak, with the head chopped off. What JWT had done was to stick to the humorous vein but to invent a mythical ingredient called Weppes which gave the drinks their special attraction. The Weppes could be of various kinds, ginger or lemon for example, thus enabling commercials and magazine ads to focus, as Holloway wished, on the different varieties available within the Schweppes range. The general opinion in other agencies was that the campaign was unimpressive, though Holloway declared himself well satisfied, and it did not last long. Eventually the Weppes were abandoned. Not, however, before some wag at OBM had pinned a large sign to the agency notice board saying 'Jesus Wepped'.

Rightly or wrongly the feeling persisted there among all who had been involved with the account that they were the victims of Holloway's personal ambition. After a little while had elapsed, OBM's managing director, Richard Venables, wrote to John Beasley, chairman of Schweppes, suggesting that he might like to discuss returning the account to the agency, the implication being that JWT's efforts were disappointing. The tone taken by Venables annoyed Holloway, and he denounced the OBM managing director as being guilty of ungentlemanly conduct.

John Beasley, however, who had been appointed to the Schweppes chairmanship in 1974 after running the Cadbury-Typhoo division of the Cadbury Schweppes empire, was himself disappointed with JWT's efforts. He hinted that if he had been in charge two years earlier things might have turned out differently. 'There's one golden rule,' he said, 'you don't change a good campaign until you know you've got something better.' The search for something better led at the beginning of 1976 to a fresh contest for the account. OBM, which by this time had acquired Canada Dry, was no longer in the running. Saatchi and Saatchi Garland-Compton emerged the winner in a decision seen by a number of people in Adland as a snub by Beasley to his deputy chairman, Holloway.

This was perhaps an unfair way of looking at things, since the two in fact agreed on the choice. What was true was that after JWT's original scheme for the 1976 campaign had been turned down, senior executives of the agency had gone to Holloway's home with revised proposals and got his backing for them only to have them too turned down by Beasley the next day.

'They came back with the guts of a good idea,' acknowledged the chairman, 'which we invited them to go away and work up. I'm convinced that if they'd stuck it out they could have got there.' But, feeling that they were caught in a power play between two strong but very different personalities and disconsolate that other agencies were being invited to submit ideas, JWT chose to resign. 'We gave them the chance to resign,' commented the blunt-talking Beasley, 'we could have sacked them.'

The Saatchi campaign for Schweppes, which broke on TV in June 1976, was written, ironically enough, by Chris Wilkins, who had first made his creative reputation at JWT. The punch line was 'You can always spot a rotter by his total lack of Schweppes', and the commercials featured characters like Jack the Rotter and Stinker Fosdyke, 'a truly dedicated rotter', who last took a bath in 1947. Beasley confidently expected the campaign to restore what he called the 'premium gift' character of Schweppes advertising, with the ads being perceived as an extra source of consumer satisfaction.

The blow to OBM's prestige of losing Schweppes was slight compared with that suffered some years previously by the agency it was to take over, S. H. Benson, when it lost the Guinness account, also to JWT.

No description, however condensed, of the British advertising industry can fail to make some mention of Guinness. Not only because it is one of the biggest advertisers (£3 million spent in 1975 alone on promoting a single product) but because its advertising, both early and recent, is a *locus classicus* for the industry's practitioners and, indeed, for its historians.

Bensons kept the account for all of 40 years, starting in 1929 with an ad in the *Daily Chronicle* which was, as its headline proudly announced, 'The first advertisement ever issued in a national paper to advertise Guinness'. The copy was in keeping with the solemnity of the occasion. 'For 150 years,' it began, 'the House of Guinness have been engaged in brewing Stout. By concentrating upon doing one thing well, they have produced a beverage which stands alone.'

The ad went on, in a style of which Claude Hopkins no doubt thoroughly approved, to speak of the product's purity, its health-giving value and its nourishing properties. 'Guinness is one of the most nourishing beverages, richer in carbohydrates than a glass of milk. That is one reason why it is so good when people are tired or exhausted.' And the ad proclaimed in words that were to become famous 'Guinness is good for you'.

But, despite this earnest informational start—or perhaps the word should be misinformational, if you don't accept the ad's statements that Guinness builds muscles and guards against insomnia—Guinness advertising very soon became famous for a completely different, quite unHopkinsite approach.

Bensons made Guinness practically synonymous with

humour. A variety of styles was employed, including pastiches of Lewis Carroll, but the ads which made the deepest impression were the two long-running series of posters originally designed by the artist Gilroy. One series, captioned 'Guinness for strength' depicted such pieces of hyperbole as a workman carrying a huge girder with one hand or popping up through a manhole to lift a steamroller, again with one hand. The other, captioned 'My goodness—my Guinness', was the animals series. A zoo keeper chased after a sea-lion balancing a glass of Guinness on its nose, a kangaroo stood to attention with a bottle of Guinness in its pouch. From the 1930s to the 1950s there were many variations on these simple themes. Lions, ostriches, toucans, kinkajous all got a look in.

Meanwhile Guinness sales in Britain grew from 750,000 barrels in 1936 to two million in 1951, aided by this happy, fun-loving advertising. When commercial television started in 1955 it was only natural that the comic menagerie should be transferred from the hoardings to the small screen, and so it was.

But *had* the sales been aided by the humour? Were the people who enjoyed looking at the funny animals the same people that went into a pub and ordered a glass of the black stuff? The Guinness company began to wonder. Market research strengthened its doubts, establishing that the typical Guinness drinker was a mature man who drank the stuff not in gay abandon but as a kind of restorative.

A change of strategy was ordered. The company, nervous that its market might run away from it—and as the only major British brewer without its own chain of pubs it couldn't afford to take the future for granted—decided that the time had come to appeal to those serious mature chaps more directly. In 1963 the first posters appeared showing a Guinness drinker. Previously the policy had always been to avoid doing so for fear of identifying the product too closely with one type of consumer when the aim was to enlist all classes and ages and both sexes. The Guinness drinker was now unveiled as a rather nondescript-looking fellow in a raincoat. 'You've earned that Guinness,' the posters told him, which was about as unhumorous as you could get.

The same dreary message (it could have been written by the research firm; maybe it was) was put across in the new TV commercials devised by Bensons. These featured dreary men in dreary bars, drinking to a background of dreary music. 'Clean, strong, dark, rewarding,' grumbled the voice-over. 'After a day's work a man needs his Guinness.'

Later films cheered up a bit, with shots of sportsmen and strolling couples and the line 'There's a whole world in a Guinness', indicating that the company's marketing brains had had second thoughts about the wisdom of concentrating on that nondescript raincoated drinker—and, my God, even if you looked like that, would you want to look like that? But, whatever the thinking behind them, the commercials failed to achieve the distinction that had been universally recognised in the great humorous poster campaigns.

Bensons lost the account in 1969. Micky Barnes, chairman of the agency at the time, recounted that there had been rumours for years that the client was getting restless, and the rumours had multiplied after his charismatic predecessor Bobby Bevan's departure in 1963. In the eyes of the poshocracy which ran Guinness, Barnes acknowledged rather touchingly, 'I, with my grammar school education and market-place soap experience, was certainly not the man to occupy Bevan's shoes.' He reckoned that there were several schools of thought in the client company at that time which variously wanted a 'hot creative shop', a strong marketing-oriented agency and an agency with which the gentlemen of Guinness could establish a 'cosy, academic relationship'. He had no doubts, recalled Barnes, that the one best able to satisfy all these requirements was the one they chose, JWT.

How far personal relationships do count in such a decision it is never possible to gauge without having been involved oneself. As in politics so in advertising, differences of opinion tend to get inextricably mixed up with differences of personality. Certainly one Bensons director in 1969 commented bitterly on his colleagues that he had never known people work so hard to lose an account. Be that as it may, Guinness got from JWT something which

Schweppes three years later did not get—a fresh burst of creative inspiration.

JWT managed to put wit and humour back into Guinness ads without forgetting to whom they were talking. The agency was perhaps helped in this task by the fact that, with the 1960 introduction of draught Guinness, the market for the black stuff had expanded. More young people and more middle-class people started drinking it. TV commercials, as befits a truly mass medium, have developed the common touch, with little comedy situations like the boy on the sunny beach who, by drinking a cold Guinness, starts a run by other thirsty holidaymakers on the pub—of which he then turns out to be an employee—or the customers who patiently explain to the man they take to be the barman exactly what kind of drink it is they're after only to discover that they're in an antique shop.

Even more admired have been the magazine ads, including a spoof *What?* report on Guinness, instructions on how to economise on the product by mixing it with champagne, and a challenge to women in the form of a full Guinness glass held in an elegantly manicured and beringed female hand—'Would you be seen out with one?' Women in fact are reckoned to account for a quarter of Guinness drinkers, though a good deal less than a quarter of the amount drunk.

Agencies can lose accounts for a variety of reasons. Sometimes because of personalities, sometimes because the advertiser is dissatisfied with the way his sales are going, sometimes—in the case of multinational accounts—when headquarters in America or wherever decide to drop one agency and hire another worldwide. (Thus Masius lost the Vauxhall account in 1973 on the orders of General Motors in Detroit after the main GM agency, Campbell-Ewald, was taken over by the Interpublic group. The account was switched to Waseys, henceforth to be called Wasey Campbell-Ewald, which was already within the Interpublic fold.) Sometimes, although not very often, the rupture occurs when the agency fires the client! This may sound rather like the rat knocking off the ratcatcher, and indeed any agency's claim to have resigned an account voluntarily without having been forced to do so is likely to provoke scepticism. However, the scepticism is not always justified. There are three main reasons for (genuine) voluntary resignations: (*a*) the account is unprofitable; (*b*) the agency refuses to give way to the client in a disagreement about advertising policy; (*c*) the agency wants to be free to go after a conflicting account which it otherwise wouldn't stand a chance of getting.

Taking (*a*) first, the profitability of an account depends partly on the amount of work it involves and partly on the size of the agency. A big agency has big overheads (wages, rent) and just cannot afford to devote time to an account which contributes less than a given amount of income. JWT, for example, made it a general rule even in the early Seventies that it wouldn't touch an account billing under £100,000 a year, and under the pressure of inflation the floor gradually rose. A smaller agency with a smaller staff and fewer overheads can often make money out of an account which it is uneconomic for a larger shop to handle, which is why JWT created a subsidiary agency, Contract Advertising, specifically to handle such accounts.

Leo Burnett, however, when the general drop in advertising spending made the financial going difficult in 1975, decided it had to get rid of its smaller accounts in a hurry. It resigned eight of them at a blow, totalling £1½ million of billing, and at the same time sacked 53 of its staff. This caused quite a shock in Adland, more because of the number of people involved than the number of accounts. The same kinds of pressure had been forcing other agencies to trim their staffs, but they had been doing so more slowly and discreetly, and although the end result might have been the same their manner appeared less brutal. Note, by the way, that admen do not by and large belong to trade unions and have only their own individual contracts to protect them against the rigours of redundancy.

That kind of clean sweep of accounts is extremely unusual. The only precedent anybody in the industry could remember was in 1969 when a smallish agency called PKL fired nine clients, spending a total of £1 million a year, and got rid of 11 of its staff of 36. PKL was a firm with a strong creative reputation and it announced that its priority was to carry on doing excellent work for a limited number of clients rather than to expand to the point where its owning directors, notably chairman Nigel Seely and creative director Peter Mayle, could no longer take a personal interest in everything that went on in it. How true this was nobody has ever been quite sure, but the publicity effect was enormous and largely beneficial to Messrs Seely and Mayle. Before very long they had replaced the £1 million of billing with an even greater amount of business more to their taste and shortly after that they sold out, at great profit to themselves, to BBDO (Batten Barton Durstine and Osborne), a big American agency with a then somewhat weak London office.

When it comes to category (*b*)—the agency with the courage of its convictions—the most memorable British example of recent years was Collett Dickenson Pearce's resignation of the £1 million Ford account in 1975. The car firm had asked the agency to prepare several alternative campaigns at the same time, from which it, the client, would choose. Colletts refused to comply with this request, regarding such a method of working as unacceptable. So, after eight years, their association ended. It was difficult for many observers to believe that, at a moment of general economic stringency, any agency, even one with as high an opinion of itself as Colletts, had actually thrown a million-pound account out of the window, but according to well-informed sources at a rival agency, J. Walter Thompson, it was true.

The reason why JWT was well informed about Ford's advertising was that it already had a slice of the company's business. JWT is in fact Ford's main agency in America and in Continental Europe, and the European campaigns are coordinated from JWT's London office. This made JWT favourite to replace Colletts as Ford's main British agency. But instead the company chose Ogilvy Benson and Mather.

There was a certain poetic justice in this decision, which seasoned admen were not slow to appreciate. Eight years before, when the Ford account had been, as the jargon has it, up for grabs, four agencies had been shortlisted: LPE (later to become Leo Burnett), which had up to that time been handling it, JWT, Colletts (which got it) and OBM (then called Ogilvy and Mather). To free themselves to compete for Ford the Ogilvy people had resigned the £250,000 Triumph car account. A vain sacrifice, as it turned out, but a neat example of reason (*c*), listed before, for firing a client.

The excitement generated when a big (or even a not so big) advertising account changes hands is due not only to the human consequences, sometimes traumatic, at the losing end but to the racetrack character of the contest to pick a new agency. Typically a client company which has decided to move its account draws up a long list of possible contenders which it then reduces by process of elimination to a shortlist of perhaps four or five. The process of elimination will certainly involve checking to see whether any of the potential candidates handles competitive business; it will probably involve contacts of some kind with some or all of them, which may take the form of visits by the marketing director or advertising manager to look around each agency's offices, meet its principals and be told something about its work, organisation and advertising philosophy. This may be done more or less informally. At its most formal, the agency's briefing of a prospective client becomes a full-scale presentation at which the heads of various departments (creative, research, etc.) deliver lectures, show him charts, entertain him with a show-reel of commercials, answer his questions and, of course, make sure that he eats and drinks his fill.

This is obviously a time-consuming business, and the number of agency presentations which any client can see within a given period is limited. For this reason some clients make a hobby of attending such presentations even when they are not in the market for a new agency. It assists the process of elimination when the day for hiring one arrives.

Other sources of information about agencies are the brochures, sometimes very glossy, which they produce about themselves, the coverage they get in the advertising trade press and a relatively new service called the Advertising Agency Register. The Register, a private commercial venture, provides interested advertisers for a fee with data on the business performance of the agencies which subscribe to it and with biographical details about their most important employees. It also keeps a library of videotapes on which agencies exhibit their work and talk about themselves.

The real excitement, however, starts when the process of elimination is over and the finalists are galloping up the straight. This is the stage at which the agencies may be asked, or may decide off their own bat, to offer speculative presentations. Mark the phrase, it is the subject of perennial controversy in Adland. A speculative presentation is no mere teach-in about an agency's merits, of the type previously described, it is the submission to the client of detailed plans for an advertising campaign which it is thought would suit him, including creative work which may range from rough lay-outs to finished TV commercials. The expense of a speculative presentation can, therefore, be very large, not only in terms of executive time spent preparing it but in terms of actual production costs.

In theory, if a client requests this kind of presentation he pays a fee to cover the expense incurred. In practice, the fee rarely covers the whole cost, which even in 1975, at the height of a period of general retrenchment in the ad industry, could run, for a big agency pitching for a big account, to as much as £10,000. Remember we are talking about money spent speculatively, i.e. with no guarantee that the account will be won.

In the old, less cost-conscious days, the amount spent could go even higher. In 1970 Benton and Bowles spent £20,000 of its own money on a speculative presentation for Martini. It was £20,000 down the drain; the account went to McCann-Erickson.

Objections to the principle of speculative presentations come from both advertisers and agencies. Many advertisers dislike the system because they suspect that it leads to their own agencies devoting executive and creative time and effort to prospective clients while neglecting existing ones. This is a view supported by numbers of agency people, who also point out that it is impossible to produce proper advertising proposals for an account with the problems of which they are only partly familiar.

There is, furthermore, a widespread feeling that it is somehow not quite dignified to do speculative presentations. Ideally an advertiser should pick an agency, it is felt, on the basis of its proven merits and not try to make it jump through hoops. Such an attitude is associated particularly with Doyle Dane Bernbach which has always set its face against speculative presentations. The ban, admirable perhaps as a proof of self-confidence, did Doyle Dane considerable harm when it first opened its office in London. It was in line for a £500,000 account, and the advertising manager of the company concerned was eager that the agency should get it. But he needed some 'pretty pictures' to show his board of directors in order to clinch the decision. The London office appealed to Bill Bernbach in New York to relax his inflexible rule and allow it to do some speculative ads. He refused, and the badly needed piece of business went elsewhere.

But time changes everything, even the most cherished principles, and more recently, when the Martell brandy account was choosing a new agency, Doyle Dane agreed to make a speculative presentation. The pitch was successful—fortunately for the agency; to compromise one's principles for gain is understandable, but to compromise them without gaining anything is merely ridiculous. The agency's chairman, Brian Waldron, explained that it had been decided to make an exception in the case of Martell because 'the problems seemed to be in the execution area'.

It hardly needs pointing out that in advertising some at least of the problems always are in 'the execution area' (even when the only execution in question is giving the bullet to the agency which has been found wanting).

Humbug apart, the controversy over speculative presentations can be summed up as follows: No advertiser likes the idea of his agency doing them for other people; when it comes to choosing a new agency for himself, they nevertheless constitute a very convenient way of comparing agencies as well as an opportunity to pick the brains of all the candidates. No agency likes the idea of spending a lot of money with no return; when the prize is great and the race is a close one, almost any agency can be pushed, or will push itself, into doing speculative work.

What is particularly galling for an agency is when it is asked to do a speculative campaign and then sees the prize go to another agency which has done no speculative work at all. This happened in the case of Stork margarine, a £1½ million account which had been held by Lintas for 40 years until 1974, when the client Van den Berghs (part of Unilever) became discontented. Lintas was asked to re-pitch for the account, and it made an expensive full presentation, as did another agency which had been invited to compete, Davidson Pearce Berry and Spottiswoode. In the end neither was chosen. The business went instead to McCann-Erickson on the basis of the work it had done on other Van den Berghs accounts which it already handled.

Another account which surprisingly moved without a pitch being made, in fact without any open contest at all, was Double Diamond beer, market leader among keg bitters and the brand for which Young and Rubicam had made famous the slogan 'We're only here for the beer'. Y & R lost the account, to its own astonishment as well as everyone else's, after Allied Breweries had appointed a new marketing manager, who decreed that a fresh approach was needed. The £800,000 account was switched to the Kirkwood Company, which already handled Allied's Long Life beer.

Perhaps *the* most curious story to do with an account switching agencies is that of the TV commercial made by Masius Wynne-Williams in 1972 for Nescafé, when it was struggling to keep the client. The commercial, described by Masius's then creative director, the late Desmond Skirrow, as 'the most effective this agency has ever produced', showed a cup of coffee in close-up, all swirling liquid and chintzy china, with a rose beside it. Background music, also swirling, was from Peer Gynt, classical but undemanding. A man's tender voice was heard saying, 'I'm going to make you a lovely cup of coffee.' Designed to pull at the heart-strings of every old-fashioned, lower-class housewife in the country. Designed, too, to correct what was seen as Nestlé's previous wrong emphasis on the coffee-ness of its instant coffee, when the British market valued instant coffee for its milkiness.

'We were going down Milk Avenue into Milk Country to correct an unintentional cock-up,' said Skirrow. 'It could,' he sighed appreciatively, 'have been a commercial for cocoa.'

The client shared the appreciation but not sufficiently to refrain from changing agencies. The problem, according to John Hamilton, who at that time was marketing manager at Nestlé, was that Masius couldn't suggest any convincing ways of following up the new idea. Jack Wynne-Williams didn't improve matters when he quipped, at a lunch meeting with Nestlé's managing director, William Manahan, that he had thought clients criticised advertising only when sales were falling. Masius was fired, and the £1½ million account went to Collett Dickenson Pearce, which tried out a variation of its usual style of downbeat humour on the brand. Two years later Manahan had been replaced by a new managing director, Tug Wilson, who didn't get on with Colletts, and the account had switched again.

The new agency was McCann-Erickson, which had been runner-up in the previous contest and had impressed Nestlé with its proposals for developing the 'lovely cup' approach. McCanns hadn't forgotten the old Masius commercial nor the fact that on a trial run in Yorkshire it had appeared to give extraordinarily good results. In early 1976 McCanns resurrected the film and announced that it would produce a new series of commercials based on the same theme, which was still 'absolutely right'. If Masius felt any bitterness it didn't show it. Managing director Peter Gwynn said he was 'delighted' at the ironic turn of events.

Let it not be thought that agencies acquire new business simply by waiting patiently until they are invited to pitch for it. That was not true even in the days, now long gone, when the Institute of Practitioners in Advertising (the agencies' own trade association) forbade its members to solicit another member's client. There are ways and means of attracting a prospective client's attention even without soliciting.

J. Walter Thompson, for one, has always specialised in spinning a social web around the men in charge of the accounts it wanted to get. Positioning its people, that is, where they have the most chance to cultivate the said prospects.

Being a large agency with a large number of business contacts is bound to help, as is having employees who play a full part in a variety of voluntary (not only ad industry) activities. Some large agencies, including JWT, have a director with special responsibility for planning where their main efforts to get new business should be made. In others, new business-getting is the job of the managing director, but whoever performs the function it is normally regarded as a vital one.

Smaller agencies, having less chance of seducing clients by subtle means, are generally more aggressive in their attempts to win accounts. Whenever the news breaks that a juicy account is on the loose—such news may vary in form from a bar-room rumour of discontent on the part of an advertiser to a fully authenticated story in the trade press that competitive presentations are to be asked for—a shoal of agencies will, uninvited, press their attentions upon the said advertiser. Even when he is not thus in the news a substantial advertiser is likely to be on the receiving end of a steady flow of mailing shots from agencies, invitations to attend a presentation or simple offers of lunch.

People being different, the importunate sometimes get sent away with a flea in their ear, sometimes they strike lucky. It's all part of the game, and is understood to be so, but agencies can still become very nervous when they learn that a client has been seen lunching with one of their competitors. The really nasty situation, which crops up not infrequently, is when a client is carrying on an affair with another agency—presentations and all—without telling his lawful wedded agency he is contemplating divorce.

For example, a report once appeared in *Adweek* that Heron Garages might be thinking of taking its account away from its ad agency, John Chesney and Associates. The magazine happened to have discovered that Heron had fixed up to see a presentation by Roe Humphreys (later to change its name to Roe Downton), although this titbit was discreetly not revealed in print. A furious Chesneys director rang the paper threatening legal action on the grounds that the report was devoid of truth and damaging to the agency's business standing. The agency declared that it had been assured by Heron that it was not proposing to swap horses. The editor advised his caller to make quite sure that his client had been completely candid. What transpired between client and agency is not known, but no more was heard of the threats of legal action. Nor did the account move, not for a couple of years that is. Whether Chesneys kept the business because of or in spite of the leak to the press is likewise unknown.

In competing for new business, agencies have over the years found it more and more important to be able to claim an international dimension for their services, not only because many of the big-billing advertisers are multinational companies but because, with the growth of the European Economic Community and the development of international trade generally, British manufacturers have become more aware of the need for advertising support in overseas markets. Very few of the top 50 London agencies are now without some form of representation in the principal West European countries. About 15 are American-owned agencies, subsidiaries of networks like Interpublic, J. Walter Thompson, Ogilvy and Mather, Young and Rubicam, Burnett, Bates, BBDO, Foote Cone and Belding, Kenyon and Eckhardt, which have offices throughout the world.

An American agency which handles an account in one country does not inevitably have the same account in every other. As we have seen, J. Walter Thompson, which has a lot of Ford business in the States and elsewhere, does not advertise Ford cars in Britain, though it has pitched for the account three times since 1960. Nevertheless, an agency always starts favourite if its parent company works for a client's parent. It is no accident that Young and Rubicam London works for Procter and Gamble, as Y & R does in the States, that Leo Burnett handles Marlboro cigarettes in both countries, that David Williams and Ketchum (a London subsidiary of the American agency Ketchum MacLeod and Grove) shares Japan Air Lines with its parent. The traffic is not all one way, though. McCann-Erickson's London office was passed the Esso and Coca-Cola accounts on a plate by New York headquarters, but it won Martini off its own bat and now Martini is a McCann account, coordinated from London, throughout Europe.

Non-American agencies belong in many cases to less monolithic groups. Masius Wynne-Williams, with its own subsidiaries in Europe, South Africa, Australia and New Zealand, is closely linked financially with the American D'Arcy-MacManus (to the extent that they are joint owners of a partnership into which all their profits are pooled). Lintas, though Unilever keeps a 51 per cent stake in it, is 49 per cent owned by the American agency SSC & B (Sullivan Stauffer Colwell and Bayles) and has subsidiaries in many countries. Its Hamburg office is in fact one of the top two agencies in Germany (with McCann) and is much more successful than Lintas London, which has been weakened in recent years by a succession of account losses and management upheavals.

There are yet other patterns of international expansion. Charles Barker, an old-established London agency, formed a partnership with the American firm N. W. Ayer and the Dr Hegemann agency of Düsseldorf and changed its name to Ayer Barker Hegemann. A number of British agencies—Royds, Osborne, Saatchi, Collett Dickenson Pearce—have acquired either controlling or minority interests in Continental agencies.

Some have been content with a much looser association, of which a prime example was the Kimpher group's co-operation with the French Havas group and the American

Needham Harper and Steers. These links brought the British group new accounts such as Moroccan oranges and ITT and enabled it to service its client Thorn-Ferguson in Europe. The relationship was upset in 1976, however, when the international advertising arm of Havas acquired a 50 per cent stake in Boase Massimi Pollitt. Since Univas is financially linked with Needham, its change of British partner also had repercussions in the American market.

12 ADVERTISING À LA CARTE

Let's go no deeper into the intricacies of advertising agency networks. Rather let us ponder the fact that, elaborate as the agency services offered to them may be, there are advertisers, even big ones, who have been asking themselves in all seriousness whether they have to employ an agency at all.

The short answer is no, they don't have to, although there may be advantages in doing so. There may also be disadvantages, and advertisers do have an alternative other than to set up their own house agency. The latter course is not generally favoured because it deprives the advertiser of one great advantage he enjoys vis-à-vis an independent agency, namely that he can fire it if it falls down on the job and hire a new one.

The remaining alternative is to seperate out the different advertising functions which would normally all be performed by an agency and entrust each of them to a specialised company. Now the two basic services provided by a so-called full-service agency, to which all its other activities are subsidiary, are to make ads and to place ads. These days it is possible to buy both these services from highly skilled professionals without using an agency.

Take first the placing of ads, the work done by an agency's media department. As was explained in an earlier chapter, a new species of company, the media broker, has arisen in the past few years to do this job and, as some would say, to undermine the whole rationale of the agency system.

The two biggest media broking firms in London—the Media Department, which is part of the Kimpher group, and Media Buying Services—have the status of agencies, and are therefore officially entitled to agency commission of 15 per cent (or whatever the rate may be in the case of the particular medium). Other brokers use the good offices of friendly agencies to get the commission even when those agencies are not involved in the accounts for which space and airtime are being purchased. Provided the forms are observed, and provided the set-up is such that they have no fear of any default on the money owed to them, the media—newspapers, TV contractors—are happy to go along with this.

The IPA, speaking for agencies as a whole, is not happy. In the words of Jim O'Connor, director of the IPA, 'To recognise media shops is wrong. They can only be in business for two reasons, to offer a cut rate and pay money back to the client.'

Irrespective of the morality of such transactions, O'Connor is correct about their purpose. A client using a media broker will find that the latter probably takes a cut of only 5 per cent of billing, the rest of the media commission being rebated to the advertiser. This money is available to pay for creative work, produced either in-house by the advertiser's own staff or, more usually, by a specialised creative consultancy. Together the fees the client pays to media broker and creative consultancy are supposed to equal the amount he would be charged by a full-service agency. In practice, as O'Connor laments, the total paid often works out cheaper.

The morality of the matter is arguable. To the IPA cut-price advertising on the lines described is an underhand way of doing down the honest folk who work in agencies. Others take the view that the recognition system under which the media owners are supposed to refuse to deal with firms which rebate commission to advertisers is nothing more nor less than a restrictive practice and point out that agency commission is a historic anomaly dating from the period when the agency acted primarily as a space sales representative of the press.

Under the 1973 Fair Trading Act restrictive practices have to be registered with the Office of Fair Trading, and this provision became applicable to commercial services in 1976. As this book went to press it remained to be seen whether the OFT would make an exception for the traditional recognition arrangements between media and advertising agencies and, if not, whether they would be banned or modified.

Whatever the decision, many people in the advertising industry, including agencies, believed it to be only a matter of time before the fee system of remuneration of agencies became universal, replacing the commission system and thus facilitating even further the use of consultancies instead of full-service agencies. Certainly in Sweden, a country which has set examples in the advertising as well as many other fields, legal interference with the arrangements forbidding rebating of commission to advertisers allowed media brokers and creative consultancies to grow into major forces. Two of the biggest names in Swedish advertising became Intermedia, a media broking company, and Stig Arbman, a creative consultancy which got so much business that it split its operations into several divisions, Arbman 1, Arbman 2, etc.

In Britain, despite all the fuss, only about £18 million of advertising expenditure went through the media brokers in 1975, a very small proportion of total media billing. There is no doubt, however, that a growing number of advertisers are becoming interested in the possibility of bypassing the full-service agency, and for two principal reasons: (*a*) economy (the advertising manager of one big company told the author he thought he could save tens of thousands of pounds a year by using specialised services and dispensing with his agencies); (*b*) what for want of a better word one might call vanity.

Vanity is a word that needs explaining. Going back 20 or 30 years one discovers a situation where a majority of advertisers had much less marketing expertise than the big ad agencies. That is to say that, though they knew something about selling their own products, they were less well equipped to analyse market trends, commission and interpret market research, compare the advantages of different marketing and advertising approaches.

Now things are different. Most big manufacturers of consumer goods have large marketing departments staffed by people who have often had experience in ad agencies themselves and who consider themselves as competent as as any agency account director to control the creative, media-buying, research, packaging and any other operations relevant to their business. So why not, such people wonder, cut out the account directors and go straight to the specialists whose work they need? Why not scrap the agency menu and order services à la carte?

Why not indeed? Of course vanity can go too far, as when Paul Clark, yellow fats manager (marge boss to you) of Van den Berghs decided, having dropped Lintas, to produce his own commercial for the relaunch of Stork margarine, or rather to have it written in-house and produced with the aid of a film company.

The commercial showed a herd of cows and used the line '... like you'd expect a soft butter to be'. It led to a complaint from the Butter Information Council that the copy was misleading and, rather more importantly, derision from admen who believed that the last way to sell marge is by showing a lot of cows. Mr Clark, who subsequently awarded the account to McCann-Erickson, may well have regretted not calling in a good creative consultancy to help him.

The number of consultancies has increased markedly, from an estimated 50 in 1970 to 74 in 1975. (During the same period the number of media brokers increased from one to 13.) Many, if not most, are one-man bands, but several are partnerships employing up to half a dozen people, while the biggest, called The Creative Business, is the size of a small agency.

The Creative Business is run by David Bernstein, one of British Adland's best known characters who was formerly on the agency side of the fence as creative director successively of McCann-Erickson (where he was responsible for the 'Esso sign means happy motoring' jingle), Garland-Compton and Bensons. Shortly after Bensons disappeared into the maw of OBM he struck out on his own, and by 1974 The Creative Business had a fee income of £300,000 and was working for companies like Beecham, which already employed several agencies as well.

London's oldest creative consultancy, John Simmons, also does a lot of work direct for advertisers, but the majority of creative consultancies still get all their work from ad agencies and would hesitate to compete with agencies for fear of cutting off their main source of income.

To the non-adman it may seem strange, when there are so many advertising agencies, each of which has its own creative department, and when the creative output of an agency is one of the main criteria on which it is judged, that any of them should require to call in freelance assistance. But, according to a survey carried out in 1975 by the Squad creative consultancy, and based on replies from 120 creative directors, more than half of all agencies sometimes use outside creative talent, including moonlighters employed by other agencies, and 49 per cent use consultancies. Of those which do hire consultancies, the vast majority expect their suppliers of creative ideas to keep quiet about the fact.

Why are consultancies used so often, Squad alone having 'ghosted' campaigns for 60 different agencies in five years? The survey didn't ask that question, but three of the reasons are: (*a*) in a tight money situation agencies have slimmed down their permanent staffs as much as they can, with the consequence that when sudden demands are made on their productivity they may not have sufficient creatives of their own on hand; (*b*) some agencies use outside help mainly on new business pitches so as not to have to pull copywriters and art directors off the accounts they are working on for existing clients; (*c*) creatives who've been working on the same account for a long time may get jaded. If the client is getting restless and asking for a fresh approach, this may come more easily from outsiders.

While reason (*a*) doesn't call for much comment, you may well reflect that the other two cases involve a degree of deception, in that a client who picks a new agency or decides to stick with his old one presumably does so at least partly on the basis of the creative work offered him. If he were to realise that this work originated outside the agency, you may think that his decision would often be different. If you do think so, you will find many to agree with you. On the other hand, it could be argued that, provided an agency comes up with the goods, it is of no real consequence where it gets them from. That's a dangerous argument, though. For, if the agency is to boast of being merely a coordinator of services provided by others, it is a short step for the client company to conclude that it might just as easily be its own coordinator and save itself some money.

All this may have given you the impression that the traditional full-service advertising agency is in danger of becoming an extinct dinosaur. Not so. Or rather, the danger, if visible, is distant. Advertisers, like other people, tend to be conservative, and the habit of using agencies is strongly entrenched. For the really big accounts, especially the international accounts, like Coca-Cola, changing the administrative pattern would involve a massive upheaval. Besides, when all is said and done, most of the best brains in advertising are still inside the agencies.

In the immediate future the likelihood is that the creative consultancies and media brokers will make further progress, and that advertisers will give more serious consideration to the à la carte alternative, but that agencies will carry on pretty much as before.

Even the much attacked commission system may have more life in it than its enemies imagine, regardless of whether the rules governing media recognition of agencies are modified by law. In the United States, where anti-trust laws have nullified the ban on rebating, the commission system has proved remarkably resilient.

Again it is likely that remuneration by fee will become more common but that it will not entirely displace the older system. After all, the 15 per cent commission figure provides a benchmark for any negotiations between client and agency over what the size of fees should be.

13 WHICH HALF IS WASTED?

Once you know something about the agency game it is easy to become absorbed in the complexities of the relationships between those who pay for advertising and those who produce it. But, fascinating as the spectacle of admen struggling for accounts may be, it is of course only a sideshow. From the point of view of society as a whole the important thing about advertising is not who is employed to make advertisements but what effects those advertisements have. Does advertising work, and if so how?

An earlier chapter mentioned several bits of evidence that advertising campaigns do in fact achieve, in some cases at least, the ends they are supposed to. How this happens is a much more vexed question. The inevitable cliché which springs to mind is the dictum attributed to Lord Leverhulme (among others) that he knew half of what he spent on advertising was wasted but he didn't know which half. Since then many very clever people have spent an enormous amount of brainpower trying to find out.

The pages that follow will tell you something about advertising research and then go on to say a little about market research in general. It's a vast subject, to which one can't hope to give more here than a sketchy introduction; unfortunately it is also one which tends to evoke little interest outside the ranks of specialists. This is not only unfortunate, it is ironic, since the work of researchers is designed not simply to sell products but to uncover fundamental truths about the way human beings behave, than which there could hardly be a subject of wider potential interest.

Research people, however, jealous of their scientific

status, have a habit of writing about their findings, when they do write about them, in a hermetic jargon, complete with graphs and statistical formulations, which repels attention rather than attracting it. They are also inhibited by the fact that a lot of their work, done for commercial clients, is covered by a vow of confidentiality which prevents them giving details of case histories until years after the event, when the information has ceased to be of benefit to competitors.

Advertising research is conventionally divided into pre-testing and post-testing. To clarify the jargon, pre-testing is what you do before the ad runs on the box, in the newspapers or wherever, and post-testing is what you do afterwards. The tests are of various kinds and seek to measure various things, including an ad's memorability, its credibility, its comprehensibility, the extent to which it arouses the respondents' interest and the effect it has on their attitudes towards what is advertised.

Now we are already faced with a problem. Research, like everything else, costs money, and to spend money on measuring any given attribute of an ad implies a conviction that it is worth measuring, which in turn implies certain preconceptions about how advertising works. For example, if the ability of people to remember an ad is irrelevant to the impact it has on their purchasing behaviour, then it is pointless for a manufacturer wishing to promote sales of his product to pay for research which tells him only how many TV viewers can describe what happened in his latest commercial.

Though it might have struck you as simple common sense to suppose that an ad's memorability and its effectiveness in influencing behaviour were positively correlated, common sense is not an infallible guide, and there are quite certainly cases in which everyone is familiar with the advertising but comparatively few people buy the product. One need only mention the example of Strand cigarettes launched by Wills in 1960 with a campaign by S. H. Benson hailed as the most memorable in Britain since the war. The accolade was deserved. The television campaign, based on the theme 'You're never alone with a Strand' and featuring a sad, lonely young man whose sole companion was his cigarette, was so successful that a *Daily Mirror* poll of teenagers resulted in the character's being elected man of the month. The actor who played him, Terence Brook, acquired a fan club. Within months the slogan was a household word. But the brand flopped. The youngsters at whom it was aimed and who loved the advertising just wouldn't buy it.

One professional researcher, Peter Macarte, managing director of Response Evaluation Services, has suggested that it is conceivable that advertisements may be more effective in influencing behaviour when they are not remembered as ads at all but when the message contained in them sticks at the back of the consumer's mind as received information the source of which has been forgotten. Macarte points out that the days are dead when anyone could say of a product, 'I believe it is highly thought of. Certainly the advertisements speak well of it.' What has to be taken into consideration is the extent to which people fed on a diet of advertising have learned to be cynical about the claims of advertisers.

Yet one of the commonest types of advertising research carried out is still the survey in which people are questioned about which of the previous evening's commercials they can remember seeing. Their answers fall into two categories: spontaneous recall (i.e. when the interviewer has not prompted them) and aided recall (when their memory has been given a jog). For press ads a widely used technique is the one called 'reading and noting' where the interviewer goes through an issue of the publication which respondents have previously seen and questions them about ads they read or noted the existence of. But as well as being widely used the technique is much criticised on the grounds that the responses are often inaccurate and that, again, it is not necessarily helpful to know whether the ads are well remembered or not.

Memorability like most other attributes can be pretested as well as post-tested. In other words, you don't necessarily have to wait until the ads have been published to try to find out how well people remember what they say. Respondents can be shown unpublished ads, in rough or finished form, and examined as to how clearly they recall them or any part of them. The same goes for television advertising, where the guinea pigs will be gathered together in a viewing theatre or in front of a TV set through which a videotape is played.

Some researchers concentrate more on finding out whether ads arouse interest when they are seen than on whether they can be clearly recalled, and a battery of non-verbal tests has been invented to counter the criticism that people, when asked by an interviewer what they think, may give misleading answers. Some of these non-verbal tests are as comical (to anyone but a professional researcher) as they are complicated. For example, equipment has been devised to measure various physiological reactions of people when watching commercials—the number of times their eyes blink, changes in the heart beat or rate of breathing, muscular tension, galvanic skin response. Such reactions are taken to be unconscious indications of emotional arousal. Other equipment measures exactly how long people look at each page of a magazine they are asked to glance through. Tests have been used in which respondents had to make some physical effort, such as pressing a knob, to make an advertising film easier to see or hear, the effort being taken with arguable logic as an indication of the degree of interest the film aroused in them.

Again, common sense might lead you to agree that interestingness, however measured, ought like memorability to be correlated with persuasive effectiveness, and you would be supported by some of the best known theories of advertising research, such as AIDA, an acronym of Attention, Interest, Desire, Action, which are supposed to follow each other in that order. Other so-called linear sequential theories are those of Dr Daniel Starch, the American pioneer of reading and noting surveys, and of a gentleman named Colley who invented another acronym, DAGMAR (Defining Advertising Goals for Measured Advertising Results). Starch said successful ads were seen, read, believed, remembered and acted upon, in that order. The DAGMAR sequence is awareness, comprehension, conviction, action.

Again not all the evidence bears out such simple models of the advertising process. Recent data suggest that in some cases attitudes to a product change after a change in purchasing behaviour rather than before it. And it is now undisputed that the effect of much advertising is, and ought to be, to reinforce existing patterns of behaviour rather than to convert anyone. Peter Macarte has even suggested, somewhat mischievously, that the best (in the sense of most effective) TV commercials may be not only the least memorable but the least interesting. His argument is based on psychological risk theory, and it is thought-provoking enough to be worth quoting at length:

'Risk theory says that there is an optimum level of psychological arousal for any individual, and that the individual will always seek to be at his optimum level. This means that when someone is below his optimum level he will seek to raise his arousal level by, among other things, taking risks. If he is above his optimum level, he will seek to lower his arousal level or will at least go to some level to avoid raising it still further; he will therefore avoid any risk.

'It follows from this that if a suggestion that he should make a decision (i.e. take a risk) is presented to someone when he is below his optimum level of arousal, he is likely to seek to raise his arousal level by accepting the decision, whereas if the same suggestion is made when he is above his optimum level he will refuse to make the decision.

'If this theory is projected on to a housewife seeing an advertisement, it would seem to indicate that she is more likely to decide to change a brand (or to reverse a decision to change a brand, if that is what the advertisement suggests) when she is at a low level of arousal than when she is at a high level. Furthermore, when she actually gets to the shop she is quite likely to be so highly aroused psychologically that she will avoid taking the new decision necessary to change her mind back.

'This in itself could account for the relative power of television, which is more often than not received in a kind of stupor, rather than the more generally accepted notion that the cause of its effectiveness is that it stimulates more than one sense at a time.

'The implications are far-reaching, particularly for television advertising. It would seem that commercials will be more effective when shown during dull, stupor-inducing programmes like opera than when shown during or after highly arousing programmes like wrestling, ghost stories and so on. The commercial itself, this reasoning would also imply, should be designed not to awake interest in, and therefore arouse, the audience, but should seek to lower the level of arousal still further, offering the suggested decision as the only possible arousal mechanism to bring relief.'

It is not certain how seriously Peter Macarte meant this to be taken, since his essential purpose was to criticise the excess of faith of other researchers in measurements which might be meaningless. Nor has he attempted any statistical demonstration that dull ads sell more goods. But, all joking aside, it is clear that some goods which sell very well have been backed by advertising which the clever boys in the creative hot shops would undoubtedly dismiss as very dull. Would it be invidious to mention Masius's Wilkinson Sword commercials or those by Benton and Bowles for Kerrygold butter, all pastoral tranquillity?

Nor is it at all certain that another attribute of ads which researchers often measure, their likeability, is all that relevant to their persuasive influence. The obvious examples are from the detergent field, where housewives often complain, when their opinion is sought, about the strident tone of the commercials yet go on buying the stuff.

So what about discarding measurements of how housewives react to ads and trying to gauge directly what impact they have on sales? Is that possible? Yes it is—up to a point. One has to start, of course, with the oft-repeated caveat, so often ignored by agency spokesmen when they are busy singing their employers' praises, that many factors beside advertising affect sales.

One cannot simply assume that, when sales of a product rise after a new advertising campaign, the rise is due to the campaign. Take Esso petrol. In the late Thirties its share of the private motorist petrol market in Britain was about 8 per cent. Then came the war during which petrol ceased to be branded, and only one variety, 'Pool', was available. The marketing of branded petrol resumed in 1953, and Esso launched an ad campaign through its agency, McCann-Erickson, featuring a tiger as a symbol of power. (Note, this was a serious, dignified beast, not the comical cartoon tiger that came out of McCanns ten years later.) Within a year the company had achieved a 25 per cent market share in place of the pre-war 8 per cent. A proof of the power of advertising, as well as of tigers? Well, no. Or rather, maybe just a tiny bit.

As business consultant Harry Henry explains—and he is in a good position to know because in earlier years he ran Marplan, the research subsidiary of McCanns—there are two other facts you have to know. First, and most important, Esso was the first petrol company in Britain to adopt a policy of tied houses, signing up garages to sell only one brand. This change in the distributive system took place in the period just before the reintroduction of brand identification at the pump, and this alone was sufficient to ensure that Esso would have 22 per cent of the market. Second, the company also priced Esso Extra one penny dearer than other premium brands, and this gave it a quality image which Henry believes helped bump up Esso's share still further. The image was backed up by the advertising, and a 'typology test' carried out around that time by Henry himself indicated that people identified Esso users as 'young and sporty' drivers.

So perhaps advertising was responsible for increasing the brand's share by 1 per cent (of course, 1 per cent of a big market like petrol still means a lot of money), and perhaps not. There is no way that anybody will ever know.

But that is to be negative. How can one positively correlate advertising with sales? Well, with one kind of advertising it is very easy, and that is mail order, where the reader who has swallowed the advertiser's story and is interested in buying the goods has to cut out a coupon and post it. This was the kind of ad that Claude Hopkins knew all about, and his rules of 'Scientific Advertising' were based on the direct responses he got to different mail order ads.

However, that doesn't take us very far, since although mail order is still important it represents only a fraction of total advertising expenditure, and in any case it is clear that the kind of approach which will induce newspaper readers to write in for, say, a cut-price radio set is likely to be very different from that which will persuade TV-watching housewives to buy a packet of Corn Flakes rather than one of Weetabix, or a packet of Frosties rather than Shreddies.

This may remind you of what Arthur Lines, advertising director of Kelloggs, was quoted as talking about earlier in this book, namely the sales increase enjoyed by Frosties in one television area after the volume of advertising there had been doubled. Though even in such a case there are bound to be doubts about the precise chain of cause and effect, one is working with data of a more concrete kind than those elicited by the aided recall or reading and noting type of research.

The same principle is taken even further when the same company runs ad campaigns of different character or different weight (i.e. frequency of repetition) in different areas. This can be done simply through ITV or the provincial press, both of which function on a regional basis. It can also be done, though slightly less simply, through national newspapers which offer split run facilities (i.e. the possibility of dividing the print run and inserting different ads in different sets of copies).

The chief snag about comparing the effects of advertising on different areas is, as always, that of controlling the variables, that is to say of making sure that the two or more areas are genuinely comparable and that there are not other factors than advertising which may be distorting the results. For example, if area X has a certain demographic composition and area Y a completely different one—say X is predominantly elderly working class and Y predominantly young middle class—then one would expect different reactions to the same campaign, let alone different campaigns.

Ingenious ways have been worked out of trying to measure the sales effect of a given commercial on a small number of people in a laboratory situation. The key name here is that of the American Horace Schwerin, who in the Fifties started getting audiences together in a New York theatre and making them sit through film shows mixed with commercials. Members of the audience were asked to choose a raffle gift they would like to win from a list of alternative brands. Their choices were recorded. After the show tickets were drawn, and winners could choose anew. The point of the exercise was to find out whether their preferences had been altered by the advertising to which they had been exposed. In a significant proportion of cases such alteration did occur.

For a time the Schwerin Research Corporation was all the rage and it established a branch in Britain. But its techniques, like other research techniques, have been much criticised on the grounds of the artificiality of the situation created and its remoteness from real life, where it is the impact of a campaign rather than of a single commercial which is at stake.

But variations of the old Schwerin method continued to be devised. In 1974 the Market Research Society conference in Bournemouth was told by John Clements of Marplan about one such variation (actually he called it a new method) called Adweight. It involved recruiting two matched samples of more than 100 housewives and showing them a half-hour TV programme of cartoons interspersed with commercials. One sample would see a test commercial, the other would not. After the show the housewives would be given a sheaf of money-off coupons to redeem in a special shop set up next to the viewing hall, and the product advertised in the test commercial would naturally be among those available. By comparing the purchasing behaviour in the shop of the two sets of women it was supposed to be possible to measure to what extent the commercial had influenced its viewers towards the product.

Clements reported that two different commercials for a certain slimming food had been tested in this way, and one had been found to be much more successful in terms of coupons exchanged for the product than the other. Written questionnaires which all the women taking part had filled in indicated that they could identify more easily with the character portrayed in the more successful film. Its superior advertising effectiveness was thereby proven. At least Clements thought so. Not all his listeners were convinced.

We are driven back to the aforementioned problem of how advertising works. The short but facile answer is that nobody knows. It is facile because, for all the doubts and controversies, there is a great deal of evidence, collected over the years, about the kinds of thing which are liable to happen in various kinds of advertising situation.

The recognition that there is more than one kind of advertising effect is the basis of the 'theory of advertisements' put forward by Stephen King of J. Walter Thompson in the monthly journal *Admap*. King, whose lucidity as a researcher probably derives from the fact that, unlike most of the breed, he was trained as neither a psychologist nor a mathematician but a classicist, has arranged the different types of advertisement on a scale according to the degree of immediacy with which they are intended to influence action. And it is clear that the hoped-for ultimate result of all advertising is action of some kind, though not necessarily a purchase.

At the most immediate, direct end of the scale comes direct response advertising, as for mail order goods. It works through a rational (even when untrue) appeal to self-interest. Further along the scale is advertising which aims, in King's words, at the 'what a good idea' response from defined interest groups, e.g. ads for remedies for specific complaints or ads for baby care products. Then comes 'that reminds me' advertising intended to keep a brand on the consumer's shortlist. Getting towards the indirect end of the scale, one finds advertising designed to modify attitudes, and King, giving an example from his own agency's work, picks on its attempts to persuade women that drinking Guinness can be elegant and fashionable. Finally comes 'I always knew I was right' advertising designed to reinforce existing preferences. Its effect is bound to be the hardest to measure.

A most important point is that the same ad may, in some cases, be trying to achieve several of the objectives King distinguishes. For each objective a different type of research test will be appropriate, but King's 'theory' doesn't pretend to make such tests any more precise than they were before. His 'theory' is in reality less of a theory than a classification and usefully reflects the growing consensus that advertising research must be modest and pragmatic if it is to be of any help to the makers of ads.

SEX IS WHERE YOU FIND IT 14

One way in which research is of great practical benefit to agencies is in helping their creative departments to understand more clearly what their projected ads communicate and where the pitfalls may lie. Such help is derived from what the trade calls qualitative research, which is a rather grand name for simply talking to people.

As distinct from quantitative research, as exemplified in questionnaire-type surveys, qualitative research aims not at producing a statistically accurate picture of how consumers actually think or behave but at obtaining insights into the way it is likely they may think or behave. If need be these insights can later be put to the test of statistical verification, but often the need doesn't arise.

Thus, if it emerges from a series of discussion groups or individual 'depth interviews' (in plain language, long conversations) that a few averagely intelligent people misunderstand the whole point of a proposed ad, the obvious conclusion is that the ad must be revised, not that a nationwide survey should be carried out to establish whether it is liable to be misunderstood by 5 per cent, 10 per cent or 20 per cent of readers or viewers.

An example, recounted by Michael West of Benton and Bowles in the book *The Effective Use of Market Research*, edited by Johan Aucamp, concerned a print ad devised by the agency for Maxim coffee. The ad included a photograph of a group of men and women dressed in furs and drinking coffee around a fire in a snowy forest setting, while their horses and carriages waited for them. The picture was supposed to convey the message that Maxim was a luxury product, but during a series of interviews with 52 housewives it was discovered that a high proportion of them were interpreting it as meaning merely that the coffee was good to drink in cold weather. The practical conclusion drawn was that the wording of the ad should be changed to emphasise more strongly the luxury story which was eluding some of the women.

This is perhaps a somewhat superficial example. At a deeper level qualitative research is concerned not with how to juggle the elements of an ad but with what advertising ought to be talking about in the first place.

An investigation carried out by Market Behaviour Ltd, a research firm run by a personable young couple called John and Mary Goodyear, used qualitative techniques on behalf of a slimming product. Respondents selected to take part in discussion groups were women who admitted thinking of themselves as overweight, though not all were really fat by any objective standard. The object of the discussions was to analyse their motives for wanting to be slimmer. It might be thought that these motives were obvious enough without having to be confirmed by expensive research, employing highly qualified people to conduct discussions and write reports (to say nothing of the money paid to respondents for giving up their time to take part). The truth turned out to be less straightforward than might have been expected. The dominant theme which emerged during the discussions was that the fat woman was thought of as a failure, someone 'who's let things go'.

The research report summarised the findings as follows: 'Women want to become slim because slimness represents an ideal state. Many women feel that by achieving this state they will become the sort of women they would like to be in other ways as well: those who crave elegance feel they will be elegant when they are slimmer, those who feel insecure consider security to be the slim woman's prerogative, those who want to exploit their husband's sexual interest feel that they can do this by becoming slim, and those who feel that they are aging expect to recapture their youth by returning to the weight they were when they were young. . . . Slimness is the secondary goal, the primary goal is success.'

The aim behind the investigation was to determine which of a number of suggested advertising approaches was the most effective. The outcome was that the company involved discarded proposed ads showing a young, slim woman and plumped instead for a picture of a woman neither extremely young nor extremely slim but who, glamorous in diamonds and fur, had obviously 'made it'. The copy line suggested that the advertised product was her friend.

Another researcher who runs his own firm, Conrad Jameson, discovered in the course of working for a pharmaceutical client that there was a type of headache sufferer who tended to deny having a headache but was, none the less, a frequent user of headache remedies. Jameson hypothesised that this type of person saw his or her headache as a physical and moral weakness. 'You can't,' he says, 'ask people directly about such matters. You can, however, still test the hypothesis by working out its consequences in terms of how the motivation will affect their preferences.

'Suppose you show such sufferers a large pill and a small one and ask them to choose between them. You would expect them to choose the small one because big pills are associated with big headaches, and they are denying the severity of their suffering. We did such an experiment, and the results came out just as we expected.

'Or suppose you show them two contrasting ads, one featuring a sufferer receiving sympathy, the other a woman recovering from her headache almost instantly. The second ad should be preferred, and another experiment showed that indeed it was.'

As well as talking to people, the skilled qualitative researcher disposes of a number of techniques, many of them borrowed from psychiatry, to probe the consumer's motivations. Among them are the thematic apperception test, in which the respondent is asked to make up a story about a picture, and the sentence completion test in which the stimulus is, instead of a picture, an unfinished sentence.

A trick of which researcher William Schlackman is

particularly fond is what he calls personification, which means getting respondents to act the part of a product. Giving a demonstration once of the way this works, he got an interviewee to pretend to be his own suit. Saying what came into his head, the man expressed resentment at the suit's wearer (i.e. himself) for failing to keep it neat and clean. Despite the jokiness of this performance, Schlackman suggested that it revealed a genuine sense of guilt on the part of the interviewee about neglecting his suit. If further research, he said, were to show such guilty feelings to be widespread, one could conceivably end with a recommendation that a suit manufacturer should market his garments on a platform of 'it only needs to be cleaned once a year'.

Bill Schlackman started his own firm after arriving in London from America some 15 years ago to run a branch office of Dr Ernest Dichter's Institute for Motivational Research in New York. Back in the Fifties and Sixties Dichter was one of the biggest names in the world of advertising and marketing, though both he and the phrase 'motivational research' subsequently fell out of fashion. His business was based on the proposition that, by the application of psychological knowledge (his doctorate, from his native Vienna, was in psychology), it was possible to discover not only what products people could be persuaded to buy but their unconscious reasons for buying them.

A classic piece of Dichterism is the theory of automobile sexuality he evolved while working for Chrysler, according to which a sports car is psychologically identifiable as a 'mistress', while a saloon car has the character of a wife. While this interpretation is widely regarded as being at least plausible, some of Dichter's other Freudian-type theories are harder to swallow.

In his *Handbook of Consumer Motivations*, published in 1964, he suggested, for instance, that skiing was a symbol of male potency, 'a raping of the virgin snow'. Rice was, symbolically speaking, a 'feminine food. It typically suggests a strong female, young, healthy and blessed with great fertility.' Tea too was classified as feminine, but coffee and potatoes were masculine. As for cheese, of the strong-smelling sort, the consumer's attitude 'is often quite closely associated with the acceptance or rejection of body odours.'

The reaction against Dichter, when it set in, was due not merely to nervousness, natural in conservative business-men, about his emphasis on sexuality (there is a possibly apocryphal story that the head of the Parker pen company stormed out of a meeting at which Dichter told him that what he was selling was not a pen but a penis) but to suspicion that many motivational researchers were taking their clients for a ride. Schlackman, who worked for him, agrees that Dichter often let his own bright ideas run away with him, to the point where he ignored 'validation and statistical procedures. He believed he had the ultimate truth. This was the source of his success and also of his "demise".'

Mind you, there are some Dichter-type ideas for which it is impossible to provide statistical verification but which just cannot be ignored by a prudent marketer. John Rowan, a British research man, did some work for the Ronson automatic toothbrush in the course of which he asked respondents how they visualised the managing director of the firm which made the product.

'He kept coming out very masculine, very virile, big moustache, drives a big red sports car. I couldn't understand why. Then I was looking at a drawing of this toothbrush, and it suddenly clicked that it was a phallic symbol. When I went back through the transcripts of all the interviews we'd done I found a lot of statements imputing very sensual qualities to this thing.'

Ronson took this conclusion seriously enough to change its advertising. Children were taken out of the ads on the grounds that the juxtaposition of children and a phallic symbol might prove too anxiety-provoking in parents. Nonsense? Perhaps. But it was safer to assume there might be something in it.

The foregoing anecdote is interesting, incidentally, in view of the widespread impression that admen are interested only in putting sex into ads, not in taking it out. Certainly quite a lot of advertising does make use of erotic themes, but these tend to be restricted to certain product categories where they are of obvious relevance.

Among those categories are naturally cosmetics and toiletries, the purpose of which is undeniably to enhance sex appeal. Thus TV commercials by Geers Gross for Hai Karate aftershave were built, in humorous style, on the proposition that wearing it makes the wearer irresistibly attractive to women. Old Spice commercials, by Dorlands, have pictured a bottle rearing up out of the sea in what it is impossible to believe is not intended as a piece of phallic symbolism.

True, Fabergé's Brut and Brut 33, which shot ahead in the male perfume market in 1975 did so with the help of commercials featuring Henry Cooper, the ex-boxer, which were decidedly unsexy. But the point of these commercials was to persuade viewers that a man didn't have to be effeminate to smother himself in the stuff; observers had long conjectured that the reason for the brand's original marketing success was the phallic appeal of the long-necked Brut bottle to women, and women make the majority of aftershave purchases (a curious but well authenticated fact).

Certain kinds of booze are obvious candidates for erotic treatment—one thinks immediately of Smirnoff and of Bacardi and Dry Cane white rum—because they are bought to a large extent by young people of both sexes and are doubtless consumed in social situations where copulation is thought about if not performed on the spot.

But flagrantly sexual appeals are few and far between, probably fewer and farther between these days than they once were. For this one can adduce three reasons:

1. The advertising control bodies have tightened up their rules, a point we've alluded to already and will come back to.

2. Sex is less fashionable than it used to be. At least it is as far as advertising creative departments are concerned, and they are very fashion-conscious. In the effort to be startling and original there was a time when creatives would stick a nude, or as nude a figure as they could get away with, in ads for anything, including heavy machinery. And when

a few years ago the first poster appeared showing a pretty coloured girl wearing only Elliott boots it did make quite an impact. So did the first full-page corporate ad by Fisons in *The Times* to depict a nude. These days they wouldn't attract much attention.

Be it noted that in Paris, whither the so-called creative revolution arrived from New York much later than it did in London, it is still the height of creative chic to hit the housewife over the head with sex. A 1975 poster for Glad plastic wrappers showed a half-clad young woman in her kitchen holding up the product. Over her bosom ran the copy line 'Women know how to keep fresh what needs to be kept fresh' ('*Les femmes savent garder frais ce qui doit rester frais*'), while the name of the product was printed in large capitals neatly over her crutch. The agency concerned, CLM/BBDO, denied with a straight face that any hint of pornography was intended.

3. From the marketing strategy point of view, more and more admen have come to the conclusion that sexual appeals can be counter-productive in the sense that, unless they are directly relevant to the product advertised, they can distract attention from it. No client company is happy if its ads become more popular than its product.

However, as with humour, it is not always easy to know when sex really is irrelevant. It might be difficult to argue that there was anything to connect cigars with a nubile, scantily clad girl running along a beach, but the Hobson Bates TV commercials which showed little else were thought to have done very well for the Manikin brand. The campaign, with its 'sheer enjoyment' punch line, was launched in 1967 when Manikin, though market leader, was under severe pressure from competitors. It stayed ahead until 1972 when it was overtaken by Hamlet, another Gallaher brand but longer and milder. For a short time the Manikin girl was withdrawn from the box while client and agency had a rethink. Eventually she returned, still nubile, still scantily clad, but this time presenting the product as well as titillating the (male) viewer.

The most notorious risqué campaign ever, the one by the

American William Free agency for National Airlines, also didn't hurt the client. Free's ads were the ones picturing pretty air stewardesses with the slogan 'Fly me' or even 'I'm going to fly you to Miami like you've never been flown before'. Women's Lib organisations loudly protested but National claimed a 23 per cent increase in passengers in the first year of the campaign.

There are, of course—shall we recap?—many factors which help to determine the success of a product besides advertising. Coming back to Dr Dichter, with whom we started this little sexual digression, it is ironic to record that a generation after he was claiming to have found the philosopher's stone of advertising effectiveness and after Vance Packard had been sufficiently impressed to write *The Hidden Persuaders*, warning the world of how the ad industry had learned to manipulate consumers any way it wanted, members of that same industry are themselves still full of doubts and uncertainties about the process which Packard thought they had mastered.

Before leaving the subject of sex, there is one story that must be told. A survey of sexual behaviour carried out in France by one of the leading French market research firms found that on average, men estimated their penises to be an inch longer than their wives did. This perfectly true story serves to show that it is not only in the complicated area of reactions to advertising that there is difficulty in establishing exactly what the facts are.

Many other research reports, rather less titillating, make the same point. For instance a survey by the British Market Research Bureau found that 22 per cent of people interviewed on filling station forecourts were unable correctly to identify the brand of petrol they had bought only moments beforehand. In an American experiment a large proportion of business executives, when asked whether they read a certain journal, said they did—although no journal of that name existed.

Such are the hazards of research. Yet the ad industry, on both the agency and the client sides, is an avid consumer of research data. It has to be, for without a pretty clear idea of the state of the various markets in which it operates it wouldn't know where to start work.

It should be made clear that the kinds of investigation described so far in this chapter form only a fraction of the total amount of market research done every year. The bulk of this is of the variety which qualitative or motivational researchers refer to, often with disdain, as 'head counting' and is aimed at finding out who actually buys what. A lot of it is *ad hoc* research carried out for particular manufacturers, but some of the most important work takes the form of continuous surveys which are paid for by a large number of subscribing clients.

Chief among these continuous surveys are two carried out by the two biggest market research firms in the country, AGB (Audits of Great Britain) and the American-owned A. C. Nielsen. Each month AGB interviews a national cross section of thousands of people about their purchases. Respondents are divided among the various ITV areas, and the survey, which is sponsored by ITV companies, is called the Television Consumer Audit. It provides the marketing director and the advertising agency account director with a continuous check on the progress or decline of his brands in relation to others.

Brand share figures thus obtained are sometimes the same, but sometimes not, as those provided by Nielsen's monthly retail shop audit. This is a packet-counting, rather than a head-counting operation, and is based on sales returns from a representative sample of stores.

Another important continuous survey, based on questionnaires sent out by post; is the Target Group Index run by BMRB (British Market Research Bureau). This correlates brand usership with the demographic and psychographic characteristics of the users and also with their newspaper reading and TV viewing habits. Examples of psychographics to explain this esoteric but useful term, are the preferences of respondents for either traditional or modern things, and their degree of adventurousness, as reflected in their shopping or cooking habits.

Other data available to TGI subscribers concern the financial expectations of respondents, the colour and condition of their hair, the frequency with which they buy groceries. Information which may strike you as being in some respects dull, but which would be vital to you if you were, say, a manufacturer thinking of launching a new shampoo or an ad agency media director trying to decide where to advertise it.

A rather different kind of continuous survey is Monitor, conducted by the Taylor Nelson research company, whose boss is a personable American lady named Liz Nelson. Monitor attempts to measure, among other things, shifts in social attitudes, which are less tangible than purchasing habits but which determine in large part the direction in which purchasing habits will move.

The guiding principle of all such surveys is that the behaviour of very large groups of people can be accurately deduced from that of much smaller representative samples. Accurately, that is, within certain margins of error. The general public knows a fair amount about sampling and margins of error because they crop up every so often in controversies about political opinion polling. The organisations which do this particular type of survey—Gallup, National Opinion Polls, Louis Harris, etc.—are all market research firms for which political polling constitutes a small, but well publicised, part of their business. Given the peculiarities of the British electoral system, in which a majority of the nation's votes does not necessarily turn into a majority of seats in Parliament, the record of the opinion polls is pretty good, but of course they have come some croppers in their time.

The fact that they have done so stands as a warning to anyone who would put too uncritical a faith in market research. The size of the sample clearly has a bearing on the reliability of the survey, and voices are occasionally raised complaining that, in their commercial work, some research firms base scientific-seeming conclusions on an inadequate number of interviews.

Winston Fletcher, managing director of the Fletcher Shelton ad agency, once told a Market Research Society conference of an incident in his experience when a survey was supposed to have established that a certain liqueur had a strongly feminine profile, meaning that two out of three people who drank it regularly were women. It transpired that of the 2,000 people in the survey sample only 15 were regular drinkers of the stuff, so that when the percentages which the research company had been so confidently putting forward were translated into absolute numbers it was seen to be talking about no more than ten women and five men. To draw marketing conclusions from such a tiny group, argued Fletcher, was absurd.

The general reaction from the assembled researchers was that the case cited was unrepresentative and that, whatever the defects of any particular set of evidence, decisions had to be based on something. Indeed they do, and that is the reason why, despite all the cautionary tales, researchers are assured of a respectful hearing in Adland.

A final tale, which you may find either cautionary or comforting, is the following. The MAS research firm carried out a survey in which a sample of 430 people were asked whether they thought the replies given to market research questionnaires were truthful. The great majority said they believed replies were truthful. Only ten per cent believed people might reply untruthfully, depending on the character of the interviewer and the convenience of the time at which she (nearly all doorstep interviewers are female) called.

MAS did not go into the question of how one could be sure that the 90 per cent who said they thought people were truthful were not themselves lying when they said so, perhaps to please the interviewer.

Something like a third of Britain's adult population has now been interviewed by researchers, so it's us they were talking about.

15 HOW TO WEIGH READERS

In the previous chapter mention was made of the Target Group Index, which correlates purchasing with reading and viewing habits and thereby assists the media departments of ad agencies (or the independent media buyers acting for advertisers) in choosing the media schedule for any advertising campaign. The media schedule is Adlandese for the detailed list of media (newspapers, magazines, TV, radio, posters, cinema) to be used and the dates, times and sizes of insertions, e.g. 30-second spots in the early evening on Thames, Granada and ATV, full pages in the *Daily Mirror* and *Sun*. And there are various other sources of data to help in that choice.

Before examining those sources, however, the first thing to understand is that when the adman speaks of media he means advertising media. To the journalist a Fleet Street paper may be a news medium, to an actor an ITV station may be a medium of entertainment, but to the agency media director working out his schedule both are primarily vehicles, which he may judge more or less efficient, for conveying messages from the advertisers whose money pays his salary to the consumers from whom more money for the advertiser has to be coaxed. This is a fact of very great consequence not only for the advertiser and the agency but for the media and for society as a whole.

Much of the passion which has suffused controversy over the role of advertising in Western countries has sprung from the opposing beliefs that it (*a*) underpins freedom of the media and, therefore, of opinion, (*b*) distorts public debate in favour of the status quo through the exercise of commercial pressure. For the moment, however, let us postpone consideration of these weighty political and moral issues and focus on the manner in which advertising actually makes use of the media.

The adman looks at the media through various sets of statistics corresponding to various sets of initials—ABC, NRS, JICNARS, JICTAR, JICRAR will do to be getting on with. They all sound fearfully dull, and if you have just been overcome by a sudden compulsion to turn the page it wouldn't be surprising. But the information they refer to is not really dull at all, even if you're not statistically minded, so please linger for a few words of explanation.

First, the press. What the adman wants to know about a newspaper or magazine, and what he wouldn't know just by glancing through it, is basically how many people and what kind of people read it. He can find the answer in the National Readership Survey (NRS) reports compiled under the aegis of the Joint Industry Committee for National Readership Surveys (JICNARS), a body supported by advertisers, agencies, newspapers and periodicals.

The NRS, like other continuous surveys described in the previous chapter, is a sampling operation in which figures for the whole nation are extrapolated from the the answers given by a representative cross-section. The actual work is done under contract by a research firm (for the three years 1977–79 Research Services Ltd., previously BMRB). The reports are issued both quarterly and yearly and tell you what, during the period concerned, was the average number of readers of any given publication and what proportion of them belonged to each of the various age groups and each of the various socio-economic categories, denoted as A, B, C1, C2, D and E.

These categories have during recent years come in for a great deal of criticism for incorporating obsolete and misleading distinctions. In theory they correspond to a hierarchy of both social standing and wealth, the two being presumed to go hand in hand. The essential criterion is occupational.

Heads of grade A (upper middle-class) households include successful businessmen, professional men, senior civil servants and people of independent means. Grade B (middle class) includes less senior executives. The C1s (lower middle class) are tradesmen and white collar workers. C2s and Ds are respectively skilled and unskilled blue collar workers. E is the poverty grade, including pensioners and casual workers.

To the adman these categories are useful only in so far as they indicate the purchasing power and purchasing habits of the people who are liable to see his ad if he puts it in a particular paper. From this point of view the conventional groupings have become less useful in recent years. Inflation and trade union bargaining power have helped to muddy the waters, making many C2s richer than (or less poor than) the C1s who come above them in the old pecking order.

However, many publications carry out their own research aimed at providing the advertiser and ad agency with a more complete readership profile than is obtainable from the NRS. Through their own advertisements in the advertising trade press, national newspapers compete in drawing attention to the advantages of buying space in them, boasting for example of the number of business executives among their readers or the proportion of them who regularly take holidays abroad.

Readership is not, of course, the same thing as circulation. Figures for circulation (normally the average per issue during a six-month period) are regularly announced through the Audit Bureau of Circulations, another body formed under tripartite auspices (media, advertisers and agencies). More than 2,000 publications belong to the ABC and the membership includes the vast majority of papers which are seriously interested in attracting advertising, whereas the NRS covers only the most important newspapers and magazines, not many more than 100 titles.

Every paper has more readers than purchasers, but the ratio between the two figures varies widely, as some kinds of publication have a much greater pass-on readership than others. Going by the NRS, national dailies usually have a ratio of three or four readers to each copy sold, but some periodicals have a much higher ratio. *Punch* has close on 10 readers per copy, thanks to the help of dentists' and doctors' waiting rooms, though it is obvious that not all those who, when questioned, claim to have read a publication have done so with equal attention.

The advantage of circulation figures is that they are precise in a way which readership surveys cannot be, since the latter are subject to the same uncertainties as is all research based on samples of interviewees. When a paper talks about the number of copies it has sold, however, it means the number it has sold, not an estimate derived from a sample. On the other hand, circulation figures can occasionally be slightly distorted, even though the ABC lays down certain rules which a paper's auditors have to observe, and the Bureau's own auditors carry out random inspections to make sure they are adhered to. In some sectors of periodical publishing, it is known—no names, no pack drill—that the figures are sometimes pushed up by such tricks as getting wholesalers to hang on to unsold copies until after the audit is over.

The rates which publications can charge for their advertising space depend not only upon the size of their circulations but on the character of their readerships. To put it crudely, advertisers pay more to talk to the rich than to talk to the poor.

The correct comparison here is not between the absolute cost of, say, a full page in the *Sun* and that of a full page in the *Financial Times*. The former in 1975 was £4,165, the latter £3,472. What media buyers are interested in is cost in relation to the number of people reached or, to use an indispensable bit of advertising jargon, cost per thousand. Note incidentally that the thousand in this case more often means thousand purchasers than thousand readers, which confirms the point made before that, though it is *readers* advertisers are interested in, circulation figures are harder, more reliable data than readership estimates.

Now try dividing the *Sun*'s page rate by three and a half million and the *FT*'s by 200,000, which in round figures were what their circulations were at the time, and you will see that it was roughly 14 times as expensive to advertise to one of the affluent and powerful company directors who took the *FT* as to one of the grubby labourers who carried his *Sun* with him to the building site.

Forgive the stereotypes. Of course not everyone who buys the *Financial Times* is well-to-do, and not only manual workers buy the *Sun*. But a sufficiently high proportion of the two papers' readers do fit the stereotype for *FT* advertisers to feel they were getting their money's worth.

Cost-per-thousand comparisons between newspapers are in fact usually expressed in terms of the single column centimetre rather than the full page, because not all ads are full-page ones, and in any case page rates differ within the same publication according to the position of the page (right-hand pages, which are supposed to get more attention, cost more) and to whether the ad is guaranteed to be printed on a specified day or not. Thus it was possible to calculate, again in 1975, that the average rate per column-centimetre per thousand circulation in Fleet Street's three quality Sunday newspapers was 1·34 pence as against 0·56 pence in the four popular Sundays. Such circulations are the breath of life to media departments.

But they must make many other calculations. Granted that they must pay more to get to certain types of reader than to others, which publications will allow them to reach their targets most cheaply, and will the use of several different publications give greater penetration of their target market than just one? How frequently should the ads appear to have the most effect, and within the limitations of the client's budget is it better to buy more small spaces or fewer large ones? Of these four questions the first two are fairly precise and mathematical, the last two land us back in the sticky area of deciding how advertising works.

In case this all sounds rather bloodless and boffin-like, it should be made clear that, in making up their minds which ads to print where, admen are also swayed by the editorial character of the different papers available to them. It is common ground that the editorial environment of the ad affects the manner in which it is perceived. If a publication's editorial columns are regarded by its readers as authoritative and trustworthy, then some of that authority rubs off on the ads it carries. The converse also applies. At least that's what admen believe, and the belief is illustrated in a rueful story told by Richard Ingrams, editor of *Private Eye*.

Some years ago, before the *Eye* had scaled the heights of respectability, it found itself at the last moment before going to press with an empty page. The crisis was resolved by taking an ad from another magazine and reproducing it, free, gratis and for nothing, in the *Eye*. (One of the advantages of offset printing is that it makes it easy to do this.)

But was the advertiser pleased? He was not. Instead, the ad agency concerned wrote to the *Eye* denouncing it for having made a gift of its space and warning it that if it were to do such a wicked thing again it would find itself in serious trouble. Even though the magazine already had at that time a healthy and growing circulation of around 50,000 and a fairly up-market readership, the advertiser considered that to appear inside it would do his product positive damage.

When publications of different character are used in the same advertising campaign, the ad agency will often vary the character of its ads to suit each paper. It is no accident that, skimming through a copy of *Penthouse*, one comes across headlines like the following: 'In the flesh it's even sexier' on an ad for a Jaguar car; 'You too can have a body like mine', for Alfa Romeo; 'Big boys don't play with cassettes', for Tandberg hi-fi equipment.

Time was, incidentally, when no decent advertiser would dream of exposing himself, or rather his product, in *Penthouse* and the other glossy skin books, or men's magazines as they like to call themselves. But God and media buyers are with the big battalions. By the mid-Seventies, when *Penthouse*, *Mayfair*, and *Men Only* had achieved circulations approaching half a million each, they began to be packed with ads and had become recognised as prime media for selling to young men with money to spend and pretensions to spend them on.

The effort to fit the ad to the publication, to make it look so to speak at home, is discernible also in the not uncommon device of presenting newspaper ads as if they were pages of news, though with the word 'Advertisement' tacked on top or in a corner to avoid deception. British Airways and the British Egg Information Service are both fond of this technique, and it was extensively used by Chrysler in

January 1976 when the car firm sought to reassure British newspaper readers that it really did have a future in the UK.

The degree to which newspapers and magazines depend on advertising for their revenue varies enormously. At one end of the spectrum are publications like the political weeklies which rub along with very little advertising and have to cover most of their costs, when they cover them at all, out of circulation sales.

At the other end of the spectrum is a large group of publications which are financed entirely by advertising. They include so-called controlled circulation journals, which are mailed exclusively to members of a certain profession (for example, accountants) or association (for example, the Institute of Directors). Because the readers of controlled circulation papers have been picked by the publishers, the latter can with confidence tell advertising agencies precisely who will be on the receiving end of their messages, and when the readerships are in advertisers' eyes valuable ones, disposing of great purchasing power or influence over corporate purchasing decisions, such papers can make a lot of money.

Then there are giveaway magazines like *Miss London*, which is handed out weekly to women office workers arriving in central London, and which has outlasted several competitors which were founded during the recruitment advertising boom of the early Seventies but did not last long. The most well-known giveaways, however—for that is what they are—are the colour supplements of the *Sunday Times*, *Observer* and *Sunday Telegraph*, which devote well over half their space to advertising but have nevertheless managed, because their production costs have risen faster than their ad rates, to lose money.

The cover prices of some publications, notably the aforementioned men's magazines, are fixed high enough to enable them to make a profit without advertising, and for them ads are the jam on their bread. For others, however, ad revenue is vital, and this is true in particular of the Fleet Street quality newspapers, all of which derive the greater part of their income from advertising. With the Fleet Street populars these proportions are reversed. Thus in the advertising boom year of 1973 the *Financial Times* got fully 80 per cent of its money from ads and *The Times* 73 per cent, while for the *Daily Mirror* and the *Sun* the percentages were respectively 31 and 26.

Women's weekly magazines depend on advertising for more than half of their revenue, and so do trade and technical journals and regional newspapers, both daily and weekly. In the same year of 1973 local weeklies are reckoned to have been on average more than 80 per cent financed by ads, including of course a great amount of classified.

Whatever the contribution advertising makes to their finances most newspapers and periodicals are anxious to maximise the number of ads they carry and to persuade admen, and in particular the agency executives responsible for choosing media, that they are a good proposition. This is especially true of new publications, which usually try to entice advertising into their pages by means of specially large discounts or even free space.

Equally usually the agencies avail themselves of such offers but don't commit themselves to full-hearted support of a publication until they are convinced it is a success with the readers they are interested in reaching. If the paper fills a gap in the market, catering for a special interest group or trade which has not previously been so catered for, that is a great advantage. When it comes to general interest publications, the adman's support is likely to be forthcoming only if their readerships are either very large or demonstrably well off.

The advertising-oriented economics of newspaper publishing have led to the extinction of titles like the *Daily Herald* and *News Chronicle* which, though both were selling over a million copies a day at the time of their deaths, fell between two stools; their readerships were neither big enough to compete with the *Mirror* and *Express* for mass-market advertising nor select enough to attract the premium-rate ads that went to the posh papers. Hence the complaint, which comes mainly from the political Left, that advertisers weigh readers rather than counting them. This, whatever you may think of the rights and wrongs of the process and the desirability or otherwise of changing it, is indisputable. In a society where purchasing power is unequal and purchasing habits differ from group to group, commercial advertising decisions are bound to be formulated on the basis of that inequality and those differences.

16 VIEW FROM THE LOO

Since 1955, when Britain saw its first real live TV commercial (for SR toothpaste), it is of course the box which has become the prime medium for mass-market display advertising. The information admen seek about TV is, as with the press, calculated to assist them in their task of communicating as efficiently and economically as possible with the greatest number of purchasers or potential purchasers of their product. But, the nature of the two types of media being so different, the information—or some of it—is collected in a rather different manner.

What one could call circulation figures—i.e. how many homes have TV sets, how many of those sets are capable of receiving ITV—have long since ceased to be of any importance. The vast majority of the population have ITV available at the touch of a knob. The questions are: How many people actually do watch it? At what times? Which are their favourite programmes? How does viewing vary from one part of the country to another? Answers to these questions are provided in the form of the so-called ratings.

Ratings are the basic data of the buyer of TV airtime. A rating is the estimated percentage of homes which at any given time have a TV set on and switched to any given programme. The estimates are based on research carried out under the auspices of JICTAR (Joint Industry Committee for Television Advertising Research), another tripartite body, composed of representatives of the ITCA (Independent Television Companies Association), ISBA (Incorporated Society of British Advertisers) and IPA (Institute of Practitioners in Advertising, the agencies' association)—

in this part of Adland you cannot move without falling over initials. The research is done under contract by AGB (Audits of Great Britain), which relies on a panel of 2,650 representative households. Each of these homes has a special TV set with a meter attached which records the time it is switched on and the channel it is tuned to.

The ratings, it should be emphasised, do not necessarily refer to the behaviour of the 8,000 individuals who make up the sample homes (although this is also monitored through diaries in which they are asked to write down details of their viewing). If, say, the sets were switched to *Coronation Street* in 50 per cent of them, then the programme would be given a rating of 50, even if every person in every house were asleep in an armchair at the time. This fact helps to explain the very large discrepancies which crop up between the JICTAR estimates of the ITV and BBC shares of the television audience and those issued by the BBC itself.

The BBC's figures are based on its own audience research, which makes no use of metered sets but relies on daily interviews with individuals carried on throughout the country by a force of part-time interviewers. Every day some 2,000 people, picked on the quota sampling method, are asked about the television and radio programmes they viewed or heard the day before. Respondents are given a list of programmes to aid recall, and the interviewer always introduces herself as working for the BBC. Critics of the method say that this is liable to distort the data by virtue of the well-known propensity of most people to say things they feel a questioner would like to hear. The BBC says, however, that experiments have shown the replies given to be largely accurate.

Why don't the two sides get together to produce agreed data? From time to time there have been talks about the possibility of doing so, and these led to a decision to conduct an experimental joint research project in 1976, but the two sides failed to agree on the methods to be used. The usual reason given for the failure to cooperate is that the BBC and JICTAR do research for different purposes and each prefers the technique best suited to its purpose. What the Corporation is mainly after is information about audience reactions to programmes. It is less interested in the minute-by-minute ratings which advertisers and their agencies demand to know when dealing with ITV companies.

According to an official BBC statement, 'It is totally untrue to suggest that the method either organisation has chosen was selected because it appears to give an advantage to that party.' It is nevertheless a fact that the discrepancies regarding total audience share have tended to come out just as a cynic would expect them to do, with BBC figures favouring the Corporation and JICTAR figures doing the opposite.

It is also a shade disingenuous to suggest that the BBC is not concerned in the way that ITV is with the exact share of the audience it gets. They may not be in competition for advertising, but the BBC has often organised its programming as if they were. Such actions are surely to be explained not merely in terms of professional rivalry but in those of financial necessity, since the Corporation's periodic requests to the Government for permission to raise the licence fees which provide its revenue are bound to be considered against the background of its general popularity.

Ratings makyth rates. In other words, the size of the audience any TV station normally gets at any particular time of day determines how much it will be able to charge advertisers for an advertising spot of any particular duration. Peak time is mid-evening, when most viewing is done. A minute of time between 7 pm and 10 pm can cost up to 13 times more than a minute before 4.30 pm.

Naturally the biggest stations, that is those serving the areas with the greatest populations like London and the Midlands, charge more for their time than the smaller ones. When in 1975 a minute of prime time on a weekday evening cost £5,200 in London (Thames) and £2,820 in Birmingham (ATV), it could be obtained for a mere £180 in Carlisle (Border TV).

These figures are very imperfect guides as to the amount of money which actually changes hands in any ad campaign.

All ITV companies charge extra for special facilities, e.g. fixed dates of transmission, fixed positions for an ad within the commercial break (you pay more for the first one put out and for the last one) and fixed times within the time band selected. So a spot guaranteed to be slotted in during a particularly popular programme is liable to cost you more than it would if it was broadcast half an hour earlier or later.

On the other hand, it is possible to secure, as with the press, a variety of different discounts. Discounts for big volume orders, discounts for packages of fixed and movable spots, discounts for test market campaigns advertising new products. And this is to mention only some of the discounts officially available according to printed rate cards. Big buyers of TV time feel ashamed of themselves if they cannot do better than that, and in practice a lot of wheeling and dealing goes on between ad agencies and TV companies, as it does indeed between agencies and newspapers. The media come under specially heavy pressure to sell space and time cheaply when the general volume of advertising contracts and it becomes a buyer's market. Some companies, notably ATV, have adopted a policy, however, of sticking to their official rates even when times are bad, arguing that it is better business to lose a few spots then to let them go cheap.

This policy can be risky since, unlike other commodities, advertising airtime cannot be stocked and sold later. Unsold time is lost for good. There is an important difference here between press and TV. Within certain limits a newspaper can increase or decrease its paging at will, so that if little advertising turns up for one issue or a series of issues, it can print fewer pages and compensate itself through lower newsprint costs for some of the missing revenue. When times improve it can print fatter issues and pack in a lot more ads. ITV companies operate under contract from the Independent Broadcasting Authority, itself bound by the Television Act, and the constraints upon their freedom of action are correspondingly more severe. In particular the ITV contractors are prohibited from carrying more than a certain amount of advertising, to wit six minutes an hour averaged over a day's programme time, with a normal maximum of seven minutes in any one clock-hour.

Television advertising suffers from certain other disadvantages apart from time restrictions, and the marketing and research departments of newspapers are only too pleased to point them out. The main alleged disadvantages are perhaps three in number:

1. You can never be sure exactly how many people have paid close attention to a commercial, even when you think you know how many TV sets were tuned to it.
2. People can't study a TV ad the way they can a press ad.
3. Many people don't watch much telly or prefer the BBC to ITV.

In the struggle between press and TV for a bigger share of advertising expenditure much has been made of all these problems. Let's consider them in order.

First, the point has already been made that the JICTAR ratings, detailed as they may be, provide information essentially about the activities of sets, not of people. JICTAR records can pinpoint what any of the sample sets was tuned to during every quarter of an hour, from noon to midnight. What isn't recorded is whether the supposed viewers were watching the commercial break during that quarter of an hour or whether they were talking, drinking tea, washing up or going to the lavatory. It is known that in quite a lot of households television is treated like wallpaper or background music; the fact that it is on doesn't necessarily mean that any attention is being given even to the programmes, let alone the ads. Many years ago research indicated that the number of housewives (for most advertisers the most important members of their households) who were viewing at any given time was no more than three quarters of the rating figure.

A survey by IPC Women's Magazines and the McCann-Erickson agency's research department, carried out in the Granada TV area and published in 1973, claimed to show that only 17 per cent of housewife 'viewers' were paying full and undivided attention during the commercial breaks.

It is, of course, undeniable that if a press ad does interest you you can read it, re-read it, cut it out and study it, which you can't do with a TV one—unless you are eccentric enough to want to record it on videotape. With certain kinds of fact-packed ad, this gives press a definite advantage. Obvious examples are cars and other expensive durable goods, about which the potential purchaser wants to know everything before coming to a decision, and investment services.

This doesn't mean, however, that TV can have no influence. Even car purchases—even?—are not based purely on rational consideration of the mechanical pros and cons, and you don't have to swallow everything Dr Dichter ever said to agree with that. What is more, if a reader's attention is not immediately engaged by a press ad he or she will immediately flick over the page and may well forget even having seen it (the truth of this contention has been demonstrated experimentally), whereas if you *are* watching the telly, however languidly, a commercial is bound to register to some extent.

Finally, the point about the inefficiency of TV advertising when it comes to communicating with the people known to admen as 'light viewers', i.e. those who don't watch much television. A good deal of research has been devoted to identifying which people are light viewers and which are heavy viewers, and it seems fairly well established that light viewers are more numerous among the higher social classes and that, as well as switching the box on less often than heavy viewers, they also tend to prefer the BBC channels to ITV. From the advertiser's standpoint viewers who entirely restrict their telly diet to BBC are not, of course, light viewers at all, they are non-viewers.

Given the class bias of heavy ITV viewing, similar to that of the popular national newspapers, the argument that advertisers must use the press as well as, or even instead of, TV if they want to get at light viewers is one which has been deployed by the posh Fleet Street papers rather than the pops. The *Sunday Times* marketing department, for instance, published an analysis of the options open to a canned beer manufacturer with £250,000 to spend on advertising and concluded that a mixed media schedule, with £50,000 spent on newspaper ads and the rest on TV, could engender about 18 per cent more opportunities to see the advertiser's message than if all the money were spent on TV alone.

The 'opportunity to see' or OTS (alas, more initials) is another useful bit of Adland jargon. The number of opportunities to see is arrived at by multiplying the number of insertions of an ad by the number of people who read the paper on the day, or have their TV set switched on at the time, when the ad is inserted.

If television has, however, become the preferred medium of most manufacturers of mass-produced repeat-purchase goods, especially groceries and toiletries, it is not only because their agencies have fallen in love with the medium (though for many younger creatives TV is what advertising is all about) but because they have found, or think they have found, that TV is very sales-effective. Whether this is because it facilitates repetition or because it is more involving, emotionally and sensuously, than the printed page we can leave it to the researchers to argue about.

CUTTING UP THE MEDIA CAKE 17

The big TV advertisers being who they are, it is not surprising that the effects of any economic downturn or upturn are reflected more quickly in TV ad expenditure than in the press. The big packaged goods manufacturers are particularly sensitive to the way the prevailing economic winds are blowing, and their advertising budgets are kept under constant review. Hard times normally mean a cut in spending, and the ad budget is the easiest to cut. Only few companies are financially able to heed the advice that those are the very times when promotional expenditure should be increased so as to carve out a bigger share of a contracting market.

Certainly in 1974, after the collapse of the advertising boom of the previous year, TV spending went down with a bump. It fell from a total of £210 million to £203 million, which in view of the rate of inflation was traumatic. Press expenditure rose in money terms from a total of £624 million to £649 million, which in real terms also, of course, represented a decline. But in 1975 TV recovered more quickly than the press, to increase its share of advertising expenditure from 22·6 to 24·4 per cent.

The press, it should be emphasised, does not mean only national newspapers. Far from it; some 5,000 publications are in question. Taking 1975 figures, national newspapers weighed in at £162 million, quite a way behind TV's £236 million. Regional newspapers took £282 million, including the lion's share of the £218 million spent on classified ads. Magazines took £79 million, while another £86 million went to trade and technical journals.

It should also be understood that advertisers' expenditure

is not the same as media revenue. The expenditure figures include agency commission and also £28 million in TV production costs.

Between them the press and TV account for the vast majority of the advertising pounds spent in Britain. By contrast the cinema, commercial radio and posters took only £53 million between them in 1975. But they deserve a word or two none the less.

Radio is, for the adman, both a newer and an older medium than TV. Newer in the sense that only since 1973 have there been any commercial radio stations operating, under the IBA's supervision, within the UK; older in the sense that since the 1920s there have been commercial radio broadcasts directed at this country from the Continent or from coastal waters. Only with the setting up of the first Government-authorised Independent Local Radio stations in 1973, however, did Britain get the kind of full-scale commercial radio service which has been a prominent feature of the advertising scene in a number of other Western countries for decades.

ILR was unfortunate in that, having been born at the height of the 1973 advertising boom, it had to contend almost immediately after its birth with the disastrous 1974 drop in advertising expenditure. Many ad agency people had, even before that, been deeply sceptical about the usefulness of the new medium from their point of view, believing that it was unlikely to attract sufficient numbers of listeners to make it worth spending money on. Such sceptics argued that the BBC had already upstaged the commercial stations by starting its own local radio network and by providing, through Radio One, the kind of fare which had made the pirates popular before the Marine Broadcasting Offences Act put most of them out of business.

The first two ILR stations, Capital and LBC, both in London, were soon appearing to live up to, or rather down to, the sceptics' predictions. Both lost money heavily and both were embroiled in controversy with the BBC over the size of their audiences. However, some of the provincial stations which followed them on to the air did much better, and Radio Clyde in Glasgow established itself in a very short time as the most listened-to channel in its area. As time went by, the stations found the prevailing economic difficulties working to their advantage as well as their detriment.

The reason was that in times of uncertainty advertisers are reluctant to commit their budgets very far ahead. This tends to hit those media with long copy dates—or, in non-jargon, those where ads have to be booked a long time in advance—such as colour magazines. The great strength of radio advertising, on the other hand, is its flexibility. A commercial can be recorded, booked and transmitted, if need be, within hours. This is what makes radio such a strong medium for retail store advertising.

Commercial radio benefited, too, from the institution of systematic audience research. A new set of initials came into existence, JICRAR (Joint Industry Committee for Radio Advertising Research), after consultations between the AIRC (Association of Independent Radio Contractors), the ISBA (advertisers) and IPA (ad agencies).

A contract was awarded to Research Services of Great Britain, a subsidiary of AGB, which went ahead with audience surveys based on the diary method. On this method a random sample of individuals aged over 15 and living within the area of the radio station concerned is selected and each individual is given a pocket diary to fill in for a week, listing his or her radio listening. There is obviously scope for controversy about the accuracy of this method, as there is about the accuracy of all research methods, but let that be.

By June 1975 this research had indicated a growth in many areas of both the number of people listening to commercial radio and the amount of time they spent listening to it. In London, 37 per cent of people were calculated to be tuning into Capital each week at some time or other. In Glasgow the figure for Clyde was 64 per cent, and in Birmingham BRMB Radio had 39 per cent.

Ad revenue of ILR stations in 1975 totalled £8½ million. The amount of advertising airtime sold has to conform as in the case of TV with IBA rules (with a maximum of nine minutes' radio advertising in one clock-hour). Radio time is, of course, much cheaper than TV time. A 60-second spot at peak time (with radio this means the morning, in contradistinction to TV) cost in 1975 £160 on Capital and £60 on Clyde, though again it must be added that all kinds of discount packages are available.

While radio may be the main medium used by a local advertiser, most national advertisers would look on it only as a back-up medium, and the same applies to posters and cinema, which accounted respectively for £35 million and £7 million of the 1975 advertising cake.

Because of the change in national habits, the cinema is thought of nowadays as principally a method of communicating with young people. As for posters, there are about 250,000 outdoor advertising sites in the UK. They are owned by a variety of contractors, but the task of booking space on them is simplified by the fact that most are organised into two consortia, British Posters and the smaller Independent Poster Sales. There are another 250,000 or so transport advertising sites, including bus panels.

The poster, whether it be a 'Tube card' in the London Underground or a giant hoarding, is a relatively cheap way of keeping a brand name or a slogan in the public eye. In 1975 it cost £17,500 to cover the country with some 2,000 largish posters for a month. But, although many classic masterpieces of advertising art are to be found in poster form—from Toulouse-Lautrec's Moulin Rouge pictures to Jean-Michel Folon's extraordinary Olivetti landscape in Waterloo station—the ad industry, as the figures show, does not think of 'outdoor' as being in the front rank of the persuasion battle. Compared with television and the press, little effort goes into devising poster campaigns and assessing their effectiveness.

We come back to the fact that in our society the two main media of commercial advertising are also the two main media for the communication of news and ideas. Willy-nilly, therefore, admen are drawn into controversies about the structure and function of broadcasting and the press. The consensus in the ad industry officially, and almost certainly unofficially too, is that things are pretty much as they ought to be, with one possible exception. The exception concerns the lack of competition in the commercial sector of television.

The attitude of the ITV programme contractors to this issue is well known. They favour a continuation of the present monopoly arrangements, whereby one company and one company alone is granted the franchise for a whole region (the London region being divided between two companies which are allocated different parts of the week) and enjoys the benefit of all TV advertising in that region. The companies, backed by the IBA, have argued that the unused fourth TV channel should likewise be allocated to them on the same region-by-region basis.

It is less well known that the Incorporated Society of British Advertisers, representing 500 companies which account between them for 60 per cent of national ad spending (excluding Government and classified advertising), takes a very different line. In its 1975 submission to the Annan Committee on the Future of Broadcasting ISBA explained that it would like to see two competitive ITV channels, not complementary ones as proposed by the contractors.

'We believe,' said the document, 'that the interests of the viewer are best served by competition. . . . When ITV was first introduced there was an immediate and significant improvement in the standard of BBC programmes.' What wasn't spelt out—it didn't need to be—was that ISBA members thought their own interests would also be served by such competition in so far as it led to cheaper rates being charged for advertising airtime.

The submission did not repeat the detailed proposals for the reform of television which had been floated two years previously in a pamphlet jointly produced by ISBA and the IPA, the ad agencies' body. This had in effect advocated that the BBC should be broken up, with BBC1 being turned into a commercial channel, competitive with ITV. In addition there would be two specialised non-commercial channels. In its submission to Annan ISBA emphasised that it nevertheless stuck by the philosophy expressed in the earlier document.

The agencies, however, had in the interim drifted away

from the client companies' view and towards that of the ITV companies, with which they naturally also have close relations.

In its own submission to the Annan Committee the IPA proposed that the fourth channel should, after all, be entrusted to the same contractors as the present ITV channel but with one proviso. Instead of each contractor—Thames, Granada or whichever—simply putting out two services, it was envisaged that the new ITV2 would be operated by a new separate company jointly owned by those contractors. It would be able to call upon the programme resources of each of its parent companies but also to engage outside artists and technicians. The ITV2 channel would aim to provide national coverage for programmes of specialised appeal, including education and the arts, and would be roughly comparable with BBC2.

It can be readily appreciated that, from the strictly advertising point of view, such a system would be of great advantage, offering agency media buyers the opportunity to use the television medium far more selectively—in the sense of targeting different ads at different types of audiences—than can be done at present, when the great majority of ITV programmes are designed to appeal to the biggest possible audience.

Also proposed was that ITV2 should have its own sales organisation, so that an element of competition would be introduced even though the profits from both ITV networks flowed back to the same companies. This was an ingenious notion for pleasing both the other parties with which the agencies do business, namely the advertisers and contractors, and comes under the heading of having your cake and eating it.

Most of us can agree that competition is a good thing: our doubts about it tend to arise when our own interests are at stake. The difference of opinion between ITV companies and advertisers is, it is perhaps not too cynical to say, illustrative of this human weakness. When it comes to the press there is no such disagreeable conflict. All three sides of the advertising triangle—advertisers, agencies and publishers—are firm in their support of the established order.

ISBA does not want to break the monopoly enjoyed by the vast majority of local newspapers in the way that it would like to break ITV's monopoly. One reason for its attitude is probably that the near-disappearance of competition from the local newspaper scene in the past few decades is due to the free working of market forces, with which the champions of private enterprise who make up ISBA's membership are loth to interfere. Breaking up ITV's state-granted, state-enforced monopolies would be a matter of introducing, not interfering with, market forces.

That, however, is not the justification given in the 1975 ISBA submission to the Royal Commission on the Press. Rather, it is said there, local papers 'are not total monopolies of news and advertising because of regional television and, increasingly, local radio coverage'. The same point could, of course, be made in reverse with regard to the ITV monopoly, but over that the advertisers, as already stated, have taken a different tack.

Both the ISBA and the IPA, in its own separate submission to the Royal Commission on the Press, argued that advertising revenue helps to ensure the survival of a wide diversity of publications by enabling them to charge a lower cover price, and thus gain more readers, than would otherwise be the case. In other respects also the two documents were, unsurprisingly, very similar.

Both flatly denied the alleged role of advertising in polarising the national press between posh papers, catering for richer, better educated readers, and pop papers with a mass following. Neither accepted that there was any evidence that the deaths of in-between papers like the *Daily Herald* and *News Chronicle* could be ascribed to advertising.

You no doubt remember that a few pages back this book did ascribe those deaths to advertising, or rather to the advertising-oriented economics of Fleet Street, and added that it was indisputable that media buyers in ad agencies 'weighed' newspaper readers (by purchasing power) as well as counting them. It *is* indisputable, as a brief glance through *Brad* (*British Rate and Data*), the monthly guide to all advertising rates, will make abundantly clear. It is equally undeniable that if the *Herald* had been able to charge the same rate per thousand circulation as *The Times* it would have made a lot of money and survived. This is not the same thing as to say that there were no other factors responsible for its demise, nor even that its demise is to be regretted. But to try to maintain that advertising revenue has no bearing on the fate of newspapers and that their readers' class and income have no bearing on that revenue is as if Cyrano de Bergerac were to shout that he had no nose at all. Far better to admit that, yes, he did have a proboscis of somewhat unusual size, but that there was nothing he could do about it and that, in any case, he was a splendid fellow.

Still, when people feel they are being attacked they often do say foolish things. Both the IPA and ISBA were on stronger ground in pointing out the press does not mean only Fleet Street newspapers and that minority viewpoints can and do get an airing in other types of publication. Behind these arguments lay the fear which they shared with publishers that pressure from within the Labour Party might lead to the imposition of new taxes on advertising.

A Labour Party discussion document, *The People and the Media*, had earlier proposed the setting up of an Advertising Revenue Board which would redistribute the money received by different papers in such a way as to iron out the advantages and disadvantages of having mainly wealthy or mainly poor readers. It is an unsatisfactory idea, since it would involve a cumbersome administrative machine and would deprive the advertisement departments of successful publications of any incentive for maximising sales. James Curran, who dreamed up the idea as a member of the study group which produced *The People and the Media*, later dropped it in favour of a simple direct levy on advertising. The proceeds of such a levy would be used to subsidise weaker papers and facilitate the launching of new ones.

The idea of using an ad tax to fund newspaper subsidies is not in fact very revolutionary. Sweden long ago introduced such a tax, levied at the rate of 6 per cent on daily newspapers and 10 per cent on other media. In Holland a levy on broadcast advertising was imposed to subsidise the press.

The pros and cons of such subsidies fall outside the scope of this book. Suffice it to say that the polemics of British advertisers and their agencies were not basically directed against the principle of subsidising the weak but against that of penalising the strong papers, on which they have come to rely as tools of their trade.

Both the IPA and ISBA also struck back at the contention that the need for advertising forces newspapers to pander to their advertisers' interests. Great, and legitimate, play was made with examples of national papers' biting the advertising hands that fed them. It was pointed out that the large amount of liquor advertising carried by the *Sunday Times Magazine* had not prevented the parent newspaper from bitterly attacking the Distillers Company over its policy on paying compensation to victims of the drug Thalidomide. Nor, despite the legal wrangle between the two sides, had Distillers threatened to cut back its advertising in the paper.

Similarly, the national press had given prominence to reports of the health hazards of cigarettes, despite the importance to them of cigarette advertising, which is barred from using television. 'Advertisers,' declared the IPA, 'will continue to advertise in the best media for their purposes irrespective of the editorial policy of those media.'

This is true—up to a point. It is truer of very strong media, those which reach a high proportion of the audience the advertiser is after and which are financially secure enough to pursue an independent line, than it is of the less strong. Many periodicals are noticeably subservient to their advertisers, though this is normally the result of self-censorship on the part of the publication.

When your survival depends on advertising revenue and you are not big enough to afford to antagonise even one sizable advertiser you think twice before running stories which advertisers are likely to find offensive. If editorial policy was irrelevant, *Private Eye* would get many more ads than it does; its circulation, after all, is roughly the same as that of *Punch*, which does very well for ads.

Ironically, media owners, who in general deny that they bow the knee to advertisers, have not scrupled to use their own power as advertisers when someone published something they didn't like. When in its first year of existence the advertising trade journal *Campaign* made a name for itself by the vigour, some would say the recklessness, with which it pursued a policy of critical independence, it was threatened with a withdrawal of advertising by at least three big newspaper groups. Whether their indignation over particular reports was justified or not is irrelevant.

The same journal later lost a certain amount of TV company advertising after publishing allegations that IBA rules on airtime restrictions had been breached. Again, whether the allegations were correct or not—and the IBA denied them—is irrelevant.

Advertisers are not obliged to take space in papers they regard as unfriendly. Indeed, unless those papers were indispensable to their advertising strategy, it would be most surprising if they did so.

18 CONSUMERISTS AND CONS

Adland may be united in its opposition to suggestions that advertising be taxed by the Government for the purpose of modifying the effect of market forces on the press, but a tax on press advertising *was* introduced in January 1975 with the full support of the ad industry. This, be it noted, is a voluntary tax, not a Government impost, and is normally referred to as a surcharge. It is payable by advertisers at the rate of 0·1 per cent of their expenditure, and the money goes to a body called the Advertising Standards Board of Finance, which was set up by the industry to increase the resources available to the Advertising Standards Authority.

The Authority itself, despite its bureaucratic sounding name, is not a Government agency but an emanation of the industry, having been established in 1964 by the Advertising Association. The Association is the umbrella organisation of the industry, consisting of all its various special interest bodies, among them the IPA, representing agencies, ISBA (advertisers), the Newspaper Publishers Association, the Periodical Publishers Association and the Independent Television Companies Association.

Before describing the structure and functions of the ASA, it should be emphasised that the issue of advertising control—that is, control of what advertisements say rather than of where they are placed or how much is paid for them —has become in the past 20 years one of central importance for the industry. Most of the attacks on advertising have been concerned not with its role in the economics of the media, despite the preoccupations of some Left-wing theorists, but with its truthfulness and its morality. The accusation that many ads, if not all ads, are designed to mislead people or to influence them in other noxious ways has by no means come from one political group. The rise of the consumerist movement, in its different forms, represents a widespread revulsion against the habit of taking the good faith of business on trust.

'Promise, large promise is the soul of an advertisement,' said Dr Johnson, and for generations a goodly number of such promises, or puffs, were indistinguishable in content from plain lies. The history of patent medicine advertising is especially disgraceful, consisting to a large extent of the deceptions practised by the unscrupulous upon the gullible, ranging from so-called cures for baldness to the allegedly health-giving properties of Simpson's iodine-impregnated socks, against which the then newly formed Advertising Association inveighed in the 1920s. Before the First World War Beecham's Pills, made from practically worthless ingredients, were advertised as a remedy for everything from constipation to ulcers.

Leaving aside such nonsense, it is not so long ago that even the biggest firms, manufacturing perfectly legitimate products, took it for granted that an ad was entitled to obey different standards of truth from those which would apply to, say, editorial material. Go back 20 years and, as Arthur Lines of Kelloggs recalls, a bowl of Corn Flakes was being advertised as better than two boiled eggs. Going merely by the number of calories provided this may have been true, but it should be evident to all but the simple-minded that, in all-round nutritional terms, the statement was absurd. The trouble is that many people are simple-minded, and perhaps most of us are far more simple-minded, in some matters at least, that we like to think we are.

Since then, says Lines, advertising has become much more honest, and he is right. The trend towards honesty was brought about by a mixture of consumerist agitation, Government pressure and, it is fair to say, a shift in opinion among admen themselves which was not entirely due to the other two factors. For the people running ad agencies and manufacturers' marketing departments today are not the same people as 20 years ago. Like the public in general, they have different attitudes from those which prevailed when few businesses took seriously the idea that they had responsibilities to anyone other than their shareholders.

The biggest landmark on Adland's road to honesty was the 1962 conference of the Advertising Association, from which stemmed the establishment of the Advertising Standards Authority and the publication of the British Code of Advertising Practice. The Code brought together the voluntary rules of a number of different bodies in one booklet, which was henceforth to serve, with periodic revisions, as the definitive work of reference on what ads could and could not say.

A Code of Advertising Practice Committee (CAP for short), comprising representatives of the various advertising and media organisations, was set up to interpret the Code under the general supervision of the ASA. This latter body was to be headed by an independent chairman (at present Lord Drumalbyn) and to have ten other members, five from the ad industry and five from outside it. The ASA and the CAP Committee were to share a joint permanent secretariat (now headed by the ASA's director, Peter Thomson).

So far so good. The machinery of the voluntary regulation system was in place. It remained to see how well it would work. Unfortunately, the good intentions spelt out in the Code often failed to be translated into practice. Critics were able to point out correctly that it was easy for advertisers and newspapers to flout the rules and get away with it, especially as no publicity was given by the ASA to complaints it considered.

Note the word 'newspapers' above. Television advertising was from the outset placed under the official control of the IBA, which issued its own Code of Advertising Standards and Practice, and there was nothing voluntary about that. With something like 25 million press ads appearing every year, however, it was inconceivable that the ASA's exiguous staff could even begin to vet them thoroughly.

These cosy arrangements—cosy from the adman's point

of view—aroused the ire not only of professional consumerists like Charles Medawar, of the Public Interest Research Centre, but of both Labour and Conservative Ministers. When Shirley Williams, as Secretary of State for Prices and Consumer Protection, told the 1974 Advertising Association conference that she was not 'convinced a voluntary code of advertising practice will suffice' she was saying very much the same as her Tory predecessor, Sir Geoffrey Howe.

The 1974 conference proved to be, like that of 1962, a major landmark. The industry's leaders went away from it, having listened to Mrs Williams and the new Director General of the Office of Fair Trading, John Methven, in no doubt that unless they took swift action they risked being landed with a statutory control system like that of Sweden.

Under the Swedish system, which dates from 1971, a Consumer Ombudsman has power to refer advertisements he considers misleading to a Marketing Court. Statements which in other countries are considered harmless hyperbole have to be verifiable in Sweden or advertisers may not publish them. In one case, for instance, an ad for an anti-perspirant showed two girls, one with a large sweat stain visible around her armpit, the other with no stain at all. The Ombudsman ordered the advertiser either to prove that his brand was totally effective in preventing perspiration, or, failing that, to modify the ad so as to show a small stain around the armpit of the girl who had previously been spotless.

To stay out of the clutches of officialdom the British ad industry agreed to the 0·1 per cent surcharge, the proceeds of which were spent partly on enlarging the ASA/CAP secretariat. Money was also found for an ad campaign, in press and posters, to tell the public about the voluntary control system and the possibility of complaining to the ASA. The campaign, by the Roe Downton agency, emphasised the first rule of the Code of Advertising Practice, which is that 'all advertisements should be legal, decent, honest and truthful'.

At around the same time the need for stricter application

of the rules was highlighted by a survey, carried out by the Consumers' Association, which found that of about 3,000 ads checked in one month about 400 were misleading and about 200 were in direct breach of the Code. Times had not changed so very much from the early years of the century as far as patent medicines were concerned. Of 78 ads in this category 42 were judged misleading. Phyllosan's claim to 'fortify the over-forties' was criticised as being relevant only to anaemic people, though this was not made clear by the advertiser. According to the survey, advertising for Iron Jelloids and Bemax flew in the face of the Code's rule that 'no advertisement for a product containing vitamins or minerals should make any claim that good looks and good health are better maintained, or that irritability, "nerviness" and lack of energy can be avoided, merely through the consumption of extra vitamins or minerals'.

An ad for Stella Artois captioned 'Europe's strongest-selling lager' was said to have conveyed to two out of five people tested the meaning that it was the strongest in alcohol, not in sales—an ambiguity which one would have to be naïve to regard as purely accidental. This ad was subsequently withdrawn.

Tobacco advertisers were especially strongly criticised for breaching their own code which forbade glamourising cigarettes. On tobacco the ASA, with its beefed-up staff (increased from about 10 to nearly 30), made a significant move. In 1975 it announced that it would vet all cigarette advertising before publication to make sure that it conformed with the rules. At the same time a new set of rules was announced which received great publicity. What most general press reports did not make clear, however, was that the new rules were very little different in essence from the old ones, enforcement of which had been entrusted to the tobacco industry's own Tobacco Advisory Committee. The almost total failure of this latter body to make sure its members complied with them had been for years the object of impassioned attacks by the Government-funded Action on Smoking and Health organisation (ASH) and its energetic young executive director, Mike Daube.

The old rules, too, had laid it down that cigarette ads should never

- appeal to 'pride and general manliness';
- feature 'conventional heroes of the young';
- 'greatly over-emphasise the pleasure' of smoking;
- use a 'fashionable social setting to support the impression that cigarette smoking is a go-ahead habit or an essential part of the pleasure and excitement of modern living';
- 'strikingly present romantic situations and young people in love'.

It was not difficult for Mike Daube, or indeed anyone else interested in the subject, to find ads which ignored one or more of these rules. The Marlboro campaign, picturing cowboys in 'Marlboro Country' and devised by Leo Burnett in America, clearly breached the 'manliness' and 'heroes of the young' provisions. (The cowboys have now disappeared, though their horses remain.) The same went for the Rothmans campaign by McCann-Erickson featuring an airline pilot at the wheel of a car. ASH found the copy line, 'When you know what you're doing', particularly objectionable, and in response to public criticism it was changed to 'When you know what you want'. Eventually the pilot, too, disappeared.

Another campaign which particularly incensed the anti-smoking lobby was that by Kensitas showing happy people in boats with the copy line 'You get more out of life with a Kensitas'. This certainly did seem to 'greatly over-emphasise the pleasure', and the line was later changed to 'More to enjoy with a Kensitas'. A Wills Slim Kings ad, captioned 'Make it a long weekend' and showing a picture of a girl on a record sleeve, was accused of infringing the 'romantic situation' rule.

And so on—and on and on. Many cigarette ads are borderline cases where the question of interpretation of the rules becomes all-important. The new rules promulgated in 1975 prohibit, for example, any claim that it is natural to smoke or abnormal not to smoke. Does the Players No. 6

campaign, showing groups of ordinary but attractive men and women and headlined 'People like you are changing to No. 6', claim by implication that it is natural to smoke? An ASH supporter might think so, but it's arguable.

In any discussion of advertising control, cigarette advertising constitutes a special category, since in the view of many the product is nothing but a poison and no method of promoting it is legitimate whatever code may be adopted. This view finds expression even within Adland. Bill Bernbach refuses to touch tobacco advertising, and the London office of Doyle Dane Bernbach was obliged some years ago to turn away the possibility of getting a sizable chunk of Gallaher business. David Abbott, of French Gold Abbott Kenyon and Eckhardt, also takes a strong moral line on the question, and his agency's policy is that it will not take a tobacco account. Abbott's own father died of lung cancer.

In general, though, ad agencies unsurprisingly hold to the view that if it is right to sell a product it cannot be wrong to promote it. This is the opinion even of Charles Saatchi, whose agency has turned out several much admired anti-smoking campaigns for the Health Education Council. All he objects to is the smallness of the budget he has had to work on compared with the enormous sums spent by the tobacco manufacturers. (In 1974–5 the HEC spent a mere £300,000 to combat the £70 million of promotional, including advertising, spending by the tobacco industry.)

A curious aspect of the controversy is that tobacco industry spokesmen have argued that total cigarette consumption is not related to the volume of advertising, which is directed by the advertisers only at increasing their own brands' share of the market. In evidence they adduce the failure of Italy's ban on all cigarette advertising, or Britain's ban on TV commercials for cigarettes, to affect consumption.

In answer to such arguments Mike Daube told the 1975 World Conference on Smoking and Health in New York that the Italian ban 'was introduced to protect the State Tobacco Monopoly (which had no budget to advertise Italian brands) in 1962, before the hazards of smoking were widely known, and has at no time been linked with an effective health education campaign'. Partial bans, like that of ITV, had been ineffective, he added, because 'the money saved has been more than compensated for in other forms of promotion'.

Daube drew attention to what he called 'the insidious way in which tobacco advertising seeks to create a favourable climate of opinion. Young people are particularly vulnerable to the pressures of attractive advertising, which so effectively counters the efforts of health educators. It is necessary for the tobacco industry to maintain a high level of advertising (and constantly to introduce new themes) in order to ensure that they establish future markets as well as maintaining current demand.'

David Abbott put it more succinctly: 'I think it's incontrovertible, though people will argue against it, that advertising things encourages people to use them. The advertising industry believes that in every other product. I don't see why the rules are any different for cigarettes.'

This brings us back to the vexed question of the general effectiveness of advertising. As we have seen earlier, there is no simple answer to that question. It is also true that advertising, in the normal sense of paid-for messages recognised as such, is not the only way, or even in some circumstances the most important way, in which products gain beneficial publicity. If that were not so Scotch whisky, to take an example other than tobacco, would not have increased its sales year by year in France, where advertising of it, under that country's complicated rules governing liquor ads, is banned.

There is a huge amount of product publicity which goes uncounted, unpaid-for and to some extent even unintended. Every time a cigarette is lit in a play or a film or a glass of Scotch is ordered in a novel or mentioned in a press article, this kind of publicity is at work.

Its effect is even less calculable than that of advertising properly so called. As for the latter, the impartial observer, having learned of the myriad uncertainties which attend the advertising process from start to finish, must still agree with David Abbott that, yes, advertising things does encourage people to use them. By its actions, if not its polemics, the tobacco industry has demonstrated that it, too, agrees.

Advertising control, whether voluntary or statutory, throws up many dilemmas, quite apart from the exceptionally knotty problem of tobacco. It has to be faced that any set of rules, however intelligently conceived and applied, must have a certain rigidity if discipline is to be maintained. When the subject matter to be regulated, however, is as diverse as is advertising, it is to be expected that there will be constant wrangles over how rigid or how flexible the rules should be.

Mention was made at the beginning of this book of the ASA's verdict that Courvoisier's humorous ads depicting an officer in a lady's bedroom should be withdrawn as contravening the rule barring suggestions that alcohol could contribute towards sexual success. The Authority stuck to its guns despite accusations of humourlessness. There have been many other cases in which sexual innuendoes caused conflict. Of the four basic criteria laid down in the Code of Advertising Practice—legality, decency, honesty and truth—there is no doubt that the most ambiguity attaches to decency, which is not to say that there can't also be plenty of Pilate-like tussles about what is truth.

Most of the rows over alleged indecency or obscenity in ads have been between ad agencies and the media and have not got as far as the control bodies. Newspapers, the cynic may note, have always had a much sharper eye for ads which might offend their readers' sexual morals than for those which might lead them falsely to believe in the efficacy of some supposed remedy for rheumatism or fatness. The *Daily Mirror*'s ad department was busy painting out nipples even after these had become acceptable on the editorial pages.

Standards in this field are indeed notoriously subject to change. Thus *The Times*, which in 1968 had no hesitation in rejecting a perfectly well-meaning ad for the magazine *New Society* because it included a stylised drawing of a nude pregnant woman (in connection with an article in the magazine on unmarried mothers), had graduated within three years to the point where it could print a full-page photograph of a real live nude in an ad for Fisons. What model Vivian Neves's delectable body had to do with Fisons no one can remember, but the sight of it did us all a lot of good.

London Transport has been in the thick of battles fought to fix the frontiers of good taste. LT has its own published code of advertising rules, the main one being that it will not accept ads 'likely to offend the general travelling public on account of the nature of the product or service being advertised or because of the wording or design of the advertisement or the possibility of its defacement'. Michael Mountain, who is in charge of London's Tube and bus advertising, says a lot of letters are received from people who find some poster or other offensive. A high proportion of them are about ads for films, and this is the category in which the most arguments take place with advertisers.

In 1974 film distributors said they were 'astounded' that London Transport had turned down posters for two films, *Sex Farm* and *On the Game*, simply because of their titles. Another sexy film, *Emmanuelle*, had a poster barred from the Tube not on the grounds that the ad was obscene but that it would attract too many graffiti artists. It depicted an object which managed to look at the same time like a female bottom and an apple, with the peel coming away and turning into a snake.

But London Transport, too, has moved with the times, not to say *The Times*. By 1975 the Tube was carrying its first poster showing a fully bare-breasted girl. It was for the play *Life Class* and included a picture of the actress Rosemary Martin, who took the part of an artist's model. All very soft focus and tasteful, but her nipples *were* clearly visible.

Incidentally, the widespread impression that the Tube is crammed with sexy ads for female underwear is much exaggerated. Underwear advertising accounts, according to Michael Mountain, for considerably less than 5 per cent of his total revenue. The bras and bikinis are noticeable largely because they are concentrated along the sides of the escalators. The reason for that is caution. Since they are behind glass and the stairs are moving, nobody can deface them. The same ads are not allowed on station platforms.

Television also adopts a conservative attitude with respect to decency, not even allowing commercials for sanitary towels. The IBA has come in for its fair share of sneers because of its conservatism, but as a statutory body with legal responsibility for everything broadcast to more than half the viewing population, including children, it cannot afford to take chances.

In the exercise of its advertising control functions the IBA is more comparable with a single newspaper than with the Advertising Standards Authority. Even if it wanted to, the ASA would be physically incapable of vetting all the millions of national and provincial press ads before publication. It has to operate mainly by laying down guidelines and considering complaints and hoping that individual newspapers and magazines will pay attention. No TV commercial, on the other hand, can be transmitted if it has not received the Authority's prior seal of approval.

In practice the IBA's advertising control department is greatly helped by the Independent Television Companies Association, which has its own Copy Clearance Department which acts as an initial filter through which all TV advertising must pass. Peter Woodhouse, the IBA's head of advertising control, previously ran the ITCA end of the job.

The IBA's conservatism relative to the press is evident in fields other than that of sexual morality. For example, it was only in 1975 that it followed the lead of the ASA in authorising what is known in the trade as 'knocking copy'—that is, comparative advertising in which rival products are actually named and criticised.

In the press knocking had already become common practice, having been pioneered by Collett Dickenson Pearce with its Ford ads. A typical tit-for-tat exchange in the press between advertisers occurred when Ford took full pages to declare, of its Cortina model, 'It's bigger than a Mini. It's faster than a Mini. It's also cheaper to run than a Mini.' To which British Leyland replied with more full pages headed 'Ever wondered why so many of them end up comparing theirs with ours?'

But when a TV campaign for the Audi 80 car was launched on TV in 1973 the Euro Advertising agency was not allowed to use film of skid tests in which its steering and braking performance were compared with that of a named competitor. The furthest it could go was to show an unidentified vehicle with its front reshaped so that it couldn't be recognised, and even that caused quite a furore. In many eyes such 'Brand X' techniques are less honest than direct knocking, which can be answered, and finally the IBA accepted this view and brought its Code into line with the general Code of Advertising Practice, administered by the ASA.

According to the Code, 'all comparative advertisements should respect the principles of fair competition and should be so designed that there is no likelihood of the consumer being misled as a result of the comparison'.

19 TRUTH COSTS EXTRA

At the same time that the IBA relaxed its rules on knocking copy it tightened them up with regard to another, and more frequent, advertising technique, the use of well-known people to endorse a product. The technique is of venerable age. One of the most famous endorsement campaigns, that by J. Walter Thompson for Lux toilet soap, goes back to long before the war. In the old days JWT used society beauties. Later they were supplanted by film stars, and with their aid Lux claimed to have become the biggest-selling toilet soap in the world.

For critics of advertising its exploitation of, and by, celebrities is one of its worst features, corrupt and corrupting in that it normalises the buying and selling of opinions. When the IBA decided, however, that 'celebrated entertainers, writers or sportsmen may not present, endorse or recommend any investment or savings offer', its aim was not to curb their spiritual prostitution but to safeguard viewers against the rash disposal of possibly large sums of money.

A similar ban on the use of celebrities in advertising for medical products was also inspired by concern for the consumer's welfare. 'There are areas,' said Harry Theobalds, the Authority's deputy head of advertising control, 'where we think decisions should be made on rational grounds, not on emotional response.'

In the specified areas the IBA ignores the distinction between endorsing a product or service, à la Lux, and merely presenting it, a distinction which it, like the ASA, otherwise treats as one of great importance. Both the IBA and the ASA insist in their codes that endorsements or testimonials must be genuine, whether they are made by celebrities or unknown people. The snag, of course, is that in most cases it is virtually impossible to determine whether they are genuine or not. Nevertheless, both the control bodies do what they can to reduce dishonesty.

The IBA demands that anyone testifying in a commercial to the satisfaction he or she has derived from a product should sign a statement confirming the accuracy of the words spoken. If an endorser has had no experience of the product before being asked to talk about it, that is supposed to be made clear in the script.

The ASA also asks for written authentication of testimonials but, owing to the impossibility of pre-vetting press ads, only in cases where doubts arise. 'Normally,' says Peter Thomson of the ASA, 'one gets a letter from the individuals concerned swearing blind that they use the product.' Can they be trusted? 'One just has to accept,' he sighs, 'that most people have certain standards of honesty and decency.'

Occasionally evidence does come to light that the protestations of sincerity are insincere. One man who swore in a TV commercial to his love of a certain brand of booze was foolish enough to tell a newspaper that he drank only milk. The commercial was ordered off the air. In another case actress Joanna Lumley disclosed in a BBC programme that she was not addicted to Supersoft shampoo, as a commercial on the rival channel made her out to be. The official view was that the code had not been breached, since she was not named in the ad, which was regarded as a playlet rather than an endorsement. As an actress she was thought to be not well enough known for her remarks to carry the force of an endorsement. An ironic outcome of the incident was that she subsequently became sufficiently known for the IBA to decree that any similar remarks from her in future commercials *would* count as an endorsement and would have to be backed up with the usual signed statement.

Such affirmations of good faith are not, repeat not, required when the celebrity who appears in a commercial or press ad is deemed to be acting merely as a presenter without giving his or her own opinion of the product. To tell which role any given individual is undertaking is not by any means always easy without detailed attention to the copy.

From the advertiser's point of view the distinction between presenting and endorsing is often purely academic. The purpose of hiring a celebrity is not usually to talk the gullible into believing what otherwise they would not but to create interest in, and good will towards, a product by associating it with an admired or trusted figure.

That purpose is nowhere clearer than in a press campaign like that for Sanderson furnishing fabrics and wall coverings, where the featured celebrities are required to say or do nothing except be photographed in their own homes against a background of the advertiser's goods. 'Very Kingsley Amis, very Sanderson,' says the caption, 'Very Peter Hall . . .', 'Very Joan Bakewell . . .' and very several other well-known people who are willing to have one room redecorated for the ad—and receive a fee.

Sanderson's ad agency, Doyle Dane Bernbach, denied a report at the end of 1975 that theatre bigwig Peter Hall had been paid £5,000 for his participation. The people used, said chairman Brian Waldron, were happy to be linked with the 'most prestigious name in interior decoration' and had been paid 'insignificant' fees. Perhaps so, wonders do happen. But if Hall didn't get £5,000 he was selling himself for under the market price.

According to Victor Labati, talent contracts manager of J. Walter Thompson and an expert on such matters, the going price for a celebrity of Hall's calibre at that time was indeed in the region of £5,000. That was for a national press campaign. In TV a top-ranking personality could get at least £10,000 and possibly as much as £15,000 for just one commercial, up to £20,000 for a series. A well-known actor of the second rank might get between £5,000 and £10,000.

Even such fees look like chicken feed compared with the money sometimes paid out. In 1976 Brigitte Bardot got £100,000 for advertising Goya's Zendiq aftershave. Three years earlier Sir Laurence Olivier was reported to have received £100,000 for telling American TV viewers that, with Polaroid cameras, 'you will feel like you are looking at the world for the first time'. You may well think that, for the greatest English actor of his time, having to murder the English language in such a manner was worth at least £100,000 in damages to his reputation alone. Sir Laurence made five commercials, all shot in Paris. None was shown on British TV, and it is not uncommon for big stars to refuse to have their advertising work exhibited on their own home ground.

Those celebrities who do condescend to plug products in this country expect to be paid more, incidentally, for endorsing them—and remember the rules say all endorsements must be truthful—than for merely presenting them. It is a curious comment on our whole society, and not just Adland, that the truth costs extra.

In contrast with the (in practice) slight restrictions on the advertising use of paid celebrities is the strictness with which the control bodies forbid the use of unpaid ones, that is when their faces appear in ads not only without their cooperation but without their consent. At one time this was a favourite trick of creative departments in this country, and it is still widely practised abroad. The usual aim is not to convey any misleading impression but simply to grab the consumer's attention.

Perhaps the most successful effort in this *genre* by any London agency was Leo Burnett's 'Red Revolution' poster campaign for Watney's Red beer. Successful, let's get it straight, in attracting attention. The ads, featuring pictures of Fidel Castro, Mao Tse-tung and Khrushchev (or rather of actors made up to look like them) were much talked about; the fact that in the end they didn't do the brand much good is another story. Whether or not it was effective advertising in the sales sense, the campaign was not held to contravene any rules.

Some people, though, judged it to be in dubious taste. And such criticism was levelled with much greater force at an ad for the Heathrow Hotel which appeared in *The Times* and which used unauthorised pictures of the then Prime Minister, Edward Heath, and several other public figures purely as attention-getters. That at least was the intention, obvious to anyone who stopped to read the words. If you didn't read the words it was just possible you might, in flicking through the paper, have gained the impression that Heath, David Frost and the others were actually placing their names at the service of the advertiser. It was not necessary to be a fervent Tory supporter to feel that the Prime Minister had the right to feel aggrieved.

There was a short but nasty row. *The Times* apologised for running the ad. The advertiser, the Lex Hotels group, fired its agency, Aalders Marchant Smith. The Code of Advertising Practice Committee went into a huddle and subsequently came up with a new ruling that no ad should portray a public figure without his or her permission. For good measure it was also laid down that actors should not be used to impersonate a public figure and that this applied even to foreigners and criminals. From now on Mao and Castro had to be left alone, as well as Ted Heath.

Not everyone in Adland, it turned out, took the trouble to read the bulletin in which the CAP Committee issued its decision and three months later, in January 1974, another ad landed its authors in hot water for perpetrating an impersonation of the Queen. The ad, for Cygnet paper plates, was headed 'Cygnet will change everyone's mind about disposable plates' and appeared to show the Sovereign seated on an ornate chair and eating off one of the products in question. The lady photographed was not, of course, the Queen but a model, Mrs Jeannette Charles, who bears a strikingly close resemblance to her. The agency responsible, Moss Clark, denied any intention of *lèse-majesté*. It had been merely trying, said Ron Moss, to change people's attitudes to the social acceptability of paper plates. It had started by looking for a 'conservative, middle-aged, traditional type of lady', but when Mrs Charles had turned up with her regal features it had decided to take advantage of them. Neither the agency nor the trade papers which ran the ad were aware that the Code was being infringed, but the CAP Committee swiftly cured their ignorance. The ad was not repeated.

Since then neither the Queen nor her Ministers have suffered from the impudence of British admen, but different rules apply in other countries. Not long after the Cygnet episode Mrs Charles was up to her regal tricks again in an Italian ad campaign for a brand of whisky.

While the advertising control system has, then, been tightened up in various ways in the past few years, one step which consumerists have advocated strongly as a sanction against errant advertisers has never been taken. That is the institution of so-called corrective advertising and counter-advertising procedures.

In Britain the worst that can happen to an advertiser who is thought to have misled the public but not to have broken the law is that he should be required to cease publishing the offending ads. Corrective advertising means obliging him to spend his own money on new ads putting right what was previously wrong and telling the public that it was wrong.

The American Federal Trade Commission has the power to order corrective advertising in certain circumstances and has indeed used that power, notably in the case of Profile bread. Profile, a product manufactured by a subsidiary of the giant ITT conglomerate, was found to have made misleading claims about its value to slimmers and was forced to run a campaign explaining its misdeeds. In France the *Loi Royer* gave the courts power to make similar orders.

By counter-advertising is meant the publication not of actual corrections but of statements challenging the impression of a product's value or usefulness given in its advertising and describing disadvantages on which that advertising remains silent. Counter-ads of this kind have been published by American consumerists.

In Britain the Public Interest Research Centre took up the idea and as an experiment drafted a counter-ad on vaginal deodorants, with which it approached the IBA, the ASA and several newspapers and magazines. The PIRC ad contrasted claims made for certain named brands of deodorant—for example, 'When a girl becomes a woman, Femfresh becomes essential'—with the views of independent investigators that such products were at best a waste of money and at worst physically harmful. In reply to the PIRC approach the Advertising Standards Authority suggested some minor alterations to the text of the counter-ad but otherwise said it had no objections to it. None of the newspapers or magazines, however, would agree to publish it. Some ad managers would give no reason for their decision, others criticised the text as unfair. As PIRC's Charles Medawar commented, what they were really saying was that they couldn't afford to offend their normal commercial advertisers.

The IBA refused to consider allowing either advertising or counter-advertising on TV about vaginal deodorants, a subject it regarded as 'offensive to public taste'. Asked for its general views on the admissibility of counter-ads, the Authority said the use of actual brand names would probably be rejected as 'unfair disparagement'. It also opined that Parliament's intention, as reflected in the Television Act under which ITV operates, was that advertising should be confined to goods and services. On this Medawar's comment was that 'the right of reply is a basic freedom of speech, and as things stand at present commerce has a complete monopoly over the supply of information about goods and services in advertising time. This is quite wrong.'

Note the qualification, 'in advertising time'. Many people would argue—the IBA did argue—that the place for consumerists to exercise that right of reply is in programme (or editorial) time. Those who support the idea of counter-ads are thereby implying a degree of faith in the psychological impact of the advertising mode of communication which many admen would be overjoyed to think was justified.

The basic consumerist objection to the advertising control system as it works in Britain is that the test of truthfulness demanded is negative rather than positive. An advertiser is asked, as Medawar complains, to demonstrate that his claim is not untrue rather than that it tells the whole truth.

As an example he has attacked an ad which, even after conceding that it was unlikely that most people suffered from vitamin deficiency, said that nevertheless such deficiency could 'happen easily' and 'Boots Plurivite M . . . taken regularly will ensure that your body gets all the vitamins and iron that it needs'. The claim can presumably be substantiated but, says Medawar, 'What matters is that no one should take these pills if they don't need to.'

It is indeed difficult to deny that, while the control bodies have set their faces with increasing severity against outright falsehood, advertisers can still get away fairly easily with the *suggestio falsi*, achieved not by direct statement but through the use of weasel words and phrases.

When a TV commercial for Signal 2 tells us that 'no other toothpaste is better at fighting decay', we can be sure we are not being lied to—the IBA and ITCA, like the ASA and CAP Committee, have panels of expert consultants upon whom they can call for advice about claims made for any type of product—but can we be sure that we are not left with a completely wrong impression of the product's efficacy relative to that of others? The copy line does *not* say, as it could, 'several other toothpastes are just as good at fighting decay'.

Should it have to? Critics like Medawar sometimes imply that they would like to see advertising cease to be advertising, i.e. commercial propaganda, and become something else, much closer to reportage. This is not, naturally enough, a sentiment shared by advertisers. Neither do the control bodies take the view that it is their duty to prevent advertising agencies from behaving as propagandists, or advocates if you prefer the word, and to insist that every ad should be an impartial *Which?*-type review of the facts. Something, sometimes quite a lot, is left to the reader's or viewer's own discrimination and good sense.

Certainly a good deal of hyperbole, or puffery, is allowed which purists may consider offends against the truth and honesty criteria of the Code of Advertising Practice. Is Harveys Bristol Cream 'the best sherry in the world'? Its advertising says it is. How do you prove, or for that matter disprove, that it is the best? What does 'best' mean anyway? Where wine is concerned can it be anything but a subjective judgment? Let us agree that it is; of course, the use of the word in an ad is intended to influence action, not be taken merely as the advertiser's private and subjective opinion.

Other advertisers are slightly more circumspect and throw in a weasel word to protect their hyperbole against the charge of dishonesty. Thus, although press ads for Dunhill cigarettes speak unequivocally of 'The world's finest cigarette' and 'The most distinguished tobacco house in the world', commercials for Dunhill lighters are more modest. '*Perhaps* the finest lighter in the world' they say (my italics).

Similarly, KMP's commercials for Carlsberg described it only as '*probably* the best lager in the world'. If you pause to think, such a formulation is devoid of any precise meaning whatsoever. However, as with most advertising slogans, the consumer is expected not to analyse it but to be persuaded by it into valuing the product more highly than he otherwise might.

The Code of Advertising Practice says: 'It is seldom possible to substantiate general claims by an advertiser that his product is of superlative quality (best, finest) in a way which is universally acceptable. Such claims, however, are permissible under the Code, provided that their inclusion in an advertisement does not create a false impression concerning any quality possessed by the product which is capable of assessment in the light of generally accepted standards of judgement.'

It adds: 'Obvious hyperbole, which is intended to attract attention or to amuse is permissible provided that it is not likely to be taken as a positive claim to superior or superlative status.' This takes care of humorous campaigns like that by Collett Dickenson Pearce for Heineken and of many ads which are not intentionally humorous at all, like this for Ambre Solaire Moisturiser: 'Created . . . to keep your face soft, summery and beautiful. Not just for one day but for ever.' For ever? No, Ambre Solaire does not guarantee its customers immortality.

Or what about this for Player's Whisky Flake pipe tobacco? 'Your finest hour begins when you light up a pipeful. . . . Here is a mature, cool-smoking tobacco that lends reassuring support to your every endeavour'. But don't be too disappointed if it gets you nowhere.

There are hundreds of ads like these. They tend to cancel each other out, since readers of women's magazines, for instance, are exposed as they flick through the pages to the exaggerations of rival brands of cosmetics, and they can't all be as wonderful as they crack themselves up to be. Anyway who takes such puffery seriously?

Well some people do take it seriously, if only to the extent of getting very angry about what the American writer Samm Sinclair Baker called 'the permissible lie'. In his book of that name, Baker, an ex-agency man himself, observed that 'the fact that the advertiser fails to fool you is no excuse for the fraud in advertising. It should not dilute your condemnation of the deceptive approach based on the permissible lie. It does weaken belief in the veracity of *any* advertising.'

It is at this point that the interests of consumerists and admen can be thought to coincide. For, notwithstanding the uncertainties about the degree to which advertising is effective and the manner in which it works, there must be some advantage to the advertiser in having his ads looked upon as trustworthy, mustn't there?

The answer given to that question by at least some admen is yes. Robin Wight, creative director of Euro Advertising, caused quite a stir in Adland in 1972 when he published a book called *The Day the Pigs Refused to be Driven to Market* in which he espoused a goodly number of the consumerist criticisms of his own industry, which he characterised as 'the irritator, the deliverer of half-truths, the uninformer, the disrespecter of persons, the social blackmailer'. He attacked, as Samm Sinclair Baker had done before him, the hyperbolic style of much advertising, condemning even such examples as 'The happiest sounds come from babies fed with Heinz', which nobody was likely to take at face value. Like Baker his declared aim was to promote a new community of interest between business and the consumer.

For his pains Wight was rebuked by reviewers from both sides of the fence. Charles Medawar accused him of trying to have his cake and eat it. Jeremy Bullmore, of J. Walter

Thompson, dismissed as naïve his assessment of advertising puffery. Research carried out by JWT has tended to confirm the view that housewives expect ads to exaggerate and that they treat them with the same kind of scepticism as they do political speeches.

Wight, being a devotee of Bill Bernbach as well as of Ralph Nader, prefers understatement to hyperbole. But, like Bernbach, he also works hard at trying to sell his clients' goods. These include Audi cars, and ironically his own agency was once ticked off by the ASA for making an unfair claim for Audi.

If the rules regarding puffery are not hard and fast, the same is not true of some other abuses which in the past have aroused complaints. Both the Code of Advertising Practice and the IBA Code are very precise about what may and may not be said and done in ads directed at children.

Among these rules (almost identical in the two Codes) is one specifying that 'no advertisement for a commercial product or service is allowed if it contains any appeal to children which suggests in any way that unless the children themselves buy or encourage other people to buy the product or service they will be failing in some duty or lacking in loyalty towards some person or organisation whether that person or organisation is the one making the appeal or not.'

When, in 1975, an ad appeared showing a boy trying to join the Airfix Gang and succeeding only after buying an Airfix construction kit, the company was publicly reprimanded by the ASA for contravening the Code.

Another hard and fast ban, which applies to television, is that on 'subliminal' advertising. The IBA Code states that no commercial 'may include any technical device which, by using images of very brief duration or by any other means, exploits the possibility of conveying a message to, or otherwise influencing the minds of, members of an audience without their being aware, or fully aware, of what has been done.' Subliminal advertising is worth a word or two not because it is or ever has been of any practical importance—its known use has been restricted to a handful of experiments—but because it helped to give some substance to the notion that admen possess powerful and sinister instruments for manipulating public behaviour without the public realising what is being done. This notion was popularised about 20 years ago by Vance Packard in his book *The Hidden Persuaders* and has been floating around ever since. Packard's chief concern was with the work of the motivational researchers, Dr Dichter and Co., to whose wilder pretensions he gave greater credence than most of their clients ever did. But his warnings appeared to be strengthened by the results of an experiment devised by researcher Jim Vicary in the late Fifties.

Vicary got a cinema in New Jersey to flash the messages 'Drink Coke' and 'Eat Popcorn' on to the screen so fleetingly (one three-thousandth of a second every five seconds) that they could not be consciously perceived. During a six-week experimental period, sales of both products at the cinema rose, conceivably but not absolutely certainly, because the words had registered subconsciously with the viewers. Sceptics criticised the uncontrolled nature of the test.

A much later experiment, by Del Hawkins, with small groups of people, compared the reactions of those exposed subliminally to the words 'Coke' and 'Drink Coke' and to a nonsense syllable. The findings were stated to indicate that 'a subliminal stimulus can serve to arouse a basic drive such as thirst'. But the command 'Drink Coke' apparently had no greater effect than the reminder 'Coke'. The experiment, incidentally, did not measure purchasing behaviour, merely the thirstiness of the respondents.

There's not a great deal more to the history of subliminal advertising. But Vicary's initiative and the publicity given to it were sufficient to inspire the IBA ban. A pity in a way. It would have been interesting to discover whether Vicary's claims really had anything in them. A lot of people in the ad business would be astonished if they did.

20 BIG BROTHER IS TELLING YOU

So far in this book we have been concerned mainly with *commercial* advertising, and most of the examples given have come from the area of branded products. But not all advertising is commercial, and not all commercial advertising is MCA (manufacturers' consumer advertising), even though that is what most of the controversies have been about. In fact, over the past decade, during which the proportion of the gross national product devoted to advertising expenditure has been falling, MCA's share has fallen even faster. In 1968 all ad spending accounted for 1·36 per cent of GNP, but by 1975 the percentage was down to 1·05. The corresponding figures for MCA were 0·63 and 0·45.

The biggest single advertiser in the country is not a manufacturer nor even in the commercial sector at all. It is the State. In 1975 total spending by the Government and the nationalised industries was £39 million. Even leaving aside the nationalised industries, Government departments spent in the same year £21 million, the greater part of which was channelled through the Central Office of Information. By 1975 the COI alone was handling over £15 million of advertising money, which put it for the first time ahead of Unilever in the ad spending stakes.

The comparison often made with Unilever is in a sense misleading. Although the Anglo-Dutch conglomerate can be said to be Britain's biggest single commercial advertiser, it does not function as a single advertiser. Each of the subsidiary companies—Lever Brothers, Van den Berghs, Birds

Eye, Elida Gibbs, etc.—is responsible for its own advertising planning, including picking its own ad agencies. The Unilever-controlled agency Lintas is, however, used as a central media-buying agency for much work it does not itself create. The commission is split with the other agencies involved.

The COI, on the other hand, in conjunction with the Government Departments concerned, is responsible for deciding what happens to all the money it handles. Its director, Henry James, and the head of its advertising division, Owen Thetford, could be seen by any agency, therefore, as the most important clients in the UK.

Their power of patronage—over agencies and media—is huge. But they do not exercise it arbitrarily nor alone. When it comes to sharing out the juicy accounts among agencies the COI consults with a special advisory committee of independent experts like Sir David Barran, of Shell, or Howard Thomas, of Thames Television. In 1975 these accounts, ranging from road safety and energy conservation to recruitment for the Services and the hospitals, were parcelled out among more than two dozen agencies. A smaller number would increase efficiency, but the Government cannot risk suspicions of favouritism. COI accounts are automatically put up for competitive presentations every five years, and on average they move from one agency to another every six or seven years, which is about the same average as for private enterprise accounts.

The COI's advertising division—with a staff of about 40, many of them former commercial admen—inspects about a dozen agencies each year with the aim of keeping tabs on the best people in the business. Its decisions are made on merit and not on the nationality of the agency's owners, and some of its biggest campaigns in recent years have been entrusted to American firms. When the Left-wing Labour MP Frank Allaun called on the Labour Government to give more of its advertising business to British-owned agencies the demand was rejected.

It was an American-owned agency, Young and Rubicam, which was responsible for the much praised 'Clunk Click' commercials in which Jimmy Savile warned the nation of the peril of not wearing seat belts (though the idea originated with Masius Wynne-Williams). The 'Save it' campaign on conserving energy came from the same firm. It was J. Walter Thompson, another American-owned agency, which earlier ran the huge public information campaign explaining the switch-over to decimal currency.

Some Government accounts present the agency with advertising problems not altogether dissimilar from those they are accustomed to dealing with in the course of their commercial work. Recruitment campaigns, which absorb nearly half the COI's budget, are basically doing a selling job, attempting to convince individuals of the benefits, material and emotional, they will derive from, say, joining the Army.

The first Government ad campaign ever to use TV was in fact for the recruitment of Army other ranks. This happened because in the early Sixties, after the ending of national service, the Forces found themselves competing for manpower in a tight labour market. Like other enterprises in a competitive situation they resorted to advertising to boost their market share. The ad agency which produced the original Army commercials, Colman Prentis and Varley, went on to market the military life under the slogan 'The Professionals'. In 1976 French Gold Abbott Kenyon and Eckhardt, the agency into which CPV had been merged, was still handling the account.

Eventually it was decided to advertise for officers as well as men, a procedure originally felt to be out of keeping with military dignity. Much admired in Adland were Collett Dickenson Pearce's press ads like the one headed 'Any young man who says he wants to be an Army officer should have his motives examined'. Frankness of this kind, which did not eschew mentioning that soldiers were likely to have to endure terrorism in Northern Ireland, did not come about by accident. Like any other big ad campaign it was based on research, including group discussions with potential recruits. The COI has a research unit of its own.

It was this research unit which carried out a series of behavioural studies to test the effectiveness of seat belt advertising. The research involved stopping cars on the road to check whether occupants were wearing their belts. The conclusion was that belt-wearing was directly stimulated by TV advertising in any given region, and that the heavier the advertising expenditure the greater the effectiveness, at least during an initial period. Later, as with product advertising, a peak was reached after which it was difficult to expand usage.

The national average of front-seat occupants wearing seat belts rose eventually to about 35 per cent, which represented only a limited success. However, it could be argued that the effect on public opinion of the 'Clunk Click' campaign was such as to increase support for legislation to make belt-wearing compulsory. If and when such legislation is finally adopted, advertising may claim some, at least, of the credit.

When it comes to campaigns like 'Clunk Click' or 'Save it', one is in the area of attempts to change social behaviour, but these are normally non-controversial. With the 1975 anti-inflation campaign, executed by Boase Massimi Pollitt, some judged that Government advertising crossed the boundary and became political propaganda. The IBA did so judge, on the grounds that the campaign was aimed at strengthening public support for Government wage restraint policy which might be accepted by most, but was not accepted by all, sectors of political opinion. It invoked Rule 9 of its Code of Advertising Standards and Practice: 'No advertisement may be inserted by or on behalf of any body the objects whereof are wholly or mainly of a political nature, and no advertisement may be directed towards any political end. No advertisement may have any relation to any industrial dispute. No advertisement may show partiality as respects matters of political or industrial controversy or relating to current public policy.'

The anti-inflation campaign, much to the agency's chagrin, was barred from the screen. Press ads, with their juxtaposition of the portraits and platitudes of industrialists and trade union leaders, ran into no such problems. The Code of Advertising Practice which the press is expected to observe allows 'the free expression of opinion in paid-for advertising space, whether by those engaged in commerce or by political parties, foreign governments, religious or charitable bodies, provided the identity of such advertisers is made clear'.

Far from interfering with political ads, the CAP Committee and Advertising Standards Authority interpret the Code as putting them beyond their competence even when the 'free expression of opinion' is coupled with the publication of statements that could be held to offend against the 'honest and truthful' principles laid down in the same Code. In recent years there have been some quite striking examples.

During the run-up to the October 1974 General Election the steel firm GKN spent £50,000 on an anti-nationalisation campaign in Fleet Street newspapers. Full-page ads, devised by agency Collett Dickenson Pearce, asked the question 'Nationalisation: Is it unwelcome to the shop floor?' The copy purported to summarise the results of two surveys. The first was carried out at GKN's Brymbo steel works, where employees were asked whether they thought the plant should continue in private hands or be renationalised. Of 66 per cent who replied, 97 per cent wanted GKN to stay in charge.

The second part of the ad dealt with a sample survey of GKN's 80,000 non-managerial employees. Copy stated that 'on the question of whether they felt that the State should take over the largest companies in Britain, 73 per cent said no'. This part of the ad attracted the editorial attention of the *Sunday Times*, which pointed out some of its shortcomings. The ad had not explained that the State ownership question had been inserted into a much longer questionnaire supposedly aimed at establishing employees' reactions to a message from GKN's chairman, Sir Raymond Brookes. Employees had not been told that their answers would be used for political purposes.

However, it was the first part of the ad, relating to the Brymbo works, to which the most cogent objections could be, and indeed were, raised. An official complaint was made to the Advertising Standards Authority by Michael Rines, editor of the monthly journal *Marketing*, who had taken the trouble to discover a number of relevant facts, to wit:

1. Brymbo was a special case in that, even while nationalised, its output had been bought mainly by GKN. The British Steel Corporation had decided that investing in Brymbo did not fit in with its long-term plans, and if it had not been sold back to GKN it would probably have been closed.

2. The questionnaire put to the workers contained three questions. The first was whether the respondent was in favour of the works continuing to be owned by GKN; the second whether he was 'in favour of the preparation of a [GKN] development plan for the modernisation and expansion of the Brymbo steel works'; the third whether he thought the works should be renationalised. (In view of the historical background and of the implications of the second question, Rines pointed out, it was hardly surprising that most of the workers opposed renationalisation, whatever their general political views might be.)

3. In a covering letter respondents were told that the questionnaire was 'not really a matter of any political opinion, but it is a matter vital to the future of Brymbo'.

None of these facts was brought out in the ad, which Rines complained 'is not only misleading but is based on a gross abuse and misuse of proper research and advertising practices'.

Lord Drumalbyn, as chairman of the ASA, ruled that, whether the complaint might be justified or unjustified, it lay outside the Authority's scope. He wrote back to Rines: 'To invite the ASA to express an opinion on whether the use in an advertisement of a response to a political question in a questionnaire or in an opinion poll accords with the Code [of Advertising Practice] is to draw the self-regulatory system inescapably into the arena of political controversy. That the ASA must resist if it is to fulfil its role, which is entirely non-political.'

Rines was not satisfied with the reply. He reiterated that he was not concerned with the expression of political opinion in the GKN ad but with the element of deception which he—and others—believed it to contain. And this, he said, could not be outside the ASA's area of responsibility. His attitude received powerful, if oblique, backing from John Methven, the then Director-General of Fair Trading, who a little later expressed disappointment at the way the voluntary control system was working and added: 'I must congratulate Michael Rines, who is prepared to speak his mind.'

In response to Methven's behind-the-scenes pressure the system was tightened up in various ways, as has already been indicated. But Drumalbyn and his colleagues continued resolutely to refuse to have anything to do with political ads even when, as in the GKN case, it was their factual content which was in dispute. As a former politician (and Conservative Minister) himself, Lord Drumalbyn does not think highly of the standards of truthfulness adhered to by anyone in politics and is fearful that once the ASA tried to do anything about them it would be drowned in a sea of recriminations.

He is almost certainly right. But that is no excuse for the complacency with which in the past some newspapers have agreed to publish ads containing distortions and even downright lies which would have been ruthlessly eliminated from their own editorial columns. For example, in 1973 the *Guardian* printed an ad from the Club of Ten, a pro-South African pressure group, stating that 'The Church of England . . . is beginning to have grave doubts concerning the support of the "Programme to Combat Racism" organised by the World Council of Churches.' Further on the ad declared that 'the victims of terrorism in South Africa are mainly innocent and peaceful Africans butchered in remote villages by terrorists indulging in murder orgies.'

It is customary for newspaper advertisement departments to clear controversial ads with the editor (who is in law responsible for all the newspaper's contents, including advertising). In the absence of the then editor Alastair Hetherington, publication of the Club of Ten ad was approved by John Ryan, assistant to the editor (and later to hold the title of executive editor). Challenged about the accuracy of the statements quoted he came up with a somewhat lame defence.

Although the Church of England had issued no official expression of doubt about the World Council programme, Ryan supposed that the ad could be interpreted as referring to the views of some people within the Church rather than to the whole institution. As for the passage about terrorism, which at that time was practically non-existent in the Republic of South Africa, he had taken it to refer to Southern Africa as a whole, including Mozambique, where a fierce guerrilla war was going on.

It was inconceivable that, as a professional journalist, Ryan would have been similarly indulgent towards editorial copy. Given his paper's particularly outspoken opposition to South African apartheid, it was ironic that he should seek any excuses at all for a piece of blatant pro-apartheid propaganda. His reasoning was that, 'provided there is a basis for the assertions made', advertisers were entitled to use the space they paid for in any way they wanted. All ads, commercial or political, 'tend to simplify the world,' he added.

The implication, though it was not spelt out, was that what is said in ads is unimportant because in the final analysis nobody of any intelligence believes them. To which the answer would appear to be that there are ads and ads. The reader responds to messages of different kinds in different ways. If it is untrue that Persil gives 'whiteness that cares' or that 'things happen after a Badedas bath' (sexual things judging by the fantasy ads devised by Allen Brady and Marsh), these are untruths which, on the intellectual level at least, fool nobody. They are like moves in a game of make-believe the rules of which are well enough understood. To assume that the same applied to the statements made in a car ad about the vehicle's mechanical specifications would be nonsensical. Such details are expected to be accurate. If they turn out not to be, the reader will be furious and the law, too, will take a dim view.

In other words, when a statement is presented as a statement of fact and not as a piece of imagery, hyperbole or fantasy it is entitled to be judged as a statement of fact and treated accordingly. Newspapers which publish such statements without regard to their accuracy simply because they are printed in paid-for space are, on one fairly charitable hypothesis, suffering from confusion of mind. The least charitable hypothesis, alas one which is sometimes raised regarding the posh but penurious journals in which ads of the Club of Ten type usually appear, is that they need the money too much to argue with the advertisers.

Newspapers themselves are likely, when challenged, to prate about freedom of speech, which is a safer line of defence than the alleged incredibility of all ads. Thus in 1974, when another Club of Ten advertisement appeared in the *Guardian* (as well as elsewhere) the paper published a leading article warning readers that the ad contained inaccuracies but nobly declaring that, precisely because the *Guardian*'s own policy was attacked in it, printing it was the right thing to do.

Even more heat was generated by the publication at various times and in various papers of virulent anti-Israel advertisements, paid for by various Arab and Arab-funded organisations. One which appeared in *The Times*, also in 1974, caused uproar in the Jewish community by implying that British Jews put support for Israel before loyalty to their own country. In the ensuing pother the paper's columnist Bernard Levin, himself Jewish, stoutly endorsed its action. He thought the ad had been 'silly, nasty and dishonest' but added that 'the point about free speech is that it has to be upheld for the nasty as well as the nice'. He then enunciated what could be called the Levin Doctrine of advertising, namely that the paper's columns were 'available to all those who will keep within the law and will pay for the space'.

As a statement of policy this had a fine, liberal-sounding ring. There was only one thing wrong with it—it happened to be untrue. Untrue not only of *The Times* but of other newspapers, almost all of which had at one time or another rejected ads which were both legal and produced by advertisers whose ability to pay was not in doubt.

Most of the many cases which over the years have found

their way into the news columns of the advertising trade press have, it is true, raised issues of sexual rather than political decency. Not so very long before Levin's piece appeared *The Times* had, for example, banned a McCann-Erickson ad for Lufthansa which showed a group of men window-shopping outside the Dr Muller sex shop at Frankfurt Airport under the headline 'You don't have to be crazy about Germany to appreciate Frankfurt'. The *Daily Telegraph Magazine* rejected the same ad as 'objectionable', although the *Sunday Times Magazine* and the *Evening Standard* accepted it. The airline said it was 'astonished' at the reaction of those papers which found the ad offensive but it didn't question their right to ban it.

But, even supposing that *The Times* had been pursuing the policy Levin ascribed to it, he did not explain what principle there was to prevent a newspaper from arguing with an advertiser, in the same way that it argues with an editorial contributor, about the details of his copy. If an ad really is judged 'silly, nasty and dishonest', why not tell the advertiser that, while he is free to publish his opinion, he must present it in a less objectionable form? Again this has frequently happened where commercial advertisers were thought to have overstepped the mark with regard to sex.

The point is that nothing, certainly not the ASA, can relieve a publication of responsibility for everything it publishes. If it chooses to publish matter which it believes to be dishonest it is a mere evasion to say it does not wish to censor advertisers. There is in logic no reason why distortions unacceptable in editorial columns should become suddenly acceptable when they are paid for—unless they are recognisable as non-factual puffery, which often cannot be argued even in the case of commercial ads.

Anyhow, within less than a year *The Times*, showing scant regard for the Levin Doctrine, *was* arguing with a political advertiser, again an Arab one. When the Iraqi Embassy submitted another strong anti-Zionist ad the paper agreed to run it but only on condition that half the copy was deleted. The *Observer* also published a censored version, but the *Guardian* ran the ad intact on the say-so of the same John Ryan whom we met earlier passing some of the wilder assertions of the apartheid lobby.

From the point of view of the ad industry as a whole incidents like the above are of perhaps small importance. If they have been dwelt on here at some length it is partly because they illustrate one way in which advertising policy can become entangled with general considerations about the function of the media. Partly also because, even within the commercial field, a growing number of companies have been using advertising not just in the old way for bragging about the goods and services they offer for sale but as a channel through which to address opinion-formers and argue a case. Here we are talking about ads which, like the Club of Ten and Iraqi Embassy efforts, are directly comparable with editorial features.

Amoco, for instance, spent £100,000 in nine days of 1975 on an ad campaign in the national press presenting its arguments for exempting North Sea gas from petroleum revenue tax. Bristol Ship Repairers ran a similar campaign explaining why it thought it shouldn't be nationalised. In the period before the referendum on British membership of the European Economic Community British Leyland (at that time in private hands) was one of the companies which bought newspaper space to give its reasons for wanting to be in the EEC. The multinational giant ITT spent £180,000 on a six-month campaign designed to convince Britishers that, far from being the sinister force reports of its allegedly subversive activities in Chile had made it out to be, it was a good corporate citizen of this country.

Advertising of this kind is called corporate, or prestige advertising. Its purpose is in fact less often polemical than to enhance and maintain a company's reputation, not only with customers but with investors, shareholders, suppliers and its own employees. Since a plenitude of words is not the only, nor necessarily the best, means of doing this, there has been a tendency in recent years for corporate advertisers to make use of television for their image-building campaigns. ICI, with its much praised 'Pathfinders' campaign illustrating some of its multifarious activities, was something of a pioneer in this respect. Philips followed it on to the box with commercials showing, through trick photography, a boy growing by stages into a man while a voice-over burbled on about the company's contributions to research, the control of pollution and the creation of a better life.

Whether or not such campaigns achieve any real effects it is obviously extraordinarily difficult to gauge, even more difficult than in the case of brand advertising where there are always the sales figures to go by, even if these are affected by other variables. In practice they are held to be successful if attitudinal research reveals a higher proportion of the public to hold favourable opinions about the company after the advertising than before it. Going by this test, both ICI and Philips have had reason to think their money well spent.

Particularly gratifying research results were obtained by the Trust Houses-Forte hotels group after its £150,000 campaign to publicise itself as having 'The biggest smile in Europe'. The proportion of respondents who understood it to be a fast-growing company rose from 33 per cent to 52 per cent. In the City the percentage of investors said to have a favourable image of TH-F rose from 50 to 77.

While some companies have learned to be humorous and modest, or at any rate mock-modest, about their products, none has tried knocking itself in its corporate advertising. Of course, there's a lot more at stake. A product's disadvantages can hardly be hidden for very long, so why not own up to them and try to win some credit by doing so (the Volkswagen ploy)? The shortcomings of a large and diverse corporation may be kept secret for years, and disclosure may cause ructions. Nevertheless, the day may yet come when a company advertises the fact that it's more interested in making money than in hastening the coming of the millennium. Who knows, it might even win some praise for doing so.

If commercial advertisers have in recent times learned to speak the language of political polemics in some of their ads, the professional political polemicists have picked up some of the tricks of the image-building trade. British political parties have come a long way in a comparatively short time towards accepting that commercial advertising techniques are applicable, and indeed even essential, to successful political campaigns.

Only 18 years ago this view was totally and explicitly rejected by the Labour Party. Before the 1959 General Election the publicity sub-committee of Labour's National Executive met to consider an offer of assistance from a group of admen with Labour sympathies. The volunteers were sent away with a flea in their ear.

That was the period in which the Conservatives for the first time employed an ad agency, and the credit for their 1959 victory was ascribed by many to CPV's slogan 'Life's better with the Conservatives. Don't let Labour ruin it'. That victory converted Labour to a belief in the positive virtues of advertising, and the party set up a voluntary publicity group of advertising and public relations people. It was these people who were to produce such campaigns as 'Let's go with Labour' and 'You know Labour Government works', which helped the party win power in the Sixties, and 'Labour has life and soul' and 'Yesterday's Men' (referring to the Tory leaders), which preceded its 1970 defeat.

Both major parties came to accept that, in the words of Brian Murphy, the former advertising copywriter responsible for 'Let's go with Labour', voters cannot be expected 'to follow closely reasoned arguments or to be automatically interested in the great issues of the day. Unless our propaganda can immediately echo a feeling or strike a subject close to their hearts, we have lost them.'

The main difference between the two parties is that while the Tories have continued to hire agencies—their account has moved in recent times from Davidson Pearce Berry and Spottiswoode to Roe Humphreys and back again to DPBS—Labour has gone on relying on volunteers and using an agency purely to place the ads they created. And that despite the fact that among the volunteers have been numbered some well-known agency directors, David Kingsley, of Kimpher, Mike Oxley, of Crawfords, Chris Powell, of Boase Massimi Pollitt.

The Labour Party view is that voluntary creative work not only comes cheaper but is guaranteed to be sincere. Perhaps another, unexpressed reason why it has never appointed an agency is that Labour supporters are very much in a minority in Adland, and there is probably no substantial agency which would like to be too closely identified with the party.

The Conservatives are troubled by no such inhibitions. As far as sincerity is concerned, the theory is that nobody who was not a Tory himself would work on the party's account whichever agency happened to be in charge of it. In practice it is not certain that this has always been true. At all events, when Norman Berry, creative director of Davidson Pearce, was asked at a time when his firm was working for the Tories which party he voted for he declined to reply, which a true Conservative zealot would presumably not have done.

Until 1970 party political advertising in Britain could be said to differ in two important respects from that in the United States, the true home of the genre: (*a*) it was confined to the press and posters; and (*b*) it did not have the sharp cutting edge of many of the American ads.

Regarding (*a*), political advertising, in the sense of spot commercials freely purchasable on the American pattern, is forbidden on ITV. All that is allowed on both the commercial and BBC channels is party political broadcasts, which all parties originally saw as simply an opportunity for some of their leaders to talk to a mass audience. As for (*b*), it used to be inconceivable that a British party, even if it were allowed to make TV spots, would produce anything like the 1968 ad, shown on American TV, in which the words 'Agnew for Vice-President' appeared on the screen to the sound of hysterical laughter. As the words faded they were replaced by another message, 'This would have been funny if it weren't so serious'.

That ad was, of course, made by the Democrats. Yet more spiteful—and funny—was a spot in which a voter was seen entering a polling booth and pulling a lever indicating support for the George Wallace-Curtis LeMay ticket. Upon which the whole world was seen erupting in a nuclear explosion. Even in the States that one was forced off the air for being too rude.

At that time publicity managers at both Transport House and Conservative Central Office agreed that personal attacks on political opponents would probably in the British context be counter-productive. Two years later, however, Labour did launch a knocking campaign in the shape of the 'Yesterday's Men' ads, in which the Tory leaders were pictured as ridiculous puppets. It may well have been counter-productive, as predicted. Certainly Labour lost the subsequent election.

In the same year of 1970 the Conservatives put a bit of pep into their party political broadcasts, giving them much more of a 'TV commercial' character than had previously been dreamed of. That was the year they brought in a professional TV advertising production company, James Garrett and Partners, and a top-notch agency creative man, Barry Day, to help make the films. Even Labour Party publicity people were impressed with their newsy format and imaginative camera work. By the October 1974 elections Labour had learned its lesson and was itself using quick-cutting techniques which, combined with throbbing music, gave to its films of party leaders out and about a lively interest all too frequently absent from the talking heads.

Meanwhile the Tories had been experimenting even more adventurously. In the February 1974 election they incorporated in one of their party political broadcasts a film clip in which Harold Wilson was portrayed as a comical dummy throwing away pound notes. It looked for a moment as if the gap between British and American political advertising methods might soon disappear altogether.

That film and another like it provoked quite a storm of indignation, as had the 'Yesterday's Men' campaign of four years before, which they recalled. This time, too, personal attack proved counter-productive, and the Heath Government lost office. But no doubt we have not seen the last bright idea from the world of advertising to be tried out in a British political campaign.

21 THE GREAT DEBATE

For many decades the advertising industry has been a subject of intense, sometimes bitter, controversy, no less so for engaging the attention of only a small minority.

A survey carried out by BMRB for the Advertising Association in 1976 indicated that only 6 per cent of the population were interested in advertising. To be precise, 6 per cent of the sample questioned identified it as one of their principal topics of conversation. This was an even smaller proportion than four years previously, when a similar survey had given advertising an 8 per cent score. In 1976 only 3 per cent said they felt strongly about advertising (6 per cent in 1972).

These figures could be a little misleading. Advertising, with a capital A, is a high-order abstraction, and it would have been surprising if a majority of ordinary people not concerned with the industry had given it much thought. This doesn't mean that they hadn't noticed and reacted to a host of actual advertisements. Among the 1976 sample 48 per cent of respondents said that they liked TV ads, 16 per cent that they disliked them, and only 36 per cent that they weren't bothered or didn't know. For press ads the corresponding figures were 36, 13 and 51 per cent.

More to the point, 73 per cent expressed general approval of advertising, an increase of six points over the 1972 figure and a source of public satisfaction to the Advertising Association. At the same time, as the AA admitted, it appeared that agreement with several propositions unfavourable to advertising had also grown. In particular, the 1976 survey indicated that 67 per cent believed ads to be 'often misleading', against 62 per cent who expressed a comparable opinion in 1972, when the finding almost certainly influenced the AA's decisions soon afterwards to update the Code of Advertising Practice and strengthen the Advertising Standards Authority.

(Curiously, fewer than half of those who in 1976 thought ads tended to mislead other people admitted that they themselves had ever been misled, but there is more than one way of interpreting this paradox.)

The most revealing finding of the 1972 survey was that, of those few people who did have strong opinions about advertising one way or the other, four times as many were anti as were pro. This puts Adland's public relations problem in a nutshell. As the survey report by BMRB said, 'It seems that advertising is in the disadvantageous position that, although very few people feel strongly about it, those few are particularly clustered among intellectuals, and nearly all tend to dislike advertising strongly.'

In case you think this is a recent phenomenon, it is worth quoting the words of L. G. Chiozza Money MP, who long before the First World War wrote that 'a most conspicuous waste in distribution is in advertising, one of the most unnecessary trades'. Individually, he conceded, those employed in advertising 'may be honest and industrious people. . . . From a national point of view they are wasting their time. It may be added that when they are pushing the sale of patent medicines, whiskies and complexion creams they are doing something worse than waste time.'

On the other side of the fence his contemporary John Hart, ad manager of *London Opinion*, took space in his own magazine to declare: 'When you buy branded and advertised goods you receive better value for money than you could possibly buy in any other way. Wares which are not advertised sell so slowly that the increased cost of production and marketing makes it necessary to sell them, quality for quality, at a higher price. Buyers of unadvertised goods pay for the advertising of those which are advertised. Moral: Choose the advertised brand and make the other fellow pay.'

Fifty and sixty years later the debate was still going on in terms which were not so very different, though perhaps slightly more sophisticated. Apart from accusations of deceptiveness and of upsetting the balance of the press, which problem we have already touched on, the intellectual critics of advertising have levelled the following charges against the industry:

1. Advertising is economically wasteful, as Chiozza Money said at the beginning of the century.
2. It puts prices up unnecessarily—the opposite of John Hart's thesis.
3. In modern conditions big firms are able to use advertising as a barrier to competition, keeping newcomers out of the market.
4. Advertising fosters false needs, and socially undesirable attitudes, such as excessive materialism.
5. It is spiritually vulgar and vulgarising.
6. It exploits human weaknesses in an unacceptable way.

These are pretty serious charges for anyone to be faced with, and it is not surprising that champions of the industry have devoted considerable time and energy to trying to rebut them. On both sides of the debate, and on both sides of the Atlantic, millions of words have been written and spoken. It needs a book simply to provide an adequate resumé of the arguments for and against, and in fact there is such a book, *The Three Faces of Advertising*, an excellent compendium published in 1975 by the Advertising Association and edited by Michael Barnes (no relation of Micky Barnes of Bensons), one of the few professional admen to have been a Labour MP. Its mere appearance was proof of the degree to which the industry had ceased dismissing all its critics as cranks, as it was once prone to do, and accepted that it ought to study carefully what they had to say.

Even that book had to leave out some of the most important contributions to the debate, notably those by Herbert Marcuse and J. K. Galbraith. So the next, and last, few pages of this book are to be taken as a very modest attempt indeed to summarise some of the relevant points.

First let it be said that in the author's opinion there are

elements of truth in all the charges listed and that, if it were not so, Adland would not have been so perturbed by them as it has been. At the same time the industry's more intelligent spokesmen have been able to show fairly convincingly that they have all been exaggerated by counsel for the prosecution.

The case regarding the alleged wastefulness of advertising expenditure was made most influentially in this country by Professor Nicholas Kaldor shortly after the Second World War. Like all the other critics he was, it goes almost without saying but we had better say it to avoid any confusion, concerned not with the totality of advertising (including classified, financial reports, Government advertising) but with the category we have learned to call MCA (manufacturers' consumer advertising), which he defined as a method of supplying customers with information about products. As such he declared that expenditure on it was exorbitant.

While he admitted that it did not amount to a high proportion of the national income, he contended that it should be judged not in relation to GNP but in relation to 'the probable cost of providing an adequate information service about commodities if this service were provided in some other manner', e.g. through editorial reviews in the press. From this he argued that a consumer information service ought to be set up and financed by a tax on advertising, an idea which was taken up by the Labour Party and incorporated in a Green Paper during its 1970–74 period in opposition. Like many other party ideas it was dropped by the Labour Government.

Another economist, the Advertising Association's research director Harold Lind, pointed out that there was something perverse about classifying advertising as a service supplied by advertisers to customers when the only real transaction which took place was between media owners, who supplied space and time, and advertisers who paid for it. From the manufacturing company's point of view advertising was just one of a number of selling 'inputs', like its delivery vans and packaging department, said Lind, who also pointed out that no hard and fast line could be drawn between production costs and selling costs. He ridiculed economists who 'talk about the "real" packaging costs which are part of productive expenditure, as opposed to "unnecessary" packaging costs to attract buyers, although no one could ever determine which is which.'

Another hard and fast line which various people have commented can in practice rarely be drawn is that between information, which Kaldor and Co. see as the only useful purpose of advertising, and persuasion. Most ads are attempting both at the same time, though clearly some are more persuasive and some more informative than others.

Whatever the cost-effectiveness of any ad campaign may be judged to be by the company paying for it, this does not disprove the contention that the economy as a whole is putting more of its resources into advertising than it needs to. This was obviously the feeling of the Monopolies Commission when it investigated the washing powder market, which is dominated by the two heavy-spending giants Unilever and Procter and Gamble. Both were required to introduce cheaper, non-advertised lines into the shops, which they did. But the sales results of the experiment were disappointing, confirming the two companies in their attitude that they need to advertise to maintain their turnover. What would have happened if both had been obliged to give up advertising *all* their washing powders it is interesting to speculate. Presumably they would either have spent the money saved in some other competitive way such as in-store displays or distribution of free samples or they would indeed have been able to lower their prices.

The classical argument linking advertising with *cheap* prices is the one we have already seen presented by John Hart but which still goes on being trotted out even today, namely that advertising increases turnover and by doing so reduces the unit cost of production. The argument obviously has a great deal of truth in certain situations but can hardly apply when a market is dominated, as is so often the case nowadays, by a handful of producers who have achieved all the economies of scale they are ever likely to. Here advertising serves to keep each other at bay, and if one manufacturer were to drop it while his rivals went on spending as heavily as before he would soon be in trouble, but it is one of the selling costs keeping prices up.

It is also one of the costs which set an 'entry price' which must be paid by any company which wishes to break into a market. Critics of advertising claim that this effectively reduces competition and thus works against the public interest. There seems little doubt that in some markets at least things do work this way. Given the level of expenditure by Unilever and Procter and Gamble on detergents nobody is likely to try to challenge their control of that particular market. But there are, as defenders of advertising point out, plenty of exceptions to prove the rule—if it is a rule.

Small firms with something special to offer continue to break into settled markets despite the weight of rival advertising and grow to the point where they become substantial advertisers themselves. One example is Wilkinson Sword razor blades, a big advertiser now but a tiddler when it knocked Gillette off its perch with the first coated stainless steel blade at the beginning of the Sixties (up till then Gillette had 85 per cent of the market). Another is Brut aftershave which, before the launch of the popular Brut 33 range, did very little advertising and concentrated on point-of-sale promotion in a limited number of prestige shops.

According to Kaldor, the process whereby many markets have fallen into the hands of a small number of big firms has itself been hastened by advertising. 'The reason for this is that the shift of the demand curve resulting from advertising cannot be assumed to be strictly proportionate to the amount spent on advertising—the "pulling power" of the larger expenditure must overshadow that of smaller ones with the consequence *a* that the larger firms are bound to gain at the expense of the smaller ones; *b* if at the start firms are more or less of equal size, those that forge ahead are bound to increase their lead as the additional sales enable them to increase their outlay still further.'

But the view that advertising is an important cause of oligopoly has been fiercely combated by such marketing experts as Harry Henry, who has written: 'It is true that we have in this country for all practical purposes only seven or eight companies selling petrol, only four or five marketing detergents, only six or seven producing breakfast cereals. But this is not a function of advertising; it arises from the fact that to build an oil refinery calls for an astronomical outlay, that detergents can only be produced efficiently in very large quantities, that the manufacture of breakfast cereals on an economical scale needs a sufficient volume of throughput to ensure that the product reaches the breakfast table fresh enough to be still edible. The factor that leads to the growth of giant enterprises in fields such as these is the physical one that modern mass-production methods cannot be applied except on a very large scale.' And Henry has also pointed out that in some product fields, such as toilet soap, two or three giants can co-exist quite happily with comparative dwarfs each with its own special corner of the market.

Of the economic charges against advertising perhaps the one most resented by admen and their allies, and the one they find the most unfair, is that made by Professor Galbraith in his book *The New Industrial State* that big firms can control the market through advertising, manipulating consumer demand to suit their own purposes rather than simply responding to consumer whims.

Against this admen never tire of pointing out that nearly a half of all new products, including those launched even by very big companies, fail within five years. A 1974 study of the grocery trade by the Kraushar Andrews and Eassie research firm found this to be the case with 6,000 food products introduced since 1960, and according to its analysis the rate of failure appeared to be increasing. And there have been some king-size flops. Strand cigarettes in 1960 and Ford's Edsel car in the US five years earlier are classic cases of heavily promoted goods which all the ballyhoo couldn't shift.

It has become part of the conventional wisdom of ad agencies that a good ad can sell a lousy product once but not twice, and even then it has to be a product the consumer has a good reason for being interested in, especially if it costs too much to be bought as an experiment, to 'see what it tastes like'.

The point was put pungently if a trifle superciliously in an essay on *Advertising and Society* by Roderick White and Judie Lannon, two executives of J. Walter Thompson. In their paper, one of *The Case for Advertising* series published by JWT in the winter of 1975–6, they wrote: 'An advertisement can only work effectively at its job—that of helping to sell goods—if it promotes a product for which real demand exists, in a way which is in tune with the mood and aspirations of people. If there was any reasonable chance of selling courses in meditation and fine art reproductions to Liverpool dockers, there would be advertisements directed to that end.'

Nevertheless, to paraphrase Shakespeare, there is no product either good or bad but thinking makes it so. That may not apply so much to a car as to a brand of chocolates or vermouth, and ads may often fail to move the consumer's thinking in the desired direction, but it would be foolish to deny that there was any truth in it or that advertising, therefore, did help manufacturers to achieve a higher degree of demand-management (in spite of all the slips and uncertainties) than they could without it.

Indeed a denial would be, as far as admen were concerned, not merely foolish but self-contradictory, for it has come to be another piece of conventional wisdom in the industry that advertising 'adds a new value to the existing value of the product'. The words are those of Martin Mayer, author of *Madison Avenue USA*, but the theory of 'added value' did not originate with him, though his phrase has become generally adopted.

Many tests have been carried out to show that when people are blindfolded and asked to compare two similar products they express quite different preferences from when they know the same products' brand names. Advertising is not the only factor here, but John Treasure of J. Walter Thompson probably speaks for all admen when he says there is no doubt that 'advertising does create quite genuine and real values for a brand which are none the less real for being subjective'.

All the economic criticisms of advertising are linked to its function as an instrument of free enterprise or, as some people would call it, monopoly capitalism. Sometimes it seems that criticisms of the instrument should more properly be directed at the system of which it is a part. The wastefulness of which some complain, for instance, when speaking of the ad expenditure of companies like Unilever and Procter and Gamble, is inseparable from the wastefulness inherent in the competitive system. You don't have to be an enemy of the system to agree that it is in some respects wasteful. Harry Henry, declaring his belief that 'freedom of consumer choice in a free society is a good thing and that this requires freedom of economic action', admits that 'the price which must be paid for all this economic freedom includes a certain amount of what might well be classified as waste—just as the price which has to be paid for political freedom is the relative wastefulness of democratic processes.'

Attention socialists, the non-competitive system breeds its own species of waste in the shape of piles of unsold goods produced according to the specifications of a central plan elaborated without the close attention to consumer tastes which profit-oriented corporations are obliged to pay. In such circumstances guess what the Russians do? Why, they advertise those goods. At one stage it was found that stocks of electric gas-stove lighters were accumulating. Soviet citizens, it appeared, were not turned on to lighters; matches were what they knew and matches were what they bought. An ad campaign was organised and stocks were cleared. When Leningrad found itself with a lot of unsold cheese an intensive campaign was launched through TV, radio and press, and 100,000 leaflets were distributed.

In Hungary and Yugoslavia, both of which practise forms of what has been called 'market socialism', with collectively owned enterprises competing for profit, consumer advertising is much more developed than in Russia. Hungary has two big advertising agencies which, though State-controlled, are run on commercial lines. Yugoslavia has a multiplicity of agencies controlled, like other Yugoslav enterprises, by their own employees.

Socialist admen, by the way, aren't above imitating the

techniques which so disgust some socialist critics of advertising in the decadent West. A Hungarian ad for a coffee brand told newspaper readers that the 'best people' drink it. A Soviet campaign for fruit compote made vague and exaggerated health claims for the product which might have had trouble getting past the British Code of Advertising Practice Committee.

The last three points in our six-point indictment of advertising are of a socio-ethical rather than economic character. Here the prosecution has been handled largely by literary academics like Professors Raymond Williams and Richard Hoggart. Basically they are concerned not with the truth or untruth of any particular claims made for any particular brands nor yet with the effect of advertising expenditure on the fortunes of corporations or the level of prices but with what exposure to commercial advertising as practised today does to people's minds.

Raymond Williams deplores the 'organised fantasy' of advertising and the fact that people 'now need the system of fantasy to confirm the forms of their immediate satisfactions or to cover the illusion that they are shaping their own lives'. In TV commercials actors 'pretend to a linkage of values between quite mundane products and the now generally unattached values of love, respect, significance or fulfilment' (1969 *Listener* article, reprinted in *The Three Faces of Advertising*).

Says Herbert Marcuse: 'Most of the prevailing needs to relax, to have fun, to behave and consume in accordance with the advertisements, to love and hate what others love and hate, belong to this category of false needs.' (*One Dimensional Man*)

Admen react to this sweeping kind of condemnation by pointing to research like that carried out by J. Walter Thompson among housewives which indicates that people understand and enjoy fantasy and wish-fulfilment in ads but are not taken in by them, that they use ads in fact rather than being used by them.

In their day-to-day work advertising agencies are, of course, bothered more by evidence that people are *not* paying any attention to their particular ads than that they are. This does not, however, disprove the contention that the effect of all ads taken together is to induce a majority of people to understand the good life in terms of material possessions and of the social and sexual status-seeking with which in so many ads they are linked.

Ads are indeed not directed to selling meditation or fine art to Liverpool dockers nor even, in the course of selling them beer and cigarettes, to suggesting that they might spare a little time from the attractive pub shown in the commercials, to visit the local art gallery. To which kind of talk admen again react with irritation, pointing out with some justification that condemnations of materialism come mostly from intellectual middle-class folk who are not so badly off themselves for material comforts, thank you very much, and that it's humbug to preach austerity for other people to practise. They point out, also with some justification, that it is futile to put the blame for all the ills or imagined ills of contemporary civilisation on advertising, which is only a cog in the machine.

As with the economic criticisms, those who attack the cultural aspects of advertising are often really opposed to the whole commercial and industrial system which it serves. But it cannot be seriously denied that, even if ads do not create any social attitudes, they reinforce certain already existing ones, though to what extent it would probably be impossible to measure. Having accepted that point, you are not, of course, obliged to agree with Raymond Williams or Herbert Marcuse about which attitudes and values might be preferable.

A very different point of view from that of Professor Williams was put in a speech to the 1974 Advertising Association conference by his namesake David Williams, the dapper and eloquent head of the David Williams and Ketchum ad agency and an active Church of England man. 'I hope,' he declared, 'more fervently that I can express, that advertising does encourage materialism.'

Our present 'benevolent affluence' had been fathered by materialism. 'Is it reasonable to suppose that, if cheap subsidised housing can be provided for an unskilled labourer, he should not indulge a burning and practical desire to buy furniture for it? But admit this and you have promoted him from the ranks of the deserving poor to the files of the headstrong materialists.

'Offer him a wage that reflects the true value of his labour and the spur to earn it, and more, by dangling material carrots before him and you vest him with ambition. Before you know it he's afforded all kinds of labour-saving devices for his wife, the means of entertainment in his own living room, a motor car, holidays abroad. . .

'The washing machine has made the scrubbing board obsolete in the majority of homes of this country. I cannot relate this to a fall in the rate of compassion in the hearts of the housewives, though I think it may be helping them to look younger for longer.'

No doubt the God to whom David Williams prays would be seen by Raymond Williams as a golden calf.

The vulgarity charge implicit in many attacks on advertising is to a large extent concerned with matters of technique. An example is an ad picked upon by one of the literary academic school of critics, Frank Whitehead, in an essay he contributed to *Discrimination and Popular Culture*, edited by Denys Thompson and first published in 1964. The ad, one of a number which incurred Whitehead's special ire, was for Knight's Castile soap and appeared in a woman's magazine. Under a romantic picture the prose was deepest purple:

> *It began long ago . . . with a letter in Sue's childish hand to her pen-friend Kim in California. She had quite forgotten Kim when years later a letter brought news of her and went on . . .'This is really to introduce my brother Pete. He's won a scholarship to study in your country and knows iust no one there. Then I thought of you. . .' and not long after Sue heard, for the first time, Pete's deep, slow voice on the telephone asking for a date. They met—and then again. His gentle manner, his disarming grin, soon made him a favourite with her set. Then, more and more, it was just she and Pete . . . alone even in a crowd, in their own private world. One golden day by the river Pete asked Sue to be his*

wife. Close to her, Pete felt Sue's cheek, warm and soft against his. 'My, you're beautiful,' he whispered. 'When they see that English complexion back home . . .' Sue is still as fresh and lovely as she was that day—thanks to Knight's Castile.

It's an old ad now but still a honey, a period piece worthy of inclusion in that National Gallery of Advertising Art which we sadly do not have. But instead of savouring it as such, Whitehead exploded: 'Obviously an important human emotion is trivialised when it is thus reduced to a single commercially manipulated aspect. . . Here are feelings which have indeed been "processed" to the uniform consistency and flavourlessness of a cheese spread.'

Whitehead was taken to task by Tom Corlett, another J. Walter Thompson director, in a pamphlet published by the Institute of Practitioners in Advertising some years later and entitled *Advertising—'Is This the Sort of Work an Honest Man Can Take Pride In?'* Happily for his career in the agency, Corlett felt able to answer the question in the affirmative. In doing so he challenged Whitehead's belief that it was possible to devalue any important human emotion by associating it with the commonplace. He could understand, though not accept, 'the charge that the toilet soap was made to seem absurd by being presented in such a lofty association; but the reverse effect—that of the human emotion itself being trivialised by its association with toilet soap—is one which I can neither understand nor accept.'

Those of us who are not directors of JWT may find it easy both to understand and to accept it, since it is a piece of perfectly normal literary criticism. The same kind of criticism could probably have been applied equally devastatingly to the editorial contents of the kind of magazine in which the ad appeared. Such incongruities are by no means confined to advertising. The pulp literature of all ages, not to mention the theatre, cinema and TV programmes, abound in them. They find a ready market because a majority of people are not aesthetes and do have more or less vulgar sensibilities (*vulgus*, after all, means the crowd).

A more telling retort might have been that Whitehead,

like others of his school, had no sense of humour. Yes, the ad trivialises love. Yes, it also makes the soap seem absurd. That's why it reads so comically. Conceivably a fair number even of its original readers found it pretty funny.

Styles have changed since the early Sixties, in advertising as well as everything else, and nowadays the incongruities are more likely to be intentionally designed to amuse, the fantasies more conscious of themselves. Perhaps even Frank Whitehead's canons of good taste would not be offended by the self-mocking style of a commercial like that by Collett Dickenson Pearce for Supersoft hair spray in which a good looking couple, obviously in love, walk on a moonlit balcony to a background of romantic music. 'Moonlight becomes you,' sings the dinner-jacketed man, 'It goes with your h. . .' Before he can get the word 'hair' out he notices that part of her coiffure has collapsed. 'Your hair,' says the voice-over, 'can sometimes let you down.' Close-up of the girl's upset face. 'New Supersoft. We'll never let you down.'

Nothing phoney as in the Knight's Castile ad. The technique is different, and phoneyness and sincerity are, as we all know or ought to, a matter of technique. But the two are appealing to precisely the same hope (love and marriage). The Collets commercial is, further, playing on precisely the same fear (If I don't buy the right toiletries to make the most of my looks, I won't catch my man) which in other, cruder ads Whitehead denounced as 'a peculiarly distasteful form of contempt for human nature'.

This brings us to the point about whether ads exploit human weaknesses. About that there can really be no argument. Yes, of course they do, although some admen may not like that wording. Rephrase it and say that ads commonly attempt to persuade people to choose or continue in certain courses of action through appeals to their appetites, fears, anxieties, hopes, aspirations. (These are all in a sense weaknesses.) The only question left is whether that is unacceptable. To that the answer surely is that advertising and other varieties of propaganda are like war—it makes all the difference which side you're on. Unless you're one of those absolute conscientious objectors who are opposed to the use of weapons at any time for any reason, you presumably believe that wars can be fought for good or for evil purposes. Most people would agree that it was wrong for Hitler to make war to conquer his neighbours, right for the Allies to make war to stop him.

If you think it is right for companies to make and sell goods at a profit you are likely to agree that they should be allowed to advertise them as persuasively as they can, within a framework of recognised rules and restrictions, and if all appeals to fears, hopes, etc., are banned that doesn't leave much of an armoury of persuasion.

If you're not too keen on the private enterprise system you may feel differently. But would you ban appeals to fear in, say, road safety advertising? Some experts are against putting a lot of horror in road safety campaigns, but only because of the suspicion, about which controversy continues, that too much fear makes people mentally switch off and is, as a propaganda technique, counter-productive.

Advertising, as Jeremy Bullmore of J. Walter Thompson never tires of repeating, consists of advertisements, which are of many sorts and can be used for many purposes in many ways. Over the past few years in Britain, as we have seen, Government advertising has grown, while manufacturers' consumer advertising, the kind that most of the fuss is about, has declined in proportion to national wealth. It may be that as time goes by the 'social marketing' ingredient in the advertising cake will gain still further in importance.

If that were to happen, in conjunction perhaps with increased collectivisation of the economy, reduced affluence, and yet tighter limitation of the claims allowed to be made for commercial products, advertising might come to be looked upon more as an instrument of state control, akin to the all-pervasive political propaganda of the Soviet Union, than as a pillar of capitalism. Criticism of the ad industry could then be expected to come more from the Right than, as at present, from the Left. That wouldn't necessarily put an end to accusations of deceptive half-truths and unjustifiable manipulation of human emotions.

So much is speculation, though not entirely idle. Meanwhile we can be sure of one thing: the great debate about advertising ends and means will continue, and admen and adwomen, more than members of any other profession, will go on arguing with each other and with the outside world about the morality of what they do for a living.

Meanwhile, too, the ads they turn out will, as ever, irritate us, disgust us, bore us, intrigue us, entertain us, enlighten us and, when we are especially fortunate, give us something to laugh about.

APPENDIX

1. Total Advertising Expenditure 1960–75

Year	*Expenditure in £ million*	*As percentage of consumer spending*	*As percentage of GNP*
1960	323	1·91	1·42
1961	338	1·90	1·38
1962	348	1·84	1·36
1963	371	1·84	1·37
1964	416	1·93	1·41
1965	435	1·90	1·38
1966	447	1·84	1·35
1967	451	1·80	1·31
1968	503	1·85	1·36
1969	544	1·89	1·39
1970	554	1·77	1·29
1971	591	1·71	1·23
1972	708	1·80	1·31
1973	874	1·95	1·39
1974	900	1·76	1·23
1975	967	1·54	1·04

Source: Advertising Association

2. *Advertising Expenditure by Media (£ million)*

	1960	1964	1968	1971	1972	1973	1974	1975
National newspapers	64	86	99	108	130	160	160	162
Regional newspapers	77	98	121	152	188	256	274	282
Magazines and periodicals	40	46	50	54	60	72	71	79
Trade and technical press	31	37	46	52	61	73	80	86
Directories	2	3	8	13	15	17	16	20
Press production costs	15	18	23	39	44	46	48	49
Total press	229	288	347	418	498	624	649	678
Television (transmission costs)	67	89	118	128	158	189	176	208
Television (production costs)	5	8	11	15	18	21	27	28
Total TV	72	97	129	143	176	210	203	236
Poster and transport	16	18	20	23	26	31	34	35
Cinema	5	6	6	6	7	7	8	7
Radio	1	2	1	1	1	2	6	11

Source: Advertising Association

3. *Advertising Expenditure by Categories (£ million)*

	1969	1970	1971	1972	1973	1974	1975
Classified	113	119	119	150	213	228	218
MCA	252	250	271	311	362	348	387
Food	64	62	70	82	88	81	89
Clothing	13	13	12	13	12	10	12
Automotive	20	19	18	23	29	23	33
Drink and tobacco	44	46	50	55	64	65	73
Toiletries and medical	33	32	35	39	48	50	53
Household and leisure	55	54	59	68	84	79	87
Industrial	67	71	70	81	95	103	111
Retail	52	56	63	84	114	134	163
Financial	26	23	28	39	39	36	36
Publishing	9	9	11	13	16	17	16
Tourism, entertainment, foreign	21	22	24	26	30	32	34
Charities and education	2	2	2	2	2	3	3
Nationalised Industries	12	12	14	16	19	18	18
Government	13	14	16	17	21	21	21

Source: Advertising Association

4. Top Ten Advertising Accounts

1975 *Top Ten*	£m	1974 *Top Ten*	£m
(*a*) *TV and press combined*			
COI, Energy Crisis	3·6	Brentford Nylons	3·3
Boots	3·3	C & A	2·8
Co-op, Local Branches	3·0	Co-op, Local	2·1
Woolworths, National	2·2	Boots	2·0
Brentford Nylons	2·1	Guinness	2·0
Co-op, National	2·0	British Airways	2·0
C & A	1·8	Co-op, National	1·7
Fine Fare	1·7	Army, Other Ranks	1·5
Allied Carpets	1·7	Fine Fare	1·4
Currys	1·5	COI, Energy	1·3
(*b*) *TV only*			
COI, Energy	2·4	Brentford Nylons	1·8
Woolworths, National	1·8	Guinness	1·6
K Tel Records	1·4	Kelloggs Corn Flakes	1·2
Kelloggs Corn Flakes	1·3	*The Sun*	1·2
Brentford Nylons	1·3	Weetabix	1·1
Allied Carpets	1·3	COI, Energy	1·0
Boots	1·2	Heinz Soups	1·0
Guinness Bottled	1·1	Ariel	0·9
The Sun	1·1	Boots	0·9
Oxo Red Cubes	1·1	Army, Other Ranks	0·9
(*c*) *Press only*			
Co-op, Local	2·4	C & A	2·0
Boots	2·1	Co-op, Local	1·7
C & A	1·8	Brentford Nylons	1·5
Co-op, National	1·4	MFI	1·3
Currys	1·4	B & H Special Filter	1·2
COI, Energy	1·2	Co-op, National	1·2
Benson & Hedges Special Filter Cigarettes	1·2	Boots	1·1
Players No. 6 Filter	1·2	British Airways	1·1
MFI	1·1	Midland Bank	1·0
Dixons Hi-Fi/Photo	1·1	Comet Discount Warehouses	0·9

Source: MEAL

5. Biggest UK Advertising Agencies in order of Turnover

Agency	Billings (£ million)		Number of Staff	
	1975	1974	1975	1974
J. Walter Thompson	41·70	40·10	796	890
Masius Wynne-Williams	32·50	30·49	500	515
McCann-Erickson	30·80	25·10	450	420
Saatchi Compton group	30·50	30·62	550	570
Ogilvy Benson & Mather	29·00	26·83	409	456
Young & Rubicam	26·00	23·90	325	410
Leo Burnett	25·00	25·90	390	430
Kimpher group	23·40	25·81	447	552
Charles Barker Group	22·90	22·15	430	417
Ted Bates	20·40	17·00	265	273
Collett Dickenson Pearce	20·10	21·52	205	210
Wasey Campbell-Ewald	18·40	15·70	273	232
Royds group	16·85	16·12	428	372
Foote Cone & Belding	14·70	12·92	281	279
Brunning group	12·60	12·73	388	415
Benton & Bowles	12·50	10·32	200	210
Lintas	12·00	14·90	154	200
Lonsdale Osborne	11·50	11·10	208	208
Dorland Advertising	11·00	10·75	186	180
Davidson Pearce Berry & Spottiswoode	11·00	10·50	158	158
Rupert Chetwynd	10·32	10·27	291	291
Doyle Dane Bernbach	10·30	8·70	121	131
Roe Downton	10·20	8·57	162	159
French Gold Abbott Kenyon & Eckhardt	9·58	7·30	94	94
BBDO	9·30	7·20	111	148
Boase Massimi Pollitt	8·00	6·20	98	98
Ayer Barker Hegemann	6·80	6·30	89	102
Allen Brady & Marsh	6·50	4·30	84	52
The Kirkwood Co.	6·48	5·23	47	45
Sharps Advertising	6·40	6·10	81	84
Geers Gross	5·90	3·60	40	40
Grey Advertising	5·80	5·78	100	131
David Williams & Ketchum	5·73	5·45	99	122
Cogent Elliott	5·70	3·60	118	114
Everetts	5·25	4·73	94	97
Norman Craig & Kummel	5·10	4·00	70	65
Graham & Gillies	4·40	3·50	75	62
Interlink	4·30	4·60	62	75
Saward Baker	4·30	3·80	83	98
W. S. Crawford	4·25	3·80	45	32
Haddons	4·00	3·60	75	75

5. Biggest UK Advertising Agencies in order of turnover—contd.

Agency	*Billings (£ million)*		*Number of Staff*	
	1975	1974	1975	1974
C. Vernon & Sons	4·00	3·70	74	86
Yeoward Taylor & Bonner	3·70	2·90	66	65
Freeman Mathews & Milne	3·60	3·34	62	68
NSW Partners	3·55	4·10	48	66
Fletcher Shelton	3·20	3·20	51	58
Euro Advertising	2·80	2·30	31	26

Source: Campaign

6. Turnover, Income, Staff, Profitability of IPA Agencies

	Total Turnover (£m)	*Total Income (£m)*	*Total Staff*	*Average pre-tax profit as per centage of turnover*
1960	225	34	19,000	2·9
1963	290	43·5	18,000	2·1
1966	355	56·5	20,000	1·8
1968	375	59·5	17,900	1·9
1969	395	63	17,200	1·8
1970	405	65·5	17,200	1·5
1971	420	68·5	15,600	1·8
1972	492	80	14,800	2·6
1973	578	91	15,700	2·4
1974	603	96·5	14,900	1·8
1975	650	105·4	13,300	1·54

Source: Institute of Practitioners in Advertising

BIBLIOGRAPHY

Advertising Association, *Advertising in Perspective*, Advertising Association, 1974.
Aucamp, Johan (ed.), *The Effective Use of Market Research*, Staples Press, 1971.
Baker, Samm Sinclair, *The Permissible Lie*, Peter Owen, 1969.
Barnes, Michael (ed.), *The Three Faces of Advertising*, Advertising Association, 1975.
Barnes, Micky, *Ad*, Bachman & Turner, 1973.
Barthélémy, *A Travers le Monde de la Publicité*, Stock, Paris, 1972.
Bernstein, David, *Creative Advertising*, Longman, 1974.
Broadbent, Simon, *Spending Advertising Money*, Business Books, 1975.
Cone, Fairfax, *With All Its Faults*, Little Brown, Boston, 1969.
Della Femina, Jerry, *From Those Wonderful Folks Who Gave You Pearl Harbour*, Pitman, 1971.
Dichter, Ernest, *Handbook of Consumer Motivations*, McGraw-Hill, New York, 1964.
Fletcher, Winston, *The Ad Makers*, Michael Joseph, 1973.
Galbraith, John Kenneth, *The New Industrial State*, Penguin, 1974.
Grundy, Bill, *The Press Inside Out*, W. H. Allen, 1976.
Hanson, Philip, *Advertising and Socialism*, Macmillan, 1974.
Henry, Harry, *Perspectives in Marketing, Advertising, Management*, Crosby Lockwood, 1971.
Hopkins, Claude, *Scientific Advertising*, MacGibbon & Kee, 1968.
Jefkins, Frank, *Advertising Made Simple*, W. H. Allen, 1973.
King, Stephen, *Developing New Brands*, Pitman, 1973.
Marcuse, Herbert, *One Dimensional Man*, Sphere Books, 1968.
Mayer, Martin, *Madison Avenue U.S.A.*, Penguin, 1961.
Ogilvy, David, *Confessions of an Advertising Man*, Longman, 1964.
Packard, Vance, *The Hidden Persuaders*, Penguin (Pelican), 1975.
Pearson, John, and Turner, Graham, *The Persuasion Industry*, Eyre & Spottiswoode, 1965.
Potter, Jack, and Lovell, Mark, *Assessing the Effectiveness of Advertising*, Business Books, 1975.
Smelt, Maurice (ed.), *What Advertising Is*, Pelham Books, 1972.
Thompson, Denys (ed.), *Discrimination and Popular Culture*, Penguin, 1973.
Thompson, J. Walter Company, *The Case for Advertising*, a collection of papers by JWT executives, J. Walter Thompson, 1976.

Turner, E. S., *The Shocking History of Advertising* (revised edn.), Penguin with Michael Joseph, 1965.
Wight, Robin, *The Day the Pigs Refused to be Driven to Market*, Hart-Davis, MacGibbon, 1972.
Worcester, Robert (ed.), *Consumer Market Research Handbook*, McGraw-Hill, 1971.

In addition, for those interested in the look of advertisements, two annual publications can be recommended: the *Designers and Art Directors Association Annual*, published by D & AD, and *Modern Publicity* (ed. Felix Gluck), from Studio Vista.

Trade Papers

Admap. Monthly to subscribers. Consists largely of experts' contributions on advertising research and the media.
Advertising Quarterly. Official journal of the Advertising Association.
Campaign. Founded in 1968, this weekly at first ruffled a lot of feathers with its 'publish and be damned' attitude to the ad industry. Has quietened down since and is, since the disappearance of *Adweek* in 1975, the main purveyor of industry news and views.
Marketing. Journal of the Institute of Marketing. Covers many advertising topics.

INDEX